Raymond Collishaw
and the
Black Flight

RAYMOND COLLISHAW

COLLISHAW

AND THE

BLACK FLIGHT

ROGER GUNN

DUNDURN
TORONTO

Excerpt reprinted from *Gunning for the Red Baron* by Leon Bennett by permission of the Texas A&M University Press. Copyright © 2006 Leon Bennett.

Editor: Britanie Wilson
Design: Courtney Horner
Printer: Webcom

Library and Archives Canada Cataloguing in Publication

Gunn, Roger
    Raymond Collishaw and the Black Flight / Roger Gunn.

Includes bibliographical references.
Also issued in electronic format.
ISBN 978-1-4597-0660-6

    1. Collishaw, Raymond, 1893-1976. 2. Fighter pilots--
Canada--Biography. 3. Great Britain. Royal Naval Air
Service--Biography. 4. World War, 1914-1918--Aerial
operations, British. I. Title.

UG626.2.C64G85 2013   940.4'4941092   C2012-904597-7

1 2 3 4 5   17 16 15 14 13

We acknowledge the support of the **Canada Council for the Arts** and the **Ontario Arts Council** for our publishing program. We also acknowledge the financial support of the **Government of Canada** through the **Canada Book Fund** and **Livres Canada Books**, and the **Government of Ontario** through the **Ontario Book Publishing Tax Credit** and the **Ontario Media Development Corporation**.

Care has been taken to trace the ownership of copyright material used in this book. The author and the publisher welcome any information enabling them to rectify any references or credits in subsequent editions.

J. Kirk Howard, President

Printed and bound in Canada.

Visit us at
Dundurn.com
Definingcanada.ca
@dundurnpress
Facebook.com/dundurnpress

Dundurn	Gazelle Book Services Limited	Dundurn
3 Church Street, Suite 500	White Cross Mills	2250 Military Road
Toronto, Ontario, Canada	High Town, Lancaster, England	Tonawanda, NY
M5E 1M2	LA1 4XS	U.S.A. 14150

This book is dedicated to all those who flew in the First World War. Let us not forget them.

CONTENTS

ACKNOWLEDGEMENTS

THIS BOOK HAS BEEN SIX YEARS IN THE MAKING. EACH SUMMER, I visited Library and Archives Canada or the Canadian War Museum's library in Ottawa and researched Raymond Collishaw. My wife Diane supported this research time, spending our entire trip visiting friends and relatives. I could not have sifted through the nine boxes of material on Collishaw made available to me if it weren't for the kind assistance of the Library and Archives Canada staff. I would like to thank David Crone, the Curator of Canada's Aviation Hall of Fame in Wetaskiwin, Alberta, for allowing me access to their research centre. Thanks also go to Emily Porter, Librarian, and to Carol Reid, Collections Manager at the Canadian War Museum, for their help and assistance.

I would like to formally and posthumously thank Raymond Collishaw and Ronald V. Dodds for their correspondence to one another in the 1960s and early 1970s. These records make for fascinating reading and show their efforts in putting together Collishaw's autobiography: *Air Command, A Fighter Pilot's Story.*

Both of these men were historians in their own right. Collishaw immersed himself in the Imperial Archives in London, collecting and researching material on the air battles of the First World War and engaged in a lengthy correspondence with fellow pilots like William Melville Alexander and Alfred William "Nick" Carter.

INTRODUCTION

CANADA IS A COUNTRY THAT UNFORTUNATELY REMAINS LARGELY unaware of its wartime heroes, both past and present. In writing this book, I hope to open the eyes of many Canadians to one of the unsung heroes of this nation's proud military history. *Raymond Collishaw and the Black Flight* is the story of the third highest-scoring flying ace of all the British and colonial pilots in the First World War, with an astonishing sixty victories. Only Billy Bishop and Edward Mannock surpassed him. This book covers the accomplished pilot's life from his humble beginnings as a ship's mate off the coast of British Columbia in the early 1900s to his wartime exploits fighting the German flyers over the skies of France in the First World War. Courage and leadership were the hallmarks of the skilled and gifted flying ace, Raymond Collishaw.

The first book that I read on First World War flyers was Quentin Reynolds' *They Fought For The Sky*. I must have been eleven or twelve years old; thus started my fascination for the First World War, and for

Library and Archives Canada, PA-118990.

Aircrew of 3 Naval Wing, RNAS. Left to right: Flight Sub-Lieutenants C.E. Burden, Gordon Harrower, H.E.P. Wigglesworth, Raymond Collishaw, J.A. Page, J.S.N. Rockey.

the pilots who flew their aircraft in that war. Around the same time in my life, I can remember one summer in a cottage my parents rented in the Ottawa Valley, my older brother and I, each with a fly swatter, pretending we were Richthofen or Bishop or Ball and trying to swat more flies than the other — increasing our number of "kills" before vacation was over and we had to return home. I read as many books as I could get a hold of on First World War flyers and their exploits, but none were devoted solely to Raymond Collishaw. I was going to fill that void.

This book was researched and written a few years before and after 2009, 100 years after the first flight of Alexander Graham Bell's "heavier than air" craft, the *Silver Dart*, flew in Nova Scotia. Just five years later, the Great War broke out. One year later, in 1915, Raymond Collishaw joined the Royal Naval Air Service (RNAS).

While not the most brilliant of student pilots, he persevered and was sent to France in September of 1916. As part of No. 3 Naval Wing, Collishaw took part in the famous raid on the Oberndorf factories in Germany. This was the Allies' first real attempt at strategic bombing. While with the 3 Naval Wing, Collishaw and his fellow British and Canadian pilots came in contact with American pilots from the famed *Escadrille Americaine.*

Library and Archives Canada, PA-207504.

Major Raymond Collishaw, circa. 1918.

Collishaw was transferred in April 1917 to No. 10 Naval Squadron. Here he led the Black Flight, a group of four to five Sopwith Triplanes. Painted black, these fast and maneuverable scouts faced the best German aces of the day, including von Richthofen's Flying Circus. In May and June of 1917 alone, No. 10 Naval Squadron accounted for over thirty enemy aircraft. Promoted to Squadron Commander in January 1918, Collishaw led what later became Squadron No. 203 (RAF). His many combats in the air showed the courage and leadership skills of this unique and gifted fighter pilot.

After the armistice Collishaw continued on with the Royal Air Force (RAF) on a permanent commission. He was sent to south Russia with a squadron of planes to fight with the White Russian counter-revolutionaries against the Bolshevik forces. He encountered many hair-raising escapades on the steppes of the Ukraine and narrowly avoided being captured and tortured.

Collishaw went on to fight in the Second World War and ended his career as an Air Vice Marshal in the RAF.

Raymond Collishaw had many close encounters with death during his lengthy and successful career and he survived them all. His bravery in combat was recognized many times with the award of decorations and praise, and in short, his legacy should not be as forgotten by Canadians as it has become. It is my hope that this book will help the reader know and better understand the exploits of this truly accomplished Canadian hero of the First World War.

≡1≡

THE EARLY YEARS

IN 1893, NANAIMO, BRITISH COLUMBIA WAS A PROSPEROUS COAL MINING town located on the southeast coast of Vancouver Island. In those days coal was king and it generated much construction and growth in the community. In the early 1890s Nanaimo saw the first telephone service established and electric lights appeared for the first time in the town. Nanaimo had an opera house, a court house, and a brick fire hall with its own aerial ladder and truck.

The coal mines of the Nanaimo area were a draw for many workers in search of employment. One such worker was John Edward "Jack" Collishaw, Raymond Collishaw's father. Originally from Wrexham, Wales, John was university educated with a music background, but had no interest in helping his father run their hotel or to devoting the rest of his life to music in England. Restless to discover other lands and opportunities, John excitedly turned his sights to Western Australia, then California, and finally on to the Klondike in search of fortune.

It is estimated that 100,000 persons had set out for the Klondike, driven by the desire to pan and mine for gold, but only 30,000–40,000 ever reached their destination. Most could not bear the primitive living conditions of living in the wilderness or the brutal weather. There were no roads or rail links to get there and you had to hack your way through the dense forests. From the early days of the gold rush in 1886 only a few hundred miners had crossed over the Chilkoot Pass and on down the Yukon River. However, during the peak of the gold rush from 1896 to 1899, thousands had journied to the Klondike, many taking odd jobs in Skagway or Dawson City to earn enough money for the equipment necessary to mine for the gold they so fiercely desired. Some have estimated that only 4,000 people actually found gold during the Klondike gold rush, a mere four per cent of those who had started out. Of those 4,000 souls only a handful of people made their fortune and were able to live the life of luxury for the rest of their days. Regardless of their fortune, in later life those who did reach the Klondike looked back on the experience fondly. John Collishaw was no exception.

"Jack" met his wife Sadie in Oakland, California, and they were married in 1892. "Jack was a coal miner who entered the United States via Ellis Island. Sadie, one of a family of eleven children, came from Newport, Monmouthshire, and had immigrated with two of her sisters to America."[1]

John was forced to take a number of different jobs to finance his penchant for prospecting, and therefore landed in Nanaimo to work in the coal mines. Their son, Raymond, was born on November 22, 1893 in Nanaimo and spent most of his early years there, attending the Nanaimo Public School. He was but a young lad during the peak of the Klondike gold rush from 1896 to 1899. Raymond followed his parents to Victoria and later to Oakland, California for schooling while his father prospected for gold in the California gold fields. John Edward Collishaw died in 1923 in Australia, still searching for the gold he never found.

Raymond completed his schooling in the summer of 1908. Because Raymond's father was a good friend of the Canadian government's Superintendent of Fisheries for British Columbia, he arranged for Raymond to obtain a position with the Fisheries Protection Service. The British government had, in 1906, withdrawn its Royal Naval Squadron from Esquimalt, leaving the Fisheries Protection cruisers as the only Canadian government ships on the Pacific coast.

> .... there had been some hope for the establishment of a meaningful naval presence when the Naval Service Act was passed by Sir Wilfred Laurier's Liberal government. Under the Act, which received royal ascent on May 4, 1910, the Dominion of Canada undertook to provide for its own naval defence. In the event of a declaration of war by Britain, Canada's naval forces would be placed at the disposal of the British Admiralty. This lodged responsibility for the protection of Canada's shores with the Admiralty as part of the overall strategic plan. A Department of the Naval Service was created and a Canadian born retired Royal Navy officer, Charles E. Kingsmill, was given the position of Director of the Naval Service. He held the rank of vice-admiral.[2]

The Fisheries Protection Service now came under Kingsmill's direction and control. Based out of Esquimalt, the crews of its ships (painted naval grey) wore naval uniforms, and the officers were commissioned by the Federal government out of Ottawa, where all crew members were paid from.

Raymond joined his first ship, the *Alcedo*, on August 1, 1908 at the tender age of fifteen. He was the cabin boy, although his duties more resembled that of a junior seaman. He was the youngest member of the crew, and like most boys of his age he was attracted to the smart uniform consisting of a blue jacket with gilt (gold-coloured) buttons and a peaked white cap with an impressive looking naval badge on the front. The CGS *Alcedo* was typical of the Fisheries Protection Services vessels of the time. Built of wood, she was 69 feet long, was registered as over 140,000 pounds, and was powered by coal-burning steam boilers. The food was good and the work was interesting.

Collishaw found his life on board the Fisheries Protection Services vessels and the work they performed reasonably good, provided you did what was asked of you and you worked hard.

The ships were based at Esquimalt near Victoria on the southern tip of Vancouver Island, but during the autumn and winter months the Fisheries Protection vessels ventured further north toward the Alaskan Panhandle. Their role was to guard the fishing grounds against poachers from other countries, mainly the United States, and to inspect all fishing boats, both Canadian and those from other nations, to ensure they complied with the rules and regulations in place at the time. Often Collishaw witnessed vessels operating illegally and was excited, as any young man would be, to come upon an unsuspecting vessel that was fishing illegally. In those cases the crew had to tow the captured boat to port and place the offenders into the hands of the authorities.

Life onboard a ship had its lonely moments and periods of boredom, especially when anchored by some desolate northern British Columbia island. Crew members had to find their own way of passing the time. For some it was taking in the spectacular scenery, for others it was playing a game of cards or telling tall tales of the sea. For Collishaw it was studying for his Mate's Certificate, which he obtained in 1911, and for his Passenger Master's Certificate, received in 1914.

On June 1, 1910 Collishaw joined the vessel CGS *Restless* as a seaman. He was made First Officer aboard the same ship on May 1, 1913. From October 1, 1913 to October 31, 1915 Collishaw was a Mate, then First Officer aboard the CGS *Fispa*. This rating brought Collishaw the privilege of dining alone with the Captain. The *Fispa* was a large, ocean-going yacht and was lavishly appointed. It was covered in varnish, making it a pain in the neck for the crew to keep looking in good form. You were considered very lucky and part of an elite group of sailors if you were a crew member of the *Fispa*.

Sometime in 1914 the *Fispa* was sent up through the Bering Straight into the Canadian Arctic, presumably in search of the vessel *Karluk*. The steamer *Karluk* was one of the vessels in the Stefansson Artic expedition, sponsored by the Canadian government. It had been crushed in the ice and sank. Some eight men were lost in this tragic disaster.

A number of publications, including current websites and books on First World War flyers, refer to Raymond Collishaw as having been a crew member on either Captain Scott's Antarctic expedition of 1910 or going with Shackleton on a similar voyage. However, none of these stories are accurate.

At the outbreak of the First World War in August of 1914, the *Fispa*, along with other vessels, was employed on examination duties, minesweeping, patrol duties, and as "lookout" ships (in addition to their fishery protection work, which became a secondary function) along the coast of British Columbia. The *Fispa* was sent to patrol the Hecate Straights in the Queen Charlotte Islands.

Collishaw applied for a more active role in the Naval Service, but to no avail. His future would lie not on the seas, but in the air.

≡2≡

RECRUITED INTO THE ROYAL NAVAL AIR SERVICE

EARLY IN 1915 RAYMOND COLLISHAW HEARD THAT THE ROYAL NAVAL Air Service (RNAS) was recruiting pilots in Canada. He couldn't apply, however, until his shipboard duties were over. Upon leaving the Hecate Straights and arriving in Esquimalt harbour, Collishaw put in an application. It was a number of months before he was given an interview by a senior naval officer.

Canada did not have an air force at the time. Some initial attempts were made by Canada's vitriolic Minister of Militia and Defence, Colonel Sam Hughes in the fall of 1914 but they failed to materialize into anything. The formation of the British Royal Flying Corps (RFC), however, dated back to 1912. The Cabinet, by Royal Warrant, on April 13, 1912 had created the Royal Flying Corps, and intended it to embrace all naval and military flying.[1]

> The apparent subservience of all forms of naval aviation to an army corps was much resented by the senior

service, and the Admiralty, independently and without authority, having developed its own training centre at Eastchurch, established an autonomous existence for its flying branch by proclaiming the birth of the Royal Naval Air Service. Such was the political clout of the Admiralty at that time that this brazen act of unilateralism went unchallenged. It was not officially recognized as the Royal Naval Air Service until July 1, 1914.[2]

Therefore, the existence of two separate air services meant that both the RFC and the RNAS were vying for the same talent pool of pilots, both in Britain and in Canada. The two separate services were also in competition for the limited resources required for the design and construction of aircraft. While the RFC built its own aircraft factory at Farnborough, the RNAS preferred to deal with the private sector and approached such firms as A.V. Roe, Shorts, Sopwith, Vickers, and Handley Page.[3] It was this proclivity to the private sector that led the RNAS to contact the Curtiss Aeroplane Company of Hammondsport, New York through one of their associates, J.A.D. McCurdy.

McCurdy, a Canadian legend in his own right, made the first successful airplane flight in Canada on February 23, 1909 when he piloted the *Silver Dart* for half a mile over the ice of Baddeck Bay. McCurdy was a friend of the family of Dr. Alexander Graham Bell, who maintained a summer home near Baddeck, McCurdy's hometown on Cape Breton Island in Nova Scotia. Bell had been experimenting there for a number of years with kites.

By 1907 his work had reached a point where he needed the help of a trained engineering staff to achieve practical results. What was known as the Aerial Experiment Association was formed under Bell's leadership. It was financed by Mrs. Bell and its aim was to "get into the air" by means of a powered, manned flying machine. The Association included two young Canadians recently graduated in engineering from the University of Toronto, John Alexander, Douglas

McCurdy and Frederick Walter Baldwin.... Both were keenly interested in aviation. The other members, both American, were Glenn H. Curtiss who had gained a reputation for building light and reliable motor cycle engines, and Lt. Thomas Selfridge, an artillery officer.[4]

It was through the Aerial Experiment Association that McCurdy and Curtiss became friends and associates. Curtiss hired McCurdy to lobby the Government of Canada to build aircraft in Canada, for the war effort.

McCurdy had made a proposal to the government of Sir Robert Borden that Canada form an aviation corps, purchasing machines from the Curtiss firm. Borden was not interested but did pass on the proposal to the British Admiralty and War Office in February and March of 1915 respectively. The War Office wasn't interested but the Admiralty was, and on March 26, 1915 placed an order for aircraft from the Curtiss Company, fifty of which were to be produced in Canada.

The Admiralty's proposition came as a direct consequence of a North American visit by Captain William Leslie Elder, Inspecting Captain of Aircraft Building in the Admiralty's Air Department. There seems little doubt that aircraft procurement in the United States was the reason — or one of the main reasons — for his mission. In fact, the Admiralty order of March 26 was probably placed with the Curtiss firm by Elder personally ... Curtiss and McCurdy must have had good reason to anticipate the decision to produce Admiralty aircraft in Canada, because on February 18, 1915 federal incorporation papers were taken out for a Toronto-based company known as Curtiss Aeroplanes and Motors, Ltd. The firm began operations on April 12 with McCurdy as its managing director.[5]

McCurdy was also instrumental in the establishment of a private flying school in Toronto, known as the Curtiss Flying School.[6]

The RNAS had begun its recruiting drive for pilots in Canada around the middle of April 1915 by placing ads in local newspapers. Arrangements were also made with the Canadian Naval Service Headquarters in Ottawa (headed by Admiral Charles Kingsmill) to recruit pilots for the RNAS, and for those accepted to obtain their flying certificates from the Curtiss School in Toronto.[7]

> Recruitment began almost immediately in Ottawa and at the naval establishments on the east and west coasts. It was limited to British subjects of "pure European descent" and preference was given to those between nineteen and twenty-three years of age, thirty being the maximum age limit. Successful applicants, having been interviewed and medically examined, were declared to be "candidates", meaning that they had been accepted into the RNAS on the condition that they obtain their pilot certificates.[8]

Raymond Collishaw answered the call for recruits in July 1915, and having been interviewed in Esquimalt, British Columbia, was sent to Ottawa in August for an interview in front of Admiral Kingsmill himself. Kingsmill was impressed with Collishaw's record of service and the interview must have gone well, as Collishaw was accepted as a Temporary Probationary Flight Sub-Lieutenant. The rank alone does not give off an air of permanence, but Collishaw was determined to learn to fly. He transferred from the Royal Canadian Navy to the Royal Naval Air Service on August 27, 1915. Collishaw was left to search out available flying schools on his own, and pay for the lessons and his room and board, wherever he ended up.

The only flying school at that time was the Curtiss School in Toronto, so Collishaw made his way there. The Curtiss School charged all students $400 for flying training, including 400 minutes of flying time. Four hundred dollars was an enormous amount at the time, which few people could afford. The Curtiss School had two locations, Centre Island just offshore from Toronto harbour and Long Branch, west of the city. The Long Branch field, where three hangars were built, may justly be called Canada's first proper airfield.[9] Centre Island airport operates to this day, and Long Branch is a suburb of Toronto surrounded by other boroughs of the Greater Toronto Area.

Library and Archives Canada, C-07117.

Flight Sub-Lieutenant Raymond Collishaw (second from right) with a group of RNAS trainee pilots.

The Curtiss school had Curtiss F-type flying boats at their Centre Island location and Curtiss Jennys, or JN-3s as they were known, at Long Branch. The Reynolds-Alberta Museum in Wetaskiwin, home of Canada's Aviation Hall of Fame, has a restored Curtiss Jenny, similar to those flown by students at the Curtiss school, hanging from the ceiling of its foyer.

Collishaw was accepted by the Curtiss School in September so he paid a $50 deposit against the required $400 fee and waited his turn to be instructed. He was number 197 on the waiting list and was told it would be four to six weeks before he could start his training.

Not to be outdone by the RNAS, the War Office sent one of its own to recruit pilots in Canada for the RFC.

On June 20 Captain Alec Ross-Hume arrived in Canada to oversee RFC recruiting. After a brief survey of the situation he reported to the War Office that there were "absolutely no trained aviators out here of any kind". He then visited the Toronto school to see if he could lure recruits into the RFC.[10]

Ross-Hume explained to the Canadian recruits the advantages of joining the RFC and promised the RNAS recruits that they would receive commissions as Second Lieutenants if they switched allegiances. Many decided to join the RFC and abandon the RNAS. Coincidently, Royal Navy Captain Elder of the Air Division of the Admiralty was visiting Toronto at the same time as Hume. He got wind of the poaching going on by the RFC representative and immediately sent a telegram to the Admiralty asking for authority to commission Canadian pilots, which was granted. Captain Elder then visited the Curtiss School and pointed out that RNAS recruits would be commissioned as Flight Sub-Lieutenants, a higher rank than army Second Lieutenants and would receive higher pay! The recruits then flocked back to the RNAS. It wasn't until 1917 that the RFC established a formal recruiting program in Canada, with its headquarters in Toronto, and its training carried out at Camp Borden, Ontario and locations in the Toronto area.

The Curtiss School graduated its first students in July of 1915, but by the fall of that year the school had a significant backlog of students waiting to commence their training. Many candidates, knowing the school was plugged with hopefuls, went to the United States in search of other flying schools. Others joined the army to get overseas sooner and then enlist in the flying corps once they reached England. It is estimated that in mid-November, 1915 there were some 100 RFC and 150 RNAS candidates waiting for certificate training, most of whom had signed up at the Toronto school.[11]

Many of the recruits were treated poorly or had little funds to stay a long time waiting for their turn to learn to fly. Those from well-to-do families had no problem, but others, who had come from long distances to train in Toronto, faced grave financial difficulties and did not have the funds to pay for their room and board. Some barely had enough money to eat. Many had given up their full-time jobs in order to learn to fly for Britain and the Empire. One RNAS candidate in particular, Hubert W. Eades, wrote to the Department of Naval Services (DNS) on October 25, 1915, of his plight.

> ... I have been in training now at the Curtiss School
> for about five weeks and the end of the course is not in

sight. We were told by the Curtiss Co. that our course would take from four weeks to six weeks. We find on arriving in Toronto, some of us from the remotest part of Canada, as in my own case, some of us with just enough money to czrry [sic] us through the supposed six weeks of training, that the course usually takes from 2 to 4 or 5 months, and many of us promise soon to be in grave financial situation. There has been no flying at the school at all for a fortnight and there promises to be practically none at all this winter, for the weather will be totally unsuited for flying of an instructional nature…. Cannot the Department do something in the matter?… As it stands now, I and many others are stranded in Toronto, and likely to be stranded for the winter unless the Department can arrange something for us…. I myself have resigned a lucrative position in Victoria B.C. to come to this school. I have sacrificed much for the opportunity of becoming a Flying Officer. Now the shadow of disappointment looms ahead. Many of us are in the same position.[12]

DNS replied that the matter would be taken up with the Admiralty, but some of the RNAS candidates could not wait any longer. It was decided that a deputation of three would travel to Ottawa to plead their case to the Minister of Defence, Mr. Sam Hughes. Hughes met the deputation and in his usual contemptuous and pompous fashion replied that they should join the infantry and there was no need for an air service. Had Hughes visited the front, he would have realized that thousands of young men were dying on the battlefield, desperately in need of air support.

So what were these trainees to do? Money was running out and the Curtiss School had suspended operations for the winter. McCurdy had thought of opening a school in Bermuda because of its milder weather, but no one would commit to getting the students there. On November 22, 1915 the Admiralty communicated by letter to Canada's Department of Naval Services outlining how it intended to handle the uncertified RNAS pilots in waiting.

Group of candidates for the RNAS aboard the HMCS Niobe. *Front row (left to right): G.E. Nash, Raymond Collishaw, Arnold J. Chadwick. Rear row (left to right): C.E. Pattison, Q. S. Sherriff, R.A. Campbell, Kenneth Y. Sinclair.*

Sir,

The following arrangements have been arrived at with the Admiralty with regard to accepted candidates for the Royal Naval Air Service:

Forty-eight will be sent to England in batches of twelve between now and the New Year and the remainder will be sent over as convenient after the New Year. It is anticipated that all will be sent to England by about the middle of March, 1916.

$1.25 per day will be paid to meet living expenses for each day, for a reasonable time, in excess of seven weeks under training at the Flying School. A form of declaration in connection with this is enclosed. If not already made out, it should be filled in and returned without delay to the Secretary of this Department.

Candidates who are already training may adopt either of the three following schemes:

Scheme 1. Remain at School to complete their training and be sent to England as Probationary Flight Sub-Lieutenants as soon as they have passed their test flights.

Scheme 2. Give up the attempt to obtain their certificates in Canada, return to their homes and await their turn to be sent to England, there to complete their training.

Scheme 3. Give up the attempt to obtain their certificates in Canada, enrol as Able Seamen in the Royal Naval Canadian Volunteer Reserve and be sent to the "Niobe" at Halifax, there to undergo a course of training in Gunnery, Signals, Seamanship, First Aid and generally obtain an insight into Naval life and routine, and then be sent to England in turn to complete their flying training.

Whilst in the "Niobe" they would receive pay at the rate of .85 cents [sic] per day, be supplied with the necessary uniform and accommodated in the ship. It should be understood that those who select to go to the "Niobe' would not be treated as Officers. They would, however, mess, drill and be instructed together.

Each accepted candidate should decide immediately which of these schemes he intends to adopt and inform the Secretary of this Department accordingly at once....

— H.C. Pinsent (Signed)
Secretary[13]

Admiral Kingsmill of DNS immediately sent off instructions from Ottawa to the Commanding Officer of HMCS *Niobe* via the Captain Superintendent HMC Dockyard at Halifax, Nova Scotia as follows:

It has been decided to raise a special company of the R.N.C.V.R. from the many applicants of the Royal Naval Air Service, who have been training in Canada.

Owing to the inclement weather the training schools have closed and the Admiralty have instructed the Department to send the candidates to England, but only in batches, which will necessitate a large number of them being left in this country for some time.

As a large number of these young gentlemen have given up their civil employment for the purpose of the training, the Department has offered to raise a company of the R.N.C.V.R. and is sending them to Halifax where they are to be trained in signalling, wireless telegraphy, squad drill, machine gun drill as far as possible, and a short course of ammunition and generally brushed up so that they may have an insight into Naval matters when they reach the other side.

It is highly desirable, without making too many invidious distinctions, that this class should be kept to themselves and treated with as much consideration as proper discipline will allow.

They are to be kitted up with sufficient uniform to keep them comfortably dressed and new winter clothing provided on loan, it being pointed out to them that any loss &c. [sic] through neglect will have to be charged against them.

It may be some time before all the men who wish to join are sent to Halifax, but a party of four or five are leaving Toronto Thursday in charge of a Petty Officer created for the moment, R. Collishaw. Everything should be ready for their arrival on board and they are to be made

Library and Archives Canada, PA-118992.

Group of candidates for the RNAS aboard HMCS Niobe. *Front row (left to right): A. C. Dissette, Raymond Collishaw, Arnold J. Chadwick, Lloyd A. Sands, H.M. Hill, Kenneth Y. Sinclair, Q.S. Shirriff, G.E. Nash. Rear row (left to right): C.E. Pattison, Gordon C. Dingwall.*

as comfortable as possible and the situation realised be [sic] the Officers of NIOBE. The drafting Master at Arms is to take this matter up.

C.E. Kingsmill,
Vice Admiral
Director of Naval Service[14]

The *Niobe* was an elderly Royal Naval cruiser that had been given to the Royal Canadian Navy by the British Admiralty. The armoured cruiser HMCS *Niobe* was the fledgling Canadian Navy's first ship. It had arrived in Halifax harbour on October 21, 1910. By then the thirteen-year-old ship, with a crew of approximately 700 RN officers and ratings and carrying sixteen 6-inch guns, was already obsolete. She was, however, the first tangible evidence that Wilfred Laurier's Naval Service Act of May, 1910, was being implemented.

With both Britain and Germany locked in an arms race to see who could build the most battleships in the shortest possible time, the British government had requested financial assistance from the Canadian government and the governments of her other dominions. Debate in Canada had raged for months over whether to provide the requested funds for the construction of new battleships or whether Canada should build her own fleet. Laurier's government, wanting a way to show its independence from Britain, passed the Naval Service Act which created Canada's independent navy. In the event of war the Canadian government would decide which of its ships would be placed under the control of the British Admiralty. In this event, the Admiralty would exercise its control for the duration of the war.

Admiral Sir Charles Kingsmill, who had recently retired from the RN and who was born in Guelph, Ontario, was asked to be the first head of the new Canadian Naval Service. He agreed without hesitation.

What was intended in the letter and the instructions given to the officers of the *Niobe* from Admiral Kingsmill, were a far cry from what actually took place. No uniforms of any kind were given out, nor was it ever mentioned to the group that such amenities were being provided. Those candidates sent to the *Niobe*, numbering about eighteen, had to obtain their Royal Navy Flight Sub-Lieutenant uniforms from local tailors at their own expense. All members of the party lived privately on shore, also at their own expense. Typical of the behaviour of the Royal Navy at the time, the Captain of the *Niobe* and her Officers did their best to ignore Collishaw and the rest of the group. The only contact Collishaw and the others had with the crew members of *Niobe* was when they took their meals on the mess deck. All instruction was given on shore at the dockyard from 9:00 a.m. until 4:00 p.m. each day. Collishaw found the instruction excellent as it provided to those who had no previous experience in the Navy, a practical introduction to its customs and operations. This basic training turned out to be useful later on when the pilots attended ground training in England.

Collishaw didn't know the contents of Admiral Kingsmill's letter to the Commanding Officer of the *Niobe* (quoted above) and was unaware he was supposed to have been appointed Petty Officer in charge of the group. To his knowledge, he was just an Able Seaman like all the other members of the R.N.C.V.R. company.

RFC/RNAS reunion. Raymond Collishaw is fourth from left.

Library and Archives Canada, C-087001.

Collishaw remained with the *Niobe* until early January, 1916 when he and another candidate were sent to Ottawa. There they found out they were being sent to England — welcome news indeed after all they had been through. Raymond Collishaw was appointed a temporary Flight Sub-Lieutenant on probation on January 10, 1916 by Admiral Pinsent, DMS secretary and sent by rail to New York City. There, Collishaw and a number of other candidates boarded the White Star liner *Adriatic* and set off for England on January 12, 1916. The other candidates included: Charles E. Pattison, Patrick S. Kennedy, Henry M. Hill, James A. Shaw, William H. Chisam, Lloyd S. Breadner, Robert A. Campbell, Ellis Vair Reid, and William E. Robinson. We will hear more about many of these young flyers later on.

These were some of the many Canadians who signed up to fly for England in the First World War. It is estimated that during 1915 and 1916 the RFC and the RNAS recruited about 650 pilots from Canada and that by the end of the war some 19,000 to 20,000 Canadians had served in the RFC, the RNAS, and the Royal Air Force (after the RFC and RNAS were merged).[15]

≡3≡

TRAINING IN ENGLAND

SHORTLY AFTER ARRIVING IN ENGLAND, RAYMOND COLLISHAW WAS sent to the naval air station at Redcar, on the northeastern English coast looking out over the North Sea, near the port of Middlesborough. There, along with P.S. Kennedy, J.A. Shaw, L.S. Breadner, E.V. Reid, and W.E. Robinson they commenced their flight training. Redcar was a small RNAS school and there was no officer's mess available, so pilots in training had to live in the village located about a half a mile from school, and at their own expense. They walked to and from the school four times a day. Redcar was one of about four training centres the RNAS had in England at the time.

Flight Sub-Lieutenant L.S. Breadner of Carleton Place, Ontario, one of the young Canadian arrivals to Redcar, wrote of his first impressions as…. "A splendid station, well equipped and we will be started flying at once …" "How clannish the Canucks are," Breadner noted, but "… we are all willing to fly on any kind of a day and that's what pleases the C.O…. he is tickled with us and is trying to get all the Canadians he can here."[1]

It was the RNAS and not the RFC that looked after the defence of the English coast. Their role, therefore, was critical in the defence of England against air attack by Zeppelin air ships or by bomber aircraft. The RNAS had other duties as well including reconnaissance for the fleet, flying anti-submarine patrols, and providing aerial protection for coastal convoys.[2] The RNAS air stations along the English coast were the first line of defence against air attack. The British public were shocked to learn that they were vulnerable to attack by Zeppelin and, later on in the war, by German Gotha bombers. The Zeppelin raids did little damage but caused panic in some cases and huge public concern. England was no longer impervious to attack.

As far as the training of pilots went, the RNAS air schools paid scant attention to any difference between a Canadian who had been trained in Canada and an untrained Canadian. Both students were required to start afresh on their training. Collishaw arrived at Redcar on February 4, 1916. At that time, Redcar was under the command of Commodore Paine. Collishaw made his first dual flight on February 10, 1916 with Flight Sub-Lieutenant Golding at the controls of a G3 Caudron. This dual flight lasted thirty minutes and the aircraft reached an altitude of 3,800 feet.

Many of the flight instructors treated the new trainees with disdain, especially if they were from the colonies! They often did not allow their trainees to touch the controls, but only watch as the instructor flew the machine. Some instructors had little interest in their charges and had received no specific training as an instructor. It was generally believed that anyone with flying experience also had the ability to teach the skill.

Imagine Collishaw's excitement as Golding started the engine! It sputtered at first, then Golding revved the engine, taxied along the grass runway and into the wind. Gradually, the Caudron became airborn. Collishaw could feel the wind in his face, looking down on the rural English countryside, and gazing off towards the horizon at the North Sea. Although he was not in control of the craft, it must have been thrilling to be able to fly like a bird a mere seven years after the birth of flight in Canada. Some have described this magnificent experience as "dancing in the air."

Two days later, Collishaw was taken up by Flight Sub-Lieutenant Roper for a fifteen-minute local flight at 2,500 feet. Collishaw was starting to learn how to use the controls, how to turn, and how to keep the Caudron stable in the air.

The French-built G3 Caudron was an ungainly looking machine that resembled a box kite with a tail at one end and two wings at the other. It had an open fuselage consisting of four rods joining the tail to the wings and engine. This was a two-seater tractor biplane — meaning the propeller was located at the front of the plane — with an upper wing that was almost twice the span of the lower.

The ground school portion of the training included such subjects as the theory of flight, engine maintenance, rigging, map reading, aerial navigation, meteorology, and cross country flying. In the latter case, students were instructed to look for significant geographical landmarks to assist them in locating where they were and how to get home. Rigging training related to the cross wires of the aircraft, which reinforced the struts and the two wings and kept everything strong and taunt. The trainees were also given lectures on the various types of engines and the particular aspects of such aircraft as the G3 Caudrons, the Avro 504c, and the Grahame-White Type XV. Although the instructors had more flying time and experience than their trainees, many were not versed in proper ways of teaching. Some just lectured, while others went through the material at such a speed that none of the trainees could follow what was being said.

Because of poor weather, Collishaw's next flight wasn't until April 21. He flew three times in April, always with either Golding or Flight Sub-Lieutenant Roper. Collishaw was given the controls and practiced handling the Caudron himself. At times Collishaw was unable to control the lateral movement of the aircraft as the left wing would dip lower than the right. The control column, or joy stick as it was later called, was used to manoeuver the machine, to raise or lower it, and to move it from side to side — it controlled the aircraft's "pitch and roll," in other words. On a number of occasions the pilot had to take over control of the machine when it was too bumpy aloft. Collishaw flew dual fourteen times in May, 1916, mostly in Caudron number 3280. He practised takeoffs, banking turns, lateral control of the aircraft, and landings, some of the latter being quite bumpy. By his own admission Raymond Collishaw was not a stellar pilot. Landings, in particular, bothered him. For example, sometimes he would flatten out too soon, meaning he would complete his dive toward the landing area and be horizontal with the ground, ready to land. Flattening out too soon could result in landing short of the runway and encountering any number of obstacles such as trees, bushes, or other obstructions that preceeded the landing area. Collishaw knew, however, the proper rate of climb and descent of the machine, and the speed at which he should make a proper landing. Knowing the theory of flight and putting that theory into practice, however, are two different things. By the end of May, 1916, Collishaw had logged over five hours of flying time. He had better control of the aircraft now and his takeoffs and landings were gradually improving. Collishaw felt stupid, though, every time he made a bumpy landing. Normally, after the trainee had completed four hours of dual instruction, the instructor would begin to consider sending the pupil off to do his solo tests. When the pupil had passed the tests he would move on to fly an Avro.

During the first two weeks of June, Collishaw was up in the Caudron doing left circuits (going around the aerodrome in a counter-clockwise direction), practicing takeoffs and landings with Flight Lieutenant Roper. Raymond Collishaw soloed on June 16, 1916, after having logged eight hours and twenty-three minutes dual time mainly in Caudrons. Finally he was on his own in the sky and totally in control of the machine. He spent a full fifty minutes flying around the countryside at 3,200 feet to Slatburn and back. As the sun was setting he landed at Redcar. It was almost 10:30 p.m. This solo flight gave Collishaw the confidence he needed to improve his flying. It must have been a thrilling experience being in control of the machine, and a great adventure for him.

Collishaw also soloed twice on June 19 and twice on June 20. On these flights he had mechanical problems with his machine, which were common, often having to do with the engine or the fuel system. Broken inlet valves and blown air intake connection pipes were common examples of such problems.

Pilots found their engines cutting out completely, and sometimes when wanting to switch the engine off, it did not respond. Pilots were trained to use a technique referred to as "blipping" or switching the ignition on and off by pressing and releasing a button known as the blip switch.

Collishaw flew an Avro for the first time on June 22, 1916 and experienced engine trouble so he had to make a forced landing that ended up damaging the undercarriage of the aircraft. The next day he was up in a different Avro 504 and at 15 feet the engine started to miss. Collishaw barely made it over two hedges before crashing in a field of crops, damaging his propeller and undercarriage. He spent the remainder of June and the first half of July flying the Avro. He began to practice cross-country flights and tried his hand at dropping Verey lights (flares which were used for signalling) on targets to simulate a bombing run.

The Avro 504 was a more advanced airplane than the Caudron G3 in that it had a fully covered fuselage and rotary 80-horsepower engine. However, its top speed was a mere 82 miles per hour at ground level and it had a rate of climb of seven minutes to get to 3,500 feet. The plane weighed 924 pounds without any load, had a wingspan of only 36 feet, and a length of 29 feet, 5 inches.[3] While at Redcar, Collishaw also flew the Grahame-White Type XV and the American-built Curtiss JN-4.

Given the broad mandate of the RNAS for coastal defence against air attack, people had to be trained to fly a wide variety of aircraft, from airships, blimps, and balloons to seaplanes, flying boats, and ship-borne aircraft. They also had to train fighter pilots for the Naval Fighter Squadrons operating with the RFC in Europe. The RFC, however, was solely tasked with training pilots for fighter and bomber duties at the front in France and Belgium. Collishaw found the instruction he received mediocre. Senior RNAS officers believed that once a pilot had received his flying certificate he could fly any type of machine.

At the time of the great Battle of the Somme, which began on July 1, 1916, Collishaw was practicing flying cross-country in northern England. On July 11 he made a cross country flight to Darlington and Northallerton, a distance of about 55 miles, but his engine stopped completely so he was forced to land in a farmer's field, partly destroying the machine's undercarriage. During the latter part of July, Collishaw flew a Curtiss JN-4 that had a wheel control, similar to the steering wheel of an automobile, instead of a control stick. Both had the same function but it was difficult for pilots to adjust to the wheel controls after being accustomed to using a stick control mechanism.

Life wasn't all work for Collishaw during his stay at Redcar. During most weekends he had time to visit relatives in London and Edinburgh, and to take in the night life, which was primarily at the music halls.

On July 16, 1916, Collishaw was transferred to the RNAS gunnery school at Eastchurch on the Isle of Sheppey at the mouth of the Thames River. He flew Curtiss JN-3s and Maurice Farman S.11 Shorthorns. The

Shorthorn was a pusher aircraft with the propeller behind the cockpit, which pushed the machine along. This two-seater aircraft could be likened to a box kite due to its series of rods joining the tail to the engine and cockpit. The Shorthorn measured 30 feet, 6 inches long and had a top wingspan of 51 feet, 9 inches. It weighed 1,442 pounds without a load and had a top speed of 72 miles per hour.[4] By this time Raymond Collishaw had logged thirty-three hours, twenty of which were solo.

When he wasn't in the pilot seat, Collishaw was in the second seat of a two-seater machine, which was the passenger or observer seat. He practiced dropping dummy bombs, Verey lights, and firing the Lewis machine gun. The students at Eastchurch were also required to perform a training manoeuver called "balloon chasing." During this exercise, the aircraft would approach a hot air balloon, used to observe troop movements and gun placements, as if it were an enemy, and get into position to fire on it. On the ground, the pilots would practice shooting the Lewis machine gun from a stationary position at targets that were moving in front of them, much like an enemy aircraft would. Collishaw and his colleagues were also taught deflection shooting, which required aiming where they expected the target to be once their bullets struck rather than aiming where the target was at the exact moment they shot.

One of Collishaw's instructors at the time was Flight Sub-Lieutenant John Alcock. He, along with Arthur Brown, would make the first non-stop flight across the Atlantic after the war. Upon completing the course at Eastchurch at the end of July, Raymond Collishaw was confirmed as Flight Sub-Lieutenant, meaning he was no longer probationary.

Collishaw's first operational posting was with 3 Naval Wing at Manston, near Margate, on the eastern-most tip of Kent some twenty miles to the north of Dover. It should be noted that a Wing consisted of a number of Squadrons, typically three or four. Manston had been created as a Royal Naval Station due to the deficiencies of two other Stations, Detling and Westgate. Detling was found to be unsuitable for night flying and Westgate had a very small landing surface, the end of which was a cliff.

In May of 1916, 3 Naval Wing moved to Manston and brought with them two BE2cs; a Short biplane, probably a 184 model; four Sopwith 1 1/2 Strutters; and a Curtiss Biplane. Collishaw's posting to Manston was effective August 2, 1916. While at Manston, Collishaw was under

Squadron Commander R. L.G. Marix, DSO. The day after his arrival, Collishaw flew a BE2c and practiced dropping bombs. It was his first experience flying a BE2c. The BE2c was a two-seater bomber with a wingspan of almost 37 feet, a length of over 27 feet, and a height of over 11 feet. This aircraft was powered by a 90-horsepower engine. The BE2c was different than previous models of the BE series in that it had staggered wings, with the top wing ahead of the lower. It also featured ailerons for better manoeuvrability. Ailerons are the movable surfaces at the trailing edge of a wing that control the rolling and banking of the aircraft.

Wing Commander W. L. Elder was in charge of 3 Naval Wing and his instructions were to take the Wing to Luxeuil, near Nancy, where they would carry out bombing missions against German targets. Elder was planning for the move to take place in July but plans were set back when the Somme offensive began on July 1, 1916. A number of Elder's Sopwith 1 1/2 Strutters were transferred to the Royal Flying Corps to be used for reconnaissance work before and during the battle.

Formed with the express purpose of bombing industrial targets inside Germany in retaliation for the German Zeppelin raids on Britain, 3 Naval Wing was the first British air unit formed specifically for the purpose of long-range strategic bombing. As such, it was the forerunner of later strategic bombing missions over Germany in the Second World War, led by Britain's RAF Bomber Command.

Most of Collishaw's flying while at Manston, during the months of August and September, 1916 was in the Short bombers. Despite its 250-horsepower engine, the Short bomber was a cumbersome machine to fly. It was a two-seater — one for the pilot and the other for the bombardier. Collishaw practiced in both roles. The bomb runs were made from Manston out to sea, dropping live bombs on pre-arranged targets. Manston was found to be a very misty place which added to the danger and difficulty of flying.

The airfield at Manston was not spacious, and the large, heavy Short bombers required as much space as was available. In order to assist the pilot, two ratings would usually hop on to the undercarriage as he taxied out to the end of the runway and then help him turn the plane around to get ready for takeoff. The ratings were members of the ground crew and were riggers or mechanics and the like. The Short had a big four-wheeled undercarriage with two sets of wheels positioned one ahead of the other. Apart from getting a blast from the propeller, hitching a lift in this fashion presented no particular difficulties.

The Short bomber was eventually found to be unsuitable for a bombing role. Although two of these types of machines were flown out to the air base in Luxeuil, France, they were never used in any of the Wing's raids. The more suitable machine was the Sopwith 1 1/2 Strutter. This biplane came in two types: the bomber, with a single seat; and the fighter version, a two-seater. Though more were on order, because of their scarcity at the time, Collishaw did not have many opportunities to fly the Strutters.

The situation that Collishaw found at Manston, in August of 1916, was that most pilots undergoing training were waiting for the additional Strutters to arrive. Collishaw was eventually selected to fly the fighter version, a decision that was to have important implications for his career during the rest of the war and thereafter.

His first experience in the Sopwith came on September 6, 1916 when he flew as a pilot with Flight Sub-Lieutenant Sharman as the gunlayer, or observer. They took off for a fifty-five minute flight out into the bay and back at 5,000 feet. For the next two weeks Collishaw practiced flying the 1 1/2 Strutters.

The 1 1/2 Strutter got its name from the arrangement of the upper wing centre section W-strut supports. Powered by a 110-horsepower or a 130-horsepower Clerget rotary engine, this two-seater biplane was armed with a fixed, forward-firing, synchronized Vickers .303 machine gun and a Lewis .303 machine gun pointing aft in the rear cockpit. The Strutters had a wingspan of 33 feet, 6 inches, a length of 25 feet and 3 inches. They had a weight of 1,305 pounds empty with a maximum weight of 2,150 pounds.[5] The fighter version was the first British aircraft to enter squadron service in France with a synchronized forward-firing machine gun. The bomber version was structurally identical but lacked the rear cockpit, its place being taken by the bomb compartment. The bomb load was stowed internally, and four 65-pounders could be carried. Most of 3 Naval Wing's Sopwith Strutters were powered by the 110-horsepower version of the Clerget engine, which gave the machine a top speed of 95 miles per hour at 10,000 feet. The aircraft had excellent endurance — more than four hours — which could be extended by fitting extra fuel tanks.[6]

Pilots of 3 Naval Wing, RNAS with Sopwith 1 1/2 Strutter aircraft. Left to right: Flight Sub-Lieutenants J.E. Sharman, H.C. Lemon, Raymond Collishaw.

On days off at Manston, the Canadian flyers would travel to Margate, a popular seaside resort town. On one trip, Collishaw and a fellow Canadian pilot met a couple of girls from a neighbouring village. They spent some time together that day and made plans to see one another soon. Collishaw and his fellow pilot accompanied the two girls to their homes and then headed back to Manston only to discover that Raymond's fellow pilot had received instructions to take one of the newly-arrived Strutters to France the next day. He quickly wrote a note to the girl he had taken quite a fancy to, explaining he had been posted away and asked Collishaw to drop it in the garden of the girl's home. To a pilot, this means flying over the house and dropping it from the plane, literally via airmail. Unfortunately for Collishaw his engine cut out just as he was over the girl's home at 50 feet and he ended up landing on the back houses behind the row of houses he was targeting. The parents of the girls were not amused.

Collishaw flew a number of practice flights in the 1 1/2 Strutter, often going out over Herne Bay, where he would test his machine gun. These flights were not without mishap, as in one instance he had to make a forced landing due to engine failure, and in doing so broke the axle of his undercarriage.

Collishaw was posted to the Luxeuil aerodrome on September 21, 1916. He and his gunner, Portsmouth, flew Sopwith Strutter number 9407, first to Paris, landing at Villa Coubly aerodrome. It was a flight of five hours and seven minutes. This was the longest cross-country flight Collishaw had yet taken. The next day they flew on to Luxeuil, which was about 65 miles south of the French city of Nancy and close to the Swiss border. With extra fuel tanks the 1 1/2 Strutter had an endurance of better than seven hours. Collishaw's navigational and cross-country flying abilities must have been excellent as there is no evidence of any problems along the way. Collishaw and Portsmouth were among the first to be posted to Luxeuil. It was not until October 14, 1916 that there were sufficient machines to allow the rest of 3 Naval Wing to follow.

3 NAVAL WING, LUXEUIL

THE ADMIRALTY HAD, AS ONE OF ITS PRIORITIES, FORMED WINGS WHOSE sole responsibility would be the bombing of German installations. This strategy brought it into conflict with the RFC, which questioned the use of Naval forces operating on the Western Front.

> The Admiralty was ... interested in a long-range bombing programme, which would employ the high-powered engines the navy virtually monopolized as the result of its agreement with the RFC at the beginning of the war. The Admiralty's preoccupation with strategic bombing heavily biased RNAS operations of 1916; moreover, it brought a confrontation with the RFC on several levels: at the level of high policy, over which service ought properly to carry out this role; at the operational level, over the question of control of

air activities on the Western Front; and at the level of production and supply, over how, and according to which priorities, aircraft and engine production ought to be shared between the two services.[1]

The British government attempted to obtain some cooperation of the two air forces by forming a Joint War Air Committee.

> It was the strategic bombing argument, combined with strong public dissatisfaction with the apparent failure of the two air services to collaborate effectively against zeppelin attacks, that led the British government to establish the Joint War Air Committee "for the interchange of ideas and the co-ordination of procedures." The committee, which consisted of Admiralty and War Office representatives, was established on February 24, 1916. It was short-lived.[2]

The Admiralty remained adamant and intransigent in regard to its plans to carry out the strategic bombing initiatives on its own. The British government's further attempts to obtain the cooperation of the Admiralty resulted in the establishment of the Air Board, whose chief architect was Lord Curzon, the former Viceroy to India.

> By that time, however, the Admiralty had unilaterally decided upon its own course of action. Nothing Curzon or the RFC representatives could say affected this. It had become clear in February that long-range bombing operations based on Dunkirk were only possible in co-ordination with and under the control of the Commander-in-Chief of the BEF (British Expeditionary Force). Nevertheless, the assumption by the RNAS of a strategic bombing role and the establishment of 3 Naval Bombing Wing at Luxeuil was a *fait accompli*. That decision had an important effect upon the capacity of the RNAS to carry out its other duties. Pilots for Luxeuil,

and for long-range operations from Dunkirk, had to come from somewhere. By the end of 1916 Luxeuil alone was employing roughly 20 per cent of all RNAS aeroplane pilots.[3]

As has been mentioned, 3 Naval Wing was the first British air unit formed for long-range strategic bombing. It was also the first British independent bombing force freed from flying against targets in direct support of immediate tactical objectives of the army or the navy.[4]

In May, 1916, the RNAS explored the idea of a joint operation with French air forces. The French had developed a similar proposal earlier, so the RNAS sent an officer to Paris to explore the willingness of the French to resurrect this plan for joint-bombing operations.

The Admiralty approved of the plan and started in June, 1916 to gather what was to be the nucleus of 3 Naval Wing at Manston. They named Elder as commander of the Wing and made him Wing Captain. Elder had set up the RNAS recruiting system back in early 1915. He was a rather big man and was nicknamed "Daddy" by the pilots because they were much younger than their commander. Wing Commander Richard Bell Davies was in charge of the Wing's overall operations and had much more flying experience than Elder, having been made a brevet pilot in 1911. Bell Davies had also flown in the Dardanelles campaign in 1915 with the original 3 Naval Wing, where he was awarded the Victoria Cross.

On June 16, 1916 a construction party consisting of one officer and 125 men left England for Luxeuil, near the Vosges Mountains, to commence erecting a camp. The ratings were billeted in the district while this work was being carried out. The Admiralty informed the French that machines would be sent to Luxeuil at a rate of six a week until a wing of 60 were formed. The plan was to eventually augment this number to 100 planes.[5]

The Air Board wrote to the Commander-in-Chief of the British army in France, Douglas Haig, asking if he had any objections to the formation of this wing which was to operate 200 miles from his command, and it is understood that a reply was received stating that there was no objection.[6]

The Admiralty impressed upon Elder that operations were not to be commenced until there were sufficient pilots and machines available to enable such operations to be effectively carried out. Elder was also provided with general instructions that the bombing objectives should be of military value and attacks on unfortified towns were not permitted.

Elder's report to the Admiralty shows the number of pilots and machines available at the beginning of each month the Wing was operating, in the following table:

Date	Number of Pilots	Machines Available
1916		
Sept.	12	12
Oct.	18	23
Nov.	40	25
Dec.	51	44
1917		
Jan.	56	43
Feb.	53	42
March	50	55
April	33	58[7]

So it wasn't until October that there were sufficient numbers for 3 Naval Wing to start carrying out bombing operations on its own. There was however, a joint French/British raid made on July 30, 1916 on the benzene stores at Mulhein. Three British and six French machines were involved and, although they were met with considerable anti-aircraft fire, they carried out a successful bombardment.[8] Two of the RNAS machines were flown by Canadians. Flight Sub-Lieutenant James A. Glen of Enderby, British Columbia, the pilot of a Sopwith 1 1/2 Strutter bomber, dropped his four 65-pounders in the target area. Flight Sub-Lieutenant Ernest C. Porter of Winnipeg, also on the raid, flew a Sopwith 1 1/2 Strutter fighter. All the raiding aircraft returned safely and French intelligence reported that "considerable damage" had been caused.[9]

Estimates vary as to the total number of Canadians with the RNAS. In his book *The Brave Young Wings*, Ronald Dodds, an RCAF historian states, "The 1915 Canadian recruiting programme had resulted in some 150 Canadians joining the RNAS and more were on the way. A large block of these recruits were finishing their service training in England and disperse [sic] them it was decided to post them to the new bombing unit."[10] S.F. Wise, in his official history of the Royal Canadian Air Force, *Canadian Airmen and the First World War*, mentions: "By December the Chief of the Naval Staff in Ottawa was enrolling pilot candidates at the rate of twenty-four a month. There were by this time some 300 Canadians in the RNAS, 230 of them among its total officer strength of 2,764. Most Canadian aeroplane pilots were with 3 Wing at Luxeuil, while most seaplane pilots were now on home stations."[11] In fact, of the seventy-four pilots who served with 3 Naval Wing, forty-four, or almost two-thirds, were Canadians and included such pilots as "Gus" Edwards, Collishaw, Redpath, Shearer, and Carter.

The French *4e Groupe de Bombardement*, under the command of *Capitaine* Felix Happe, shared the Luxeuil aerodrome with 3 Naval Wing. Happe was a big man, measuring over 6 feet tall with a black bushy beard parted in the middle and big black eyebrows. To complete the look he wore the black uniform of the French artillery. Very popular with his men, he commanded their loyalty with his significant experience as a pilot. He was popular with the officers of 3 Naval Wing who got to know him well. Although very imposing and fierce-looking, he had a gentle nature to him and a healthy sense of humour.

The Bombing Group consisted of three *escadrilles* (squadrons) including F. 29, flying Farman XLiis; F. 123, also equipped with Farman XLiis, and B.M. 120, which had Breguet-Michelin IVs, some nineteen machines in all. Assigned to escort Happe's bombers was *Escadrille N.124*, nicknamed the *Escadrille Americaine*. This squadron flew Nieuports and contained such notable flyers as Raoul Lufbery, Norman Prince, and Kiffin Rockwell, who was shot down a few weeks after Collishaw's arrival at Luxeuil.

Though in 1916 the United States had not yet entered the war and had declared itself to be neutral, many American flyers wanted to fight in the war alongside the French. Some Americans, like Kiffin Rockwell, fought in the French Foreign Legion, while others, like James McConnell, joined ambulance units. Norman Prince, a Harvard-educated lawyer, was intent on forming an American squadron in France. Prince, who had learned to fly in 1911, sailed to France on January 20, 1915. He lobbied the French government in Paris for the creation of the *Escadrille Americaine* but got a cool reception. By October 1915, there were seventeen Americans flying with various French squadrons which Prince wanted to consolidate into one united squadron. By April, 16, 1916 the *Escadrille Americaine*, or N 124, was a reality. Because the United States had declared themselves as neutral, the name of the squadron caused a stir in German diplomatic circles. Why was there an American squadron flying for France? Following such uproar, the name was swiftly changed to the *Lafayette Escadrille*. The squadron was led by French *Capitaine* Georges Thenault.

The squadron began its operational life at Luxeuil-les-Bains, a spa town dating back to Roman times. In 1916, the town had less than 1,000 inhabitants. Over the centuries this quaint French location was the vacation destination for nobility, including King Francis I, and later on, Louis XV and his court.

The role of *Escadrille* N 124 was to escort French bombers on bombing runs. Initially fitted out with Nieuport 11s, this machine, nicknamed Bebe, had a wingspan of 24 1/2 feet and a top speed of 100 miles per hour. It was powered by either an 80- or 110-horsepower Le Rhone engine, and equipped with a Lewis gun, which was mounted on top of the upper wing so the bullets would be fired above the propeller. The squadron was later equipped with the more powerful Nieuport 17.

Relations were good between the Canadians and the Americans in *Escadrille* N 124. If the weather was reasonable in between flights they played baseball, taking on each other in games. Sometimes, to pass the time, they played "no limit" poker, but on other occasions there was a five- or twenty-franc limit. Some players ran up winnings of up to 5,000 francs. Having run out of money, players would often scribble IOUs on pieces of toilet paper, which they threw into the pot.

Flight Sub-Lieutenant Stearne T. Edwards, a pilot in 3 Naval Wing from Carleton Place, Ontario, was a shrewd poker player and walked around with a bulge of toilet paper in his tunic. He was killed later in the war. Nothing more was heard of the IOUs.

Library and Archives Canada, PA-198357.

Sixteen Canadian flyers at Luxeuil-Les-Bains.

THE OBERNDORF RAID

By the end of September, both the French and the British had a sufficient enough stock of machines to plan a raid across the Rhine River into the German industrial heartland. The following quote is from Wing Commander R. Bell Davies's report to the Admiralty describing the Oberndorf raid.

> …. the French had three squadrons of Farmans and one of Breguet-Michelins fit for work, and Happe planned a long range attack on a German munitions factory at Oberndorf. We could by then contribute two fully trained flights of Strutters (10 bombers and 2 fighters). These constituted the Red Squadron. One flight very newly trained (5 bombers and 1 fighter) of Strutters, the first flight of the Blue Squadron. And one flight of Breguets, also very newly trained. We had adopted this Red and Blue organization for identification in the air. Each aircraft had a different design painted on the fuselage in the squadron colour.[12]

Red Squadron planes, for example, would have a white square painted on the side with a red diamond, diagonal bar, square, or rectangle within the white square to differentiate it from other planes. The Blue Squadron had a similar painting scheme only they had a blue shape within the white square. The Breguet V bombers were a completely different type of machine than the Strutters so they could be easily distinguished from the others. The Breguets were purchased from the French as a stop gap measure, because the Strutters were only trickling in to Luxeuil.

Captain Elder had acquired these Breguet V bombers on a trip to Paris. They were big lumbering machines, two-seaters, but the gunner/bombardier sat right at the front of the nacelle with the pilot behind. The engine was a 220-horsepower Mercedes-Renault, but loaded with bombs they could hardly reach 13,000 feet. The outdated Breguet took twice as long as the Sopwith to reach altitude (forty-nine minutes to 10,000 feet) and was about 15 miles per hour slower than the British machine. It was unstable fore and aft, slow on turns, and almost impossible to fly on instruments. This machine did have one virtue, however — a good arc of fire from the forward nacelle.[13] Four Breguets were shot down on the Oberndorf raid and after that no one wanted to fly them.

On September 3, 1916, the order was given to Captain Happe by his commander, Lieutenant Colonel Barres, to bombard the Mauser Factories of Oberndorf, accompanied by the English and protected by the American Squadron and the Fighting Squadron of the 7th Army. The expedition was delayed by some of the French machines not being quite up to pitch and by bad weather.[14]

Between his arrival at Luxeuil on September 21 and the date of the Oberndorf raid on October 12, 1916, Collishaw put in his time by carrying out training flights. As the Wing waited for the arrival of machines they got to know the countryside and practiced formation flying, gunnery, and bombing. By then Collishaw had built up quite a number of hours on the 1 1/2 Strutter. Much time was spent practicing rendezvous and formation flying, as these skills were critical to the success of the mission. Sufficient cover by the fighter escort was needed without impeding the progress of the bombers. The solution adopted by the British was as follows:

> In a formation of six, including a single fighter escort, the Sopwiths were staggered in height, increasing by 150 feet towards the rear, with the fighter about 750 feet above the leader in the opening of the 'V' behind the formation. The Breguets, in flights of six, formed a triangle with the machines staggered downwards in height so that they could cover each other. The formation gave these slow aircraft the maximum amount of mutual protection, buttressed by two or more fighters stationed behind and above them.[15]

Captain Happe, each morning, sent out a reconnaissance plane over the Black Forest to check on the weather conditions. For several days the weather was too bad to commence the raid. By October 11 all was in readiness, but the weather turned out to be too poor for flying.

> At last the early morning plane reported signs of the break up of the heavy cloud. Happe sent out another reconnaissance plane, and it was afternoon before he reported that the air was clearing over the Black Forest. We had agreed that the French Squadrons should take off first, then the Strutters, and then our Breguets. As the Breguets were likely to be the shakiest of our party, I had decided to go with them. It took time to get the French Squadrons off, and our party had time for lunch.[16]

The following list shows the flights and crews of the British planes sent on the Oberndorf raid from Air Ministry files and confirmed by the research of Ronald Dodds. Dodds also shows the hometown of the Canadian flyers, as well as the fate of some of the pilots and their machines.

RED SQUADRON

A Flight (scheduled take off time 1300 hrs.)	Machine Flown	Number
Flt. Lieut J.D. Newberry	Sopwith Fighter	9722
Gunlayer* Rees		
F/S/L J.A. Glen, Enderby, B.C.	Sopwith Bomber	9657
F/S/L S.T. Edwards, Carleton Place, Ont.	Sopwith Bomber	9655
F/S/L F.C. Armstrong, Brockville, Ont.	Sopwith Bomber	9666
F/S/L P.G. McNeil, Toronto	Sopwith Bomber	9742
F/S/L E.C. Porter, Winnipeg, Man.	Sopwith Bomber	9738
F/S/L W.S. Wilson (failed to form up and returned)	Sopwith Bomber	9736

*Gunlayer refers to the gunner of a two-seater bomber or fighter plane

B Flight (scheduled take-off time 1400 hrs.)	Machine Flown	Number
Flt. Lieut. C.B. Dalison	Sopwith Fighter	9744
Gunlayer Sub. Lieut. F.E. Fraser, Winnipeg		
F/S/L R. Collishaw, Nanaimo, B.C.	Sopwith Fighter	9407
Gunlayer Portsmouth		
F/S/L G.R.S. Fleming, Toronto	Sopwith Bomber	9664
F/S/L G.G. MacLennan, Eugenia, Ont. (crashed at Corbenay on return)	Sopwith Bomber	9741
F/S/L C.H.S. Butterworth, Ottawa (brought down in Germany)	Sopwith Bomber	9660
F/S/L A.B. Shearer, Neepawa, Man.	Sopwith Bomber	9669

BLUE SQUADRON————————————

A Flight (scheduled take-off time 1415 hrs.)	Machine Flown	Number
Flt. Cdr. R.H. Jones (landed at Villersexel on return)	Sopwith Fighter	9654
Gunlayer Sub. Lieut. C.N. Downes		
F/S/L .E. Smith, Mystic, P.Q.*	Sopwith Fighter	9708
Gunlayer Clegg		
F/S/L J.E. Sharman, Oak Lake, Man. (returned after 55 min.)	Sopwith Bomber	9670
F/S/L C.E. Burden, Toronto (returned after 28 min.)	Sopwith Bomber	9745
F/S/L N.M. Macgregor	Sopwith Bomber	9733
F/S/L F.S. Cotton, Australia (returned after 25 min., crashed at Faucogney)	Sopwith Bomber	9652

*P.Q. stands for "Province of Quebec"

B Flight (scheduled take-off time 1350 hrs.)	Machine Flown	Number
Wing Cdr. R.B. Davies	Sopwith Fighter	9667
Gunlayer Pinchin		
F/S/L R.F. Redpath, Montreal	Sopwith Fighter	9739
Gunlayer Dell		
F/S/L P.E. Beasley, Victoria	Breguet Bomber	9196
Gunlayer Sub. Lieut. L.V. Pearkes		
F/S/L J.S.N. Rockey, South Africa (brought down in Germany)	Breguet Bomber	9181
Gunlayer Sturdee		
F/S/L C.D. Newman, South Africa (brought down in Germany)	Breguet Bomber	9176
Gunlayer Vitty		

F/S/L L.H. Parker, Leeds Village, P.Q. (crashed at Buc on return)	Breguet Bomber	9175
Gunlayer Allen		
F/S/L J.H. Keens, Toronto	Breguet Bomber	9180
Gunlayer Allatson		
F/S/L H.E.P. Wigglesworth	Breguet Bomber	9178
Gunlayer Sinclair[17]		

Therefore, twenty-six British planes were involved in the Oberndorf raid, involving some eighteen Canadians.

> Oberndorf lies on the Neckar River, more than 100 miles northeast of Luxeuil, although the route laid down for 3 Naval Wing's aircraft to follow brought the distance to target and back to 223 miles. After bombing, the aircraft were to fly several miles northwest from Oberndorf and then were to turn to the southwest for the return flight. The return route swung northwest to the target and was roughly curved, with changes of direction to port to be made at the Alsatian town of Schlettstadt (now Selestat) and Corcieux, behind the French lines. To draw German fighters from the area, a diversionary raid on the town of Lorrach, to the south near the Swiss border, was planned by aircraft from the French Seventh Army. In all, more than eighty aircraft were to take to the air.[18]

Their target, the Mauser works, consisted of a portion called the Lower Works which was constructed of brick, stone, and masonry, and stood four storeys high. A few hundred metres away was the Outside Works also constructed of the same material. The third part of the complex was the Upper Works, located about a half a mile from the Outside Works. The factory built the standard German infantry Mauser rifle.

As planned, the French squadrons took off first, starting with F.29 from 1:15 p.m. to 1:20 p.m. The Farman machines began to roll down the dusty airfield, gaining speed and enabling their 53-foot wings to help the craft become airborne. Two of the Farman machines had to return to base due to minor troubles. Four made it to the target and bombarded for ten minutes. Squadron F. 123 was next and it too had two Farman bombers forced to return before crossing the front lines — another two were brought down by German Fokkers. Only one plane reached the objective. Given the limited range of the French and American escorts in their Nieuport fighters, they could not provide protection for the bombers all the way to the target. However, Corporal de Gaillard, who was in one of the escorts, brought down a Fokker. Eight pilots in Squadron B.M. 120 took off around 1:45 p.m. Only four machines reached the target and bombed it at an altitude of 2400 metres.[19]

The British Strutters were next to take off. Compared to the slow, lumbering French bombers the Strutters seemed to race along the airfield and were aloft in no time. Red Squadron's 'A' Flight Sopwiths took off at around 1:30 p.m. followed by the other RNAS formations. 'A' Flight of Blue Squadron was the last of the Strutters to leave at 2:15 p.m.[20] 'B' Flight, the Breguets, were the last to take off.

At this point, Wing Commander Bell Davies began to worry if there would be enough daylight to fly the round trip of 223 miles for 'B' flight. He took his fighter up to meet them and escort them to the target site. Commander Bell Davies described the journey in this way:

> A cloud layer had formed over the aerodrome, and I took my Strutter fighter up through it. When I got into the sunshine, above it, there was nothing in sight. Presently I saw a disturbance in the white layer below, and the top plane of a Breguet appeared. They came out one by one, looking like a string of hippos emerging from a pool. They picked up formation and I brought the fighter into position just behind the "V" and the leader headed for the Rhine valley. But when near to the front, they had not yet reached operational height and the leader turned back. That was quite correct and in accordance with his orders, but it delayed the start and meant a late return. While circling and climbing, we were joined by the fighter(s) of the Blue Flight and I deducted that the

Flight had failed to pick up formation, owing to the bad cloud layer and that the bombers had returned to base in accordance with their orders. There were now two other fighters beside mine with the Breguets, and I felt happier about them.[21]

The bombers of Blue Squadron had in fact failed to get into formation, so they returned to Luxeuil. Red Squadron's 'A' Flight, its five bombers all flown by Canadians, crossed the enemy lines at 10,000 feet and was met by intermittent anti-aircraft fire. The flight reached Oberndorf at 3:30 p.m., bombed the target and returned by the prescribed route to Luxeuil. All the flight's aircraft returned safely and landed at 5:00 p.m., just as dusk was drawing in.[22]

The Oberndorf raid was Collishaw's first flight against the enemy. He was flying Sopwith Strutter 9407, the same one he and Portsmouth had brought out from Manston. The Sopwith broke through the clouds and formed up with the rest of the flight. Collishaw was certainly nervous, as any pilot would be facing the enemy for the first time. He constantly checked his instruments and ensured there were no problems with his engine and fuel. As they flew on toward the target, they had no time to be afraid — they were too busy being concerned with the reliability of the aircraft.

Red Squadron's 'B' flight, with Collishaw and gunner Portsmouth providing part of the bomber escort function, had crossed the Rhine at 10,000 feet when they were pounced upon by three Fokker D.IIIs from the "Grasshopper" Squadron, flown by Lieutenant Otto Kissenberth and Sergeants Hilz and Ludwig Hanstein flying out of Colmar in Alsace. Hanstein singled out a Strutter bomber flown by Flight Sub-Lieutenant Charles Butterworth. Collishaw saw that Butterworth was being attacked so he entered the fray. He dove on the D.III, firing his Vickers machine gun as he approached the enemy plane. The Fokker turned away, and as it did Collishaw's engine cut out. By the time he got it started again, the Clerget engine failed to turn over at full power. Now he had lost considerable altitude and was unable to rejoin his flight, so he was forced to turn back to Luxeuil. Collishaw and Portsmouth barely made it back to the aerodrome. After landing they discovered that a lead wire had carried away from one of the spark plugs had disconnected and the distributor had developed a fault.[23]

Butterworth, it turned out, had been wounded in the neck but had managed to land safely at Freiburg. He recovered in a German hospital and spent the rest of the war as a prisoner. The rest of Red Flight carried on to Oberndorf and after bombing the target, returned to Luxeuil. Flight Sub-Lieutenant George G. MacLennan, unable to find the field, put his machine down in an open area north of the aerodrome, without injury.[24]

It was Hanstein who had wounded Butterworth. He had followed Butterworth down and narrowly escaped after landing not far from his victim, almost being killed by his own trigger-happy anti-aircraft machine gunners. Hanstein rose to command *Jasta* (squadron) 35 and survived the war with sixteen victories to his credit.

Blue Squadron's Breguet Flight, now under the direction of Wing Commander Bell Davies, crossed the Rhine and encountered AA (anti-aircraft) fire, but no damage was incurred. Commander Bell Davies continues his report of the raid as follows:

> Nearing Freiburg, a single German single-seater appeared and started to dive at the port wing Breguet, but I was able to get a burst at him with the front gun and he promptly dived away. Several other Germans appeared, but evidently did not like the look of the close locked formation, and after flying with us for a time, cleared off.[25]

By this time the flight was over the Black Forest and a small town was seen below. Though Commander Bell Davies did not recognize it as Oberndorf and thought the flight had wandered too far south of the intended target, the Breguet machines lined up in single file and commenced their bombing run. It was later discovered that the town was Donau-Eschingen, located south of Oberndorf.

Navigation was also difficult on the return voyage. The flight continued to go in a south-westerly direction. Bell Davies describes what happened next.

> I could see the line of the Alps and presently made out the deep gorge of the Rhine where it forms the

Swiss frontier. I had visions of the whole party getting themselves interned in Switzerland. I was still in the rear of the flight and was debating what to do about it, when I saw the other fighter, piloted by Redpath, one of the original Canadians, get in front of the leader and then make a sharp turn to starboard. The leader followed him round, so we kept clear of Switzerland.[26]

Before crossing into France the flight lost a Breguet due to engine failure. It broke formation and glided down into the Rhine valley east of Mulheim. It landed safely and the crew were taken prisoners. Although it was dark by the time the flight reached Luxeuil, most managed to land safely thanks to the flares that lined the runway.

Twenty-six British machines, sixteen French bombers, and numerous French fighter escorts took part in the raid. The British lost three machines; Butterworth in his Strutter and Flight Sub-Lieutenants Newman and Rocky along with their Gunlayers Vitty and Sturdee in Breguet machines all became prisoners of war.[27] The French lost six machines, including two Farman planes, one over Colmar and the other near Emmendingen. Another of their losses was *Escadrille Americaine* flyer Norman Prince, who flew a Nieuport.

Lufbery and Prince, having escorted some of the French bombers back across the front lines, were running low on fuel so they headed for the small airfield outside of Corcieux. Lufbery was the first to land. He waited for Prince, who had terrible depth perception. As Norman Prince commenced his approach, Lufbery noticed Prince was coming in too fast. Just clearing the trees, his Nieuport hit some high-tension cables at tree-top level, flipping the Nieuport and sending Prince flying out of the cockpit. He broke both his legs on impact and died later on of a blood clot in the brain. The founder of the *Escadrille Americaine* had tragically passed away at the young age of twenty-nine.

The French claimed they brought down four German machines but the Germans had no record of losing any machines that day. A total of 3,867 pounds of bombs were dropped by the RNAS, but not all of them were on target. The French dropped a similar amount. The losses incurred by the French caused *Capitaine* Happe to abandon further daylight raids in favour of night attacks.[28] Bell Davies was of a contrary view. He thought the newly trained pilots would lose their way in the dark and that a well-locked formation with fighter support would be difficult for the Germans to attack. He therefore favoured daylight raids.

Opinions vary on the extent of the damage caused by the Oberndorf raid. French intelligence reports obtained from an escaped French prisoner indicate that the new works building had suffered severe damage. One of the anti-aircraft batteries also appeared to have been hit. A furniture factory and a motor works facility were reported as being severely damaged by fire.[29]

Collishaw himself doubted that the Mauser arms works proper were badly hit. Was the raid worth the nine lost aircraft and their crews?

The Oberndorf raid was significant. It was the first time a joint British and French strategic bombing raid had been carried out into the German heartland. Four nationalities were represented: Canadian, British, French, and American. Despite its limited bombing success and high losses, the Oberndorf raid proved that such missions were possible and should be continued.

OTHER RAIDS BY 3 NAVAL WING ——————

Following the Oberndorf raid, Captain Happe moved his forces northward to the Plateau aerodrome near the town of Nancy to be closer to the Saar basin and northern Lorraine. From Nancy, enemy targets were between 30 and 70 miles away, whereas the targets from Luxeuil had been between 60 and 100 miles distant. He suggested the British do the same. On October 22, Collishaw along with six other fighters and thirteen bombers made the move to the new field. That night the French bombed the Thyssen steel works at Hagendingen, situated between Metz and Thionville, and 3 Naval Wing bombed it again the next day. Collishaw was part of Red Flight, the second of two flights dispatched. As they approached their target they broke from the "V" flying formation into single file so that each bomber could bomb the target in turn. Collishaw was the last one over the target and at 12,000 feet could see none of it as the area was blanketed with smoke. On the return flight they encountered little flak.

Library and Archives Canada, PA-118320.

Flight Sub-Lieutenant Raymond Collishaw (right) and Gunlayer Townsend with Sopwith 1 1/2 Strutter aircraft of 3 Naval Wing, RNAS. Ochey, France, 1916.

Close to 3,000 pounds of bombs were dropped on this raid and according to French intelligence authorities, three out of five blast furnaces were completely put out of action.[30]

The Plateau aerodrome proved to be too crowded for 3 Naval Wing as it contained not only Happe's group but also the French army co-operation unit. So Happe's bombing group and 3 Naval Wing shifted to the base at Ochey, some 15 miles southwest of Nancy. Wing Headquarters still remained at Luxeuil looking after administration, supply, and major repairs. Elder had the field at Ochey fitted out with huts for the officers and workshops for the mechanics and riggers.

On October 25, 1916, Collishaw was dispatched to ferry one of the Sopwiths from Luxeuil to the new forward base of Ochey. Since this was a simple transport mission Collishaw did not take along his gunner Portsmouth with him. This decision almost cost Raymond Collishaw his life. When ferrying planes to Ochey, 3 Naval Wing pilots would take the most direct route which brought them close to the German lines. Collishaw did no different. To make matters worse, he strayed further east due to the prevailing westerly winds, and over Luneville he was attacked by six enemy aircraft. Machine-gun fire from the EA passed close to his face with one bullet smashing his goggles, spraying glass into his eyes. Collishaw could barely see. With Portsmouth not there to protect him, Collishaw flew like a madman, throwing his machine all over the place, hoping to escape the deadly fire of the enemy. Blood blurred his sight as he dove to avoid the six enemy machines. Close to ground level he was attacked by a German pilot who misjudged how close he was to the ground and collided with a tree. Collishaw managed to fire at one of the Germans who took evasive action. Suddenly, as fast as the attack happened, it was over. The enemy machines had probably gotten low on fuel as Collishaw's machine was as well. Trying to gain altitude and with the setting sun over his left shoulder he set a course to what he hoped would be a friendly aerodrome. He finally spied one, but as he landed and taxied along he noticed the markings on the nearby aircraft were not the red, white, and blue roundels of French or British machines but were the black and white Maltese crosses of the Germans. Collishaw had landed at an enemy aerodrome! Gunning his engine to escape, he narrowly missed the trees at the end of the field. Collishaw flew on toward the front line trenches and eventually landed at a French aerodrome near Verdun.

Collishaw spent three days at the French aerodrome nursing his eyes with a tea leaf solution. The French officers could not believe what had happened to him. His eyes regained their normal vision and he returned to Ochey, 70 miles to the southeast.

The first raid for 3 Naval Wing from Ochey took place on November 10. Nine bombers and eight fighters took off for the steel works at Volklingen, located near Saarbrucken 70 miles away. Almost 2,300 pounds of bombs were dropped and they did serious damage.[31] Collishaw and the other Strutters were attacked by five hostile aircraft during the raid. One Hun aircraft picked out Flight Sub-Lieutenant Shearer, a Canadian flying the Sopwith 5088, but Lieutenant Newberry came to his rescue and between the two Strutters managed to shoot the German plane down. Two more enemy aircraft were shot down during the raid.

The next day, fourteen bombers and seven fighters went after the same target, bombing the iron foundry and blast furnaces of Volklingen. Collishaw and his loyal gunlayer Portsmouth were among them, flying in Sopwith number 9730. That day the bombers dropped 3,640 pounds of explosives. Again, serious material damage was done.[32] Three Hun machines attacked and Collishaw and Portsmouth managed to keep them at bay, fighting them on the return flight all the way back to the lines. Three Wing claimed three German attackers "brought down" and two others "driven down" on the two raids.[33]

The third raid in three days for the Wing took place on November 12, but Collishaw and Portsmouth did not take part. This time the target was the blast furnaces at St. Ingebert, also near Saarbrucken. Nine bombers and seven fighters took part with 2,275 pounds of bombs dropped. Reports from French intelligence stated that Swiss factory workers refused to continue working due to the threat of further bombing, so the factories had to be manned by the military.[34]

It wasn't until November 24, 1916 that 3 Naval Wing took off, this time for the blast furnaces at Dillingen, also in the Saar area. Flying with Collishaw was Sub-Lieutenant H.C. Lemon, a Royal Navy Volunteer Reserve observer officer. In all, nine bombers and seven fighters took part, dropping 2,000 pounds of bombs. Pilots saw their bombs falling amongst the factories of Dillingen. No losses were suffered by 3 Naval Wing and a German scout was shot down.[35]

On some raids, the Three Wing bombers released their load of bombs while flying in "V" formation, but the most commonly used procedure was for them to approach the target in such formation, escorted by the fighters, and then to form into a single line and go in to bomb. The pilot of the leading bomber, employing a crude type of bomb sight, would let his bombs go and as he did so the pilots following behind him would drop theirs. The bomber pilots were then supposed to re-form and head back to base, again under close escort, but some bombers went off on their own searching for enemy fighters after releasing their bombs. Without their bomb loads they were lighter than the two-seater fighters meant to protect them. The bomber pilots did manage to knock down a number of German planes, much to the embarrassment of the fighter pilots.

Wing Captain Elder was so confident of the accuracy of his bombers that he convinced a group of high-ranking French officers to watch a demonstration of how the 1 1/2 Strutters could instantly create a trench for emergency defence purposes. Elder had the officers sit in the stands of a nearby football field for the observation. On signal, the Strutters made their bombing run, but when doing so they flew too close to the football stands, clearing them instantaneously as the French officers scrambled for cover.

By the end of November, 1916, 3 Naval Wing was still under scheduled strength. At the time of the Dillingen raid Collishaw estimates there were forty aircraft and about fifty pilots that couldn't be put to use because of bad weather. Fog and mist hid potential targets, or the rain pelted the aerodrome making it a sticky mess. Then it turned extremely cold. To amuse themselves the French army went on boar hunts in the nearby forests. Apparently no boars were killed, but some French soldiers were injured by their own officers who shot at anything that moved.

When the weather got really cold the Canadians set up an ice rink inside one of the hangars. With the players inventing their own rules, the games were much more violent than today's game: rule one being hit the player with or near the puck as many times as you could.

Members of the Wing also had the opportunity to visit the city of Nancy in their off hours. This majestic French town was home to the Palace Stanislas, which resembled Versailles, and the Grand Hotel, and was a frequent location for dinner parties among the Wing members. To one particular party, a very successful one by all counts, the Wing invited Commandant Happe, his officers, and members of a nearby unit of the *Chasseurs Alpins*. Toast followed toast as the party got more noisy and rowdy by the minute, when suddenly in walked the *Commandant de Ville*, the provost marshal in charge of the behaviour of all troops in the area. The Canadians, not to be intimidated by this authority figure, or perhaps not knowing who he was, shoved a drink in his hand and demanded he make a toast, which he did, to England and France, before promptly leaving.

During the latter half of December Collishaw was having mechanical problems with his machine. For example, on December 24 on a flight from Luxeuil to Ochey his joy stick came off in his hands upon landing. Despite the mechanical problems with his aircraft, Collishaw did partake in the last flight of the year for 3 Naval Wing on December 27. Eleven bombers and five fighters, Collishaw among them, took off to bomb the blast furnaces of Dillingen. Due to the haze and low cloud, the flight flew 4,000 to 5,000 feet below the usual altitude, but still managed to drop over 2,300 pounds of bombs.[36]

Getting lost on the way back from a raid was a very real possibility, and some pilots, fearing they would land in enemy territory, went to great lengths to avoid doing so. One pilot continued to fly westward all the way to the Spanish border after his mission was over and ended up landing his machine on a racetrack. After he and his machine had been found by the recovery party he took off for Paris and landed on another racetrack. His machine had to be repaired again, and finally, after the repairs were complete, he took off toward the front lines only to crash before reaching his destination. Where? You guessed it, on another race-track — this time killing two horses. It's quite possible that this flyer just wanted to gamble at the track rather than fight a war.

Poor weather conditions including heavy snow in early 1917 greatly hampered the activities of 3 Naval Wing. The unheated hangars at Ochey made servicing the machines next to impossible. Stearne Edwards's log book contains an entry in January where he conducted an experimental test flight to see if oil would freeze at altitude. The temperature that day was 20 degrees Fahrenheit.[37] No mention was made of the results of the test flight.

The first raid of 1917 for 3 Naval Wing took place on January 23. The blast furnaces at Burbach in the Saar region, only a couple of miles from Saarbrucken, were attacked. Due to the extreme cold, out of twenty-four machines that took off only ten bombers and six fighters managed to get to the target[38]; the rest had engine trouble and had to turn back. Two thousand six hundred pounds of bombs were dropped at an altitude of 7,000 feet. They were shelled heavily by anti-aircraft fire and the flight was attacked by about a dozen German machines. Collishaw was attacked directly by a Fokker D.III on the return trip but without any serious consequences. He and his trusted gunlayer Portsmouth ran low on fuel on the return flight so they had to land at Nancy where he re-fueled and returned to Ochey. This was to be Collishaw's last flight with 3 Naval Wing.

Other pilots in the Wing had their own fights to contend with that day. Charles Pattison, who had been with Collishaw on the *Niobe*, and who had accompanied him to England, had to fight off a German Roland. With the help of his gunlayer, Bert Hinkler, he managed to drive off the Roland even though it was a faster plane than the 1 1/2 Strutter. Ronald Redpath of Montreal and his gunlayer were jumped by three hostile aircraft, but managed to make it home safely. John Sharman shot down a monoplane — probably a Fokker D.III — and Ernest Potter shot down one of four enemy aircraft that attacked him, but his Strutter was badly shot up and he was forced to land just beside the French lines.

Author's Collection.

The French Croix de Guerre (with palme), similar to the one awarded to Collishaw.

Not all members were so lucky, though. Maurice Stephens of Toronto, the last bomber to land, put down on the ground as two ratings ran out to assist him, each of them hanging on to a wing tip. What they and Stephens were not aware of was that one of the 65-pound bombs had failed to drop during the raid and was hung up near the tail of the aircraft. The nose of the bomb had fallen clear off the bomb rack enough to permit the safety prop to unwind, thus fusing the bomb. A violent explosion killed the two ratings instantly. A third rating was badly injured and later died. Stephens miraculously survived, though he was severely injured. He remained in hospital until late November of 1917 and ended up re-qualifying as a pilot with only one leg and continued to serve in a staff capacity until mid-1919.

The day after the raid on Burbach, January 24, 1917, Raymond Collishaw was awarded the French Croix de Guerre, *avec palme*. The citation for this award, dated March 5, reads: *"S'est a maintes reprises, distingue par sa bravoure en venant au secours d'avions de bombardment au cours de raids a grande distance."* In English this translates to: "Many times he showed his bravery by coming to the aid of bomber planes during long distance raids."

The Croix de Guerre was established in 1915 and is a bronze cross, within which is a pair of crossed swords. The obverse medallion shows the female head of the Republic. The reverse medallion shows the date of award (1914–1915, 1914–1916, 1914–1917, or 1914–1918). The ribbon is green with five equally-spaced red stripes and edges of red.

The beginning of the end of 3 Naval Wing came in the form of a letter from the Admiralty's Director of Air Services to Wing Captain Elder, directing that nine of 3 Naval Wing's best pilots be transferred to Dunkirk. There they would form RNAS Squadrons, which would then be flown to the Western Front. They were required to assist the RFC at the request of General Trenchard, head of the Royal Flying Corps. Trenchard disagreed with the RNAS conducting its own bombing raids and wrote to the British cabinet saying fighters were the first importance in order to achieve command of the air in the spring of 1917. If that was not achieved, then neither reconnaissance machines nor bombers would be of much help, he argued.

Of the nine pilots sent, seven were Canadians and all were Flight Sub-Lieutenants. They were: Raymond Collishaw, Percy McNeil, Fred Armstrong, James Glen, Arthur T. Whealy, Joseph S.T. Fall, and John J. Malone. Elder called these pilots into his office and told them that they were to go forthwith to join 3 Naval Squadron, which was then under the operational control of the RFC on the Somme front. Wing Captain Elder, in his report to the Admiralty, outlines the consequences of this decision.

> The result of these pilots being taken away just at the commencement of the spring had the double result of reducing the efficiency and upsetting the organization for squadron flying. These officers were taken from various flights and their places had to be filled by pilots unused to co-operate [sic] with the other pilots in the flight.[39]

Since arriving in France, Collishaw had taken part in all but one of the raids flown by 3 Naval Wing, up to and including January 23, 1917.

On February 25 and March 4, 1917, 3 Naval Wing carried out more raids on Burbach. However, their frequency came to a halt when Elder received more orders to transfer pilots and their planes to Dunkirk. On March 7, nineteen pilots, six Sopwith 1 1/2 Strutters and 100 ratings left the Wing, but 3 Naval Wing carried on in spite of their reduced numbers. Six bombers and three fighters dropped 1,560 pounds of bombs on the aerodrome at Morehingen, 23 miles southeast of Metz, on March 16. Another 3 Naval Wing raid took place on March 22 when the same number of bombers and fighters bombed Burbach for one last time, dropping 1,560 pounds on that target.[40]

The final nail in the coffin of 3 Naval Wing came on March 25, 1917 in the form of an Admiralty telegram instructing Elder to disband the Wing. One last raid took place on April 14 on the City of Freiburg, just across the Rhine to the east of Luxeuil. The French bombing group and 3 Naval Wing combined to send twenty-one bombers and sixteen fighters in a reprisal attack for the torpedoing the Germans had carried out the previous month on the British hospital ship *Asturias*.[41]

While in France, 3 Naval Wing carried out eighteen long-distance bombing raids into Germany, dropping 38,617 pounds of bombs. They had not lost a single man or aircraft to enemy action and all the pilots were convinced that they had the better of the German aircraft.

What was the impact of 3 Naval Wing on the German war effort? Were all those long-range missions worth the effort? In the words of S. F. Wise, "Yet the wing and its work did have considerable significance. It was created partly as a result of the influence of public opinion upon policy, it operated independently of other fighter arms; it directly co-operated with an allied force, the French Air Service; and it specialized in one thing: strategic bombing."[42]

Looking back it seems as though the establishment of 3 Naval Wing had been just an experiment in strategic bombing. Little attention was paid by the Admiralty to the lessons learned.

The breakup of 3 Wing meant the loss of many pilots experienced in long-distance bombing to quite different tasks at the front. Nor was any advantage taken by the Admiralty of the knowledge acquired by the officers who had led the wing…. Bell Davies had been transferred to flying operations with the Grand Fleet; Elder reverted to general service in an obscure sea command.[43]

=5= NO. 3 NAVAL SQUADRON
1917

I~N~ ~RESPONSE~ ~TO~ ~THE~ ~REQUEST~ ~BY~ ~THE~ RFC ~FOR~ ~ASSISTANCE~ ~ON~ ~THE~ Western Front, the naval flying arm formed from its Dunkirk units, a new fighter squadron called No. 8 Naval Squadron, which arrived on the Somme front on October 26, 1916 to serve under RFC command. Of its eighteen pilots, five were Canadian. The RFC made a further request for pilots and planes, so four more naval fighter squadrons were formed. The first of the additional units was No. 3 Naval Squadron, which came to Vert Gallant to relieve No. 8 Naval Squadron.[1]

Collishaw and the eight other transferees from 3 Naval Wing travelled from Ochey to Paris by rail and then on to Calais. Most of them had to stand in the coach corridors for the majority of the time as the train was crammed with French military and piles of luggage. They were then put on a motor bus from Calais to Dunkirk while their luggage stayed on the train. Upon arriving at Dunkirk they discovered that their new squadron, No. 3 Naval Squadron, had recently moved to Vert Galand on

Collishaw in front of Nissen huts at aerodrome, probably Vert Galand.

the Somme, and that they were desperately required there. They climbed into a motor tender and started the trip south over snow-covered roads. It was late January, 1917, bitterly cold, and all of the pilots had left their warm clothing on the train. After many hours of suffering from the cold and bumpy ride, they arrived at Doullens, where they spent the night. The so-called "Officers Rest House" where they were billeted for the night turned out to be nothing more than chicken wire beds with wooden frames. After a less-than-restful night they re-boarded the tender for the last leg of the trip to their new squadron.

Once they reached Vert Galand they were given a warm welcome. No. 3 Naval Squadron had been formed the previous November from one of the units of 1 Naval Wing at Dunkirk. No. 3 Naval Squadron was one of the RNAS squadrons formed especially to assist the RFC and was placed under the operational control of RFC's 22nd Army Wing under V Brigade. On February 1, 1917, the date of Collishaw's transfer to No. 3 Naval Squadron, its location had shifted from the aerodrome at St. Pol, near Dunkirk, to Vert Galand on the Somme.

Vert Galand, also known as "Vert Galand Farm," was located north of Amiens and to the northwest of Albert. Leonard H. "Tich" Rochford, a British pilot who had just finished his pilot's training, and, new to the squadron, described the living conditions there in his book *I Chose the Sky.*

> Our mess was an Armstrong hut constructed of wooden frames over which canvas was stretched after these frames were bolted together. In the centre of the hut was an iron stove with a chimney rising through a hole in the roof. One could sit or stand close to the stove and be scorched in [sic] from it but remain frozen behind. Our sleeping quarters consisted of Nissen huts each fitted out with an iron stove but the ratings slept in a barn which, they told me, had holes in the walls and was therefore very cold and draughty. They were sometimes troubled with rats.[2]

Collishaw with an unknown child on the steps of a Nissen hut, probably Vert Galand.

Library and Archives Canada, PA-002793.

Major Raymond Collishaw and Captain A.T. Whealy.

By the first week of February, half of the squadron's twelve pilots were Canadian; Flight Sub-Lieutenants R. Collishaw; P.G. McNeil, and A.T. Whealy, both from Toronto; J.P. White of Winnipeg; and Flight Lieutenant H.R. Wambolt of Dartmouth, Nova Scotia. The sixth was No. 3 Naval Squadron Commander Redford "Red" H. Mulock. Red Mulock was the son of a prominent barrister in Winnipeg. A graduate engineer from McGill, Mulock was part of the First Canadian Contingent to go overseas in October 1914. He then joined the RNAS in early 1915 at the ripe old age of twenty-eight.

Mulock was the first pilot in both the RNAS and RFC to have attacked a Zeppelin over England. Early on the morning of May 17, 1915 he volunteered to take up an Avro 504B and pursue the Zeppelin LZ 38 that had been spotted over Westgate. Night flights were considered quite dangerous at the time and very few flyers had attempted such a feat. Mulock planned to drop two bombs and two hand grenades on the airship. As he closed in on the Zeppelin, it fired its machine guns at Mulock and then rose rapidly out of the reach of the Avro. Mulock pursued LZ 38 out to sea, but eventually lost it in the clouds.

On July 8, 1915 Mulock transferred to 1 Naval Wing at St. Pol, in the Dunkirk area. His duties there included fighter patrols, bombing, visual and photographic reconnaissance, and directing the fire of British warships bombarding targets on the German-held coast of Belgium.

Mulock was awarded the Distinguished Service Order (DSO) on June 9, 1916 and his citation read in part: "This officer has been constantly at Dunkirk since July, 1915, and has displayed indefatigable zeal and energy."[3] Mulock continued to fly with 1 Naval Wing through the summer and early autumn of 1916 and in addition to his skill and determination as a pilot he impressed his superiors with his qualities of leadership, leading to his promotion as commander of a fighter squadron.[4]

Three other Canadians joined No. 3 Naval Squadron after the initial group of six. They were Flight Sub-Lieutenants F.C. Armstrong of Toronto; J.S.T. Fall of Hillbank, British Columbia; and Flight Lieutenant J.J. Malone of Regina.

> They were all decorated for service with the squadron during the following months. Fall and Armstrong received the DSC (Distinguished Service Cross) and Malone, who was killed in April, was posthumously gazetted a DSO (Distinguished Service Order). Another notable group arrived in March, including Flight Sub. Lieutenant L.S. Breadner of Carleton Place, who succeeded to command one of the three flights a month later.[5]

Several other Canadians arrived later from 3 Naval Wing: Gordon Harrower and George Anderson from Ottawa, Norman Hall from Victoria, British Columbia, and Alfred W. "Nick" Carter from Calgary.

Included amongst the squadron's pilots was Lieutenant Horace Wigglesworth, an Englishman who had conducted himself with great bravery during the raid of 3 Naval Wing on January 23, 1917. He was attacked by six German Halberstadts, which he and his gunlayer managed to fight off, driving down one machine.

Some of the new flyers thought they would receive their pick of all the new machines being produced at the time. They were shocked then, to find that they were going to fly Sopwith Pups, left at Vert Gallant by No. 8 Naval Squadron. They were in poor condition, having been flown for many hours. The first production of Pups was delivered to the RNAS in September 1916. This little scout was powered by an 80-horsepower Le Rhone rotary engine and was armed with one .303 Vickers machine gun. Its weight empty was a mere 787 pounds and it was only a little over 19 feet long with a wingspan of 26 1/2 feet.[6] Because of its lightweight it was a very manoeuvrable aircraft and Collishaw enjoyed flying the little machine despite its drawbacks.

Some had referred to the Sopwith Pup as the thoroughbred of machines because of its sleek lines and its ability to outclass the Fokker D.III. The Pup by all accounts was a delightful aircraft to fly and was a match for the new Halberstadt and Albatros scouts. The Pup was fast and nimble, and could be just as manoeuvrable at maximum height as it was at lower altitudes. During the fall of 1916 and the winter of 1917, those flying Pups racked up a considerable number of victories.

The Pups used by No. 3 Naval Squadron had been inherited from No. 8 Naval Squadron. A number of the machines had been flying since the autumn of 1916 and were reaching the end of their service.

Collishaw took one of the Pups up on a practice flight on February 8. For the next five days as part of 'C' Flight, Collishaw carried out "formation line patrols." On line patrol, pilots flew back and forth above the front line trenches protecting artillery observation aircraft from enemy attack. They also flew on "offensive patrols," entering enemy airspace behind the German lines. Collishaw's first combat with No. 3 Naval Squadron was on February 14. He took off in Sopwith Scout No. 6160 at 12:15 for a line patrol between Warlencourt and Rossignol. At 14,000 feet over Vaux, Collishaw's flight commander attacked a German two-seater that came into range. Collishaw dove for another two-seater that appeared just below him. Getting into position behind the enemy aircraft, Collishaw fired his Vickers only to have it jam. He peeled off to fix the jam when another German aircraft, this time a single-seater scout (fighter) came to the aid of the German two-seater. Collishaw managed to clear the jam just in time to get a burst off in the direction of the single-seater. His gun jammed again so he had to turn back to Vert Galand.

The next day, February 15, 1917 proved to be more fruitful for Raymond Collishaw. Again on line patrol to Cambrai, he attacked a two-seater that was painted speckled grey with a red cross on the surface of the upper wing. This encounter was indecisive as neither pilot got the better of the other. A few moments later, two enemy scouts were spotted flying toward them. Collishaw immediately went after one of them. He fired his single Vickers machine gun about 200 feet from the enemy aircraft, sending the German machine down in a spin. During the fight Collishaw's motor had been shot at and had ceased to function. He managed to land the Pup just north of Albert. The RFC communique which reported the engagement spelled Collishaw's name incorrectly, but nonetheless it was still his first victory!

It was not a straightforward matter determining whether a pilot had shot down an opposing plane. Rarely did they follow the damaged plane down to witness it crash because they were too busy defending themselves from attack by the enemy or coming to the aid of a fellow pilot. Often all the pilot witnessed was the plane going down "out of control" (OOC) or that the plane had been "driven down" with mechanical problems or with smoke coming from the machine. Many "kills" had to be confirmed by other pilots who had seen the enemy plane crash or by troops on the ground confirming the plane had in fact crashed. Many combats were referred to as "indecisive" by either the RNAS daily operations reports or by RFC communiqués.

Another major change the pilots from Three Wing had to get used to was the number of missions they flew. Instead of the normal bomber-unit schedule of performing a raid every week to ten days, No. 3 Naval Squadron was in the air every day and sometimes two times a day because their purpose was to support air reconnaissance as well as go on offensive patrols inside enemy territory. Collishaw flew nine patrols from February 8 to February 15, 1917. The cocky young pilots from 3 Naval Wing had to adjust to the increased intensiveness of combat. It was like a young hockey player going from a farm team to the National Hockey League. Though they did get plenty of action, encountering a wide variety of skill levels in the German pilots they faced. Some seemed inexperienced, while others were masters of their machines.

Library and Archives Canada, PA-002789.

Baron Manfred Von Richthofen wearing the Pour Le Merite around his neck.

In particular, amongst their regular opponents was the famous *Jasta* 11 of Manfred von Richthofen, the Red Baron. In the autumn of 1916, the German air force was made up of a couple dozen *Jagdstaffeln*, or *Jasta* for short. These *Jastas* were the same as RNAS or RFC Squadrons, or the

French *Escadrilles*, though the make-up of each *Jasta* was much smaller in overall size. Sometimes the pilot strength consisted of no more than eight or nine men, with perhaps the same number of airplanes. This also led to the continuance of the overall defensive role of the *Jastas*. RNAS and RFC Squadrons had between fifteen and eighteen aircraft and were divided up into "Flights" of between four and six planes each. Squadrons were grouped into Wings, and Wings into Groups.[7]

> The tactics developed by men such as Boelcke during the late summer and autumn of 1916 centred on the *Jastas* waiting until front line observers had telephoned to say that an Allied formation had crossed, or was about to cross, the German lines, or that an Allied Corps machine was over the front directing artillery fire. Most *Jastas* had their bases close to the front line, so it took only a few minutes for the pilots to gain height and intercept the enemy.[8]

Richthofen's *Jasta* 11 was stationed near the town of Douai. In early 1917 most of its pilots were inexperienced. Lothar von Richthofen recalled his brother's early combat missions with Karl Allmenroder and Kurt Wolff:

> At the time both had no experience at all and in aerial combat beginners have more fear than love of the Fatherland. In the first days, my brother flew out with them, attacked numerous British [aircraft], and his machine received an enormous number of hits, without successes to make up for it, and both of them did not help. Of course my brother came back somewhat annoyed, but did not reproach them; on the contrary, he did not say a word about it. As Wolff and Allmenroder ... told me, that influenced them more than the harshest dressing down.[9]

Much of No. 3 Naval Squadron's work in February and March of 1917 involved offensive patrols into enemy territory, involving flights of four or five machines flying at altitudes of between 12,000 and 16,000 feet. They also escorted reconnaissance and bombing aircraft over an area from the Scarpe to St. Quentin. The weather was often bitterly cold, causing their Vickers machine guns to freeze. Nothing could be more frustrating for a pilot than finding himself in a position to shoot down a hostile aircraft (HA), only to have his gun jam after the first bullet fired. Not only did the guns freeze, but so did the pilots. Flying open cockpit biplanes exposed pilots to all types of weather, plus the cold of being at 10,000 to 16,000 feet. In the first half of the First World War, pilots wore a long leather coat with large gauntlet-style gloves, boots, and a helmet. The problem of pilots getting frostbite was solved quite fortuitously by an Australian RNAS pilot named Sidney Cotton.[10]

> In the very cold winter of 1916/17, Cotton was tuning up the engine of his Sopwith 1 1/2 Strutter, dressed in dirty, begrimed overalls, when he and others were despatched [sic] in a hurry to intercept an intruder. They saw nothing, but when they collected together afterwards everyone was frozen stiff except Cotton. "That's funny," he said, "I'm quite warm." He hadn't had time to don flying kit and was still wearing his dirty overalls. On examining them he found they were saturated with oil and grease and must have acted as an airtight bag and kept the body heat in. He asked for leave, went to London, and had a flying suit made up to his own design. It had a lining of thin fur, then a layer of airproof silk, then an outside layer of light Burberry material, the whole being made up in one piece like overalls. The neck and cuffs had fur pieces sewn inside them to prevent the warm air escaping. Deep pockets below the knee allowed pilots seated in cramped cockpits to reach down into them easily for maps and accessories. After searching tests the Sidcot suit, as it was eponymously known, came into general use, replacing the old-fashioned boots and coats.[11]

It was the role of the Sopwith scouts to escort the bombers, to their target and back. Formation flying was in its infancy in the First World War, so the escorts had a number of challenges. One was to convince the bomber aircraft to stay in close formation. The more spread out they became the easier it would be for enemy aircraft to pick off the stragglers, or those machines at the end of a formation. The number of flights No. 3 Naval Squadron would send up with the bombers varied, and so too did the number of Pups in each flight. Normally two or three Pups formed a flight, and if there was only one flight of Pups providing the escort, they tended to stay close to the bombers. If there were two or three flights as escort, the second flight was positioned a few thousand feet above, behind, and to one side of the first flight. If there was a third flight it would fly at a higher altitude still, on the opposite side of the formation and closer to the rear. The Germans usually attacked the uppermost portion of the flight rather than attacking planes below, which posed the risk of being attacked from above by the escorts. The upper flight was dubbed the "Sacrifice Flight," and if there was a flight above that one, it was called the "Super Sacrifice Flight." Because Collishaw was new to the Squadron he was often assigned to the "Sacrifice Flight."

At times, Collishaw and the other scout flyers also escorted BE2cs on bombing raids. These planes, in order to carry their standard load of two 112-pound bombs, had to take off without the observer. In the BE2c the observer sat in front of the pilot closest to the engine, his Lewis gun pointing back toward the airplane's tail. Without the observer, the BE2c was defenceless if it became separated from its escort. BE2cs were slow, lumbering machines that had a top speed of only 72 miles per hour. They had a wingspan of over 36 feet and a length of over 27 feet. The maximum altitude of a BE2c was 10,000 feet, but in normal conditions they could only reach heights of between 5,000 and 8,000 feet. They made a perfect target for the anti-aircraft crews on the ground.

During the month of February, 1917, the German infantry began their retreat to the Hindenburg Line, and in doing so straightened out their line of defence. The German high command, Generals Hindenburg and Ludendorff, did not want to face another offensive on the Somme. The Battle of the Somme began on July 1, 1916 and lasted for the remainder of 1916. It cost both sides tens of thousands of casualties.

During the retreat to the Hindenburg Line air activity increased. Reconnaissance missions had to be flown to record the enemy's movements and its strength. This increased the need for escorts as well. On February 28, 1917 No. 3 Naval Squadron moved its base of operations to Bertangles, about 8 or 9 miles southwest of Vert Galant and just about 5 miles north of the city of Amiens. Tich Rochford described Bertangles as a much more comfortable camp to live in than Vert Galand. The aerodrome was extensive, the hangars were large corrugated-iron buildings, and it had sound, wooden-hutted accommodation for both officers and ratings.[12]

On the lighter side of the war, the parties held by No. 3 Naval Squadron were even more rowdy and intense than those thrown by 3 Naval Wing. Officers from other squadrons were often invited to these parties with the goal of trying to see how drunk the host squadron could get them. Anything from the bar in any mixture possible was the order of the day. By the end of the festivities most visitors had to be carried to waiting tenders to take them back to their aerodrome. Those on dawn patrol the next morning were faced with the daunting task of trying to get their machines off the ground, let alone complete their mission. Needless to say, many accidents resulted from the incapacity of the hungover or still-drunk pilots.

In order to survive, pilots needed to be keenly aware of what was going on around them in the air at all times. The reason that many pilots wore the trademark silk white scarf was to avoid rubbing raw the skin of their neck as they swivelled their head from side to side, trying to watch for enemy aircraft behind them that could be on their tail. No. 3 Naval Squadron even experimented with installing round rearview mirrors on some of the Pups.

By the middle of February, Collishaw had logged over 144 hours of flying time to date. During the latter half of the month the squadron had conducted offensive patrols over Bapaume and had flown escort missions, protecting FE2b bombers. On a number of occasions the No. 3 Naval encountered HA (hostile aircraft). In one instance Collishaw encountered a hostile enemy (HE) machine that damaged one of his left wings, resulting in a forced landing upon his return from the air battle.

On the first of March the squadron moved from Vert Galand to a new aerodrome at Bertangles. March 4, 1917 dawned cold but sunny and clear weather — perfect for flying. Two flights of Pups, including Collishaw's, took off late-morning to escort some FE2bs from No. 18 Squadron on a long-range reconnaissance mission to the Cambrai area. Over enemy territory they were attacked by a number of German Halberstadts. Collishaw found himself in a scrap with three of the hostile enemy planes. He was able to quickly turn his manoeuvrable Pup and get behind one of them, firing bullet after bullet at the German machine around the cockpit area. Eventually, after firing a full drum of ammunition at the Halberstadt, Collishaw saw it falter and then spin out of control.

RNAS operations reports out of Dunkirk credited Collishaw with the victory, his second in the war, saying: "Collishaw damaged one hostile scout and drove it down to the ground, near Bapaume."[13] This time they got his name right.

During the same scrap John Malone from Saskatchewan was worrying about the Halberstadt he was tangling with. He manoeuvred into firing range and sent off a number of rounds into the enemy machine, sending it down. Vernon and Wigglesworth each shot down an EA as well. Another Pup pilot who was victorious over a German plane that day was Leonard Rochford, nicknamed "Tich." He stood only a bit over 5 feet tall. A mild mannered, unassuming gentleman on the ground, Tich, when he got into the cockpit of a fighter, was absolutely ferocious. He fought off five German machines, sending one down out of control. It was his first victory and his first scrap in the air.

V Brigade later reported that the mission had been very successful. The FE2bs were able to take important photographs of suspected enemy lines and back areas. No. 3 Naval Squadron lost two pilots though, that day, both Canadian. James White and Harry R. Wambolt were on a line patrol when their flight was attacked and they were shot down and killed. L.A. Powell, of 'B' Flight was badly wounded but managed to crash land behind allied lines. Sadly he died in hospital three days later.

The Squadron continued to fly offensive patrols and escort missions throughout the month. Tich Rochford described one particular patrol as follows:

During the morning of 17th March our three flights carried out an operation to clear the sky of EA on the 5th Army front so that FE's of No. 18 Squadron, RFC could carry out a reconnaissance. This could be called an Offensive Sweep and Escort combined. 'A' Flight patrolled at the lowest height and just above the FE's, 'B' Flight flew above 'A' Flight and 'C' Flight were stacked above them at 17,000 feet. On this patrol many fights with EA took place. Bell shot down an EA in flames, Casey one out of control; Malone was most aggressive and shot an EA down in flames and two out of control.[14]

To distinguish the aircraft of the three Flights the pilots painted their engine cowlings different colours. Some pilots even named their machines, as Tich Rochford explains.

Mack's pup was named Black Tulip and of the other machines in 'C' flight mine was Black Bess, Collishaw's Black Maria and Whealy's Black Prince. All 'C' Flight's engine cowlings were painted black, 'B' Flight's red and 'A' Flight's blue. It is reported that Collishaw, when he became Flight Commander of 'B' Flight in 10 (Naval) Squadron, had the cowlings of his Sopwith Triplanes painted black and named his machine "Black Maria", as [sic]a result the Flight became known as "Black Flight."[15]

On March 24 the weather was particularly cold. Raymond Collishaw was flying an early morning offensive patrol to Cambrai at 17,000 feet. The flight was attacked by several German fighters, during which Collishaw was shot at. He was badly hit and his goggles were smashed, just like the year before while flying with 3 Naval Wing. Collishaw threw off his goggles and helmet. Glass again had got into his eyes, but without his goggles on, the intense cold, especially at that height, caused frostbite on his face. After landing at Bertangles, his face had swollen such that he could barely see. Due to the severity of the frostbite his commanding officer sent him to England on sick leave.

Twice Raymond Collishaw almost lost his life in less than six months. Thus was the condition for pilots in the First World War. You never knew when your time would be up. Skill played a large part in whether you lived or died, but, then again, so did uncontrollable factors like weather and the reliability of your aircraft, including your machine gun.

Collishaw, due to his convalescence in England, was absent for the Allied offensive in April 1917, which included the famous battle of Vimy Ridge on April 9. He also missed most of Bloody April, a dark period for most Allied squadrons due to their high number of losses. It seems that during the month of April, No. 3 Naval Squadron saw many victories and few losses of pilots and aircraft.

S.F. Wise sums this time up well.

> It was through the naval squadrons that Canadians made some of their most significant contributions in the spring offensive. Pride of service made the naval authorities anxious for their squadrons "to put up a good show with the RFC". One outstanding example was 3 (Naval), commanded by Squadron Commander R.H. Mulock of Winnipeg and equipped with Sopwith Pups. During the heavy fighting in March and April it was one of the few allied squadrons which gave out more punishment than it received. Its success was attributable in large measure to Mulock's ability as a leader and organizer and his extensive knowledge of aeroplanes and engines.[16]

NO. 10 NAVAL SQUADRON AND THE BLACK FLIGHT

APRIL AND MAY, 1917

IN LATE APRIL, AFTER HIS SICK LEAVE IN ENGLAND DUE TO FROSTBITE was complete, Raymond Collishaw returned to France. But, he did not return to No. 3 Naval Squadron, his old unit. Instead he was transferred to No. 10 Naval Squadron, flying out of Furnes, just east of Dunkirk and about six miles inland from the Allied-held Belgian coast. Formed originally on February 12, 1917 near Dunkirk at St. Pol, and under the command of Squadron Commander Charles D. Breeze, R.N., No. 10 Naval Squadron came under 1 Naval Wing. It was one of the RNAS squadrons formed to help the RFC on the Western Front.

> By the end of 1916 the Board of Admiralty had formally approved Trenchard's request for four additional naval squadrons on the Western Front. He already had 8 (Naval) at his disposal, and the others arrived at intervals between February and May. Three

of the squadrons, Nos. 1, 8, and 10, were equipped with Sopwith Triplanes.[1]

Initially the squadron flew Nieuport scouts and Nieuport two-seaters, but by the time Collishaw arrived on April 26 they only flew Sopwith Triplanes. Once the Squadron was up to organizational strength and was prepared for active operations, No. 10 Naval Squadron moved to Furnes on March 27, 1918 and came under 11 Naval Wing. It also had a new Squadron Commander, Bertram C. Bell.[2]

Bell had been one of the flight commanders under Mulock at 3 Naval Wing and arrived at No. 10 Naval Squadron on April 21, 1917, just days before Collishaw. At first, Collishaw was given command of 'C' Flight, one of three flights in the squadron. Each flight was comprised of five Sopwith Triplanes.

The Sopwith Triplane was unique in that it was the only three-winged airplane to see service in the British forces in the First World War and it was used exclusively by the RNAS. Less than 150 were built and the "Tripes," as they were nicknamed, had a short history, seeing action from March to November 1917. Initially powered by a 110-horsepower Clerget, most Triplanes had a replacement 130-horsepower Clerget rotary engine in them.[3] This more powerful engine gave it a top speed of 116 miles per hour and a service ceiling of 20,000 feet. Like the Sopwith 1 1/2 Strutter and the Sopwith Pup, the Tripe's armament was the single Vickers machine gun. The fuselage and tail unit of the Triplane were similar to those of the Pup, and had a length of 19 1/2 feet and a wing span of 26 1/2 feet.[4] Joining the three wings on each side was a single, broad strut, which went from the top wing through the middle wingspan and joining the lower wing. Two centre section struts joined the top and middle wing at the fuselage.

Collishaw's first flight in a Sopwith Triplane came the day he arrived on April 26, 1917. He, like the other pilots who flew the Triplane, found it a joy to fly. It had strong stability, good control response, and was in a class of its own compared to its contemporaries. Many pilots preferred it to the Sopwith Pup. The Triplane also had an adjustable stabilizer that allowed the pilot to fly virtually hands-free. The controls were light and easy to manipulate and the aircraft responded to them magnificently. It was also equipped with both an altimeter and an airspeed indicator. The pilot's seat was lower than in other Sopwith machines, yet had a wide field of vision so the pilot could see both forward and downward for landing and takeoff. The aircraft had quick acceleration and, unlike other machines, had no tendency to swing from side to side during takeoff. Its rate of climb was exceptional, turning the aircraft produced no skip or slide, and landings seemed effortless. With three wings or "planes," as they were referred to at the time, the Sopwith Triplane was without a doubt the most manoeuvrable machine in the air at the time.

No. 10 Naval Squadron initially practiced formation flying before it got into action escorting bombers from 4 Naval Wing to targets such as Zeebrugge Ostend, on the Belgian coast; and Bruges further inland. The squadron also provided air coverage for naval operations off the coast and carried out offensive patrols against hostile aircraft. On April 26, flying Triplane No. 5490, Collishaw and his flight escorted bombers to Zeebrugge at 15,000 feet. They had a minor scrap with some enemy fighters but were driven off, despite the all-too-familiar jamming of the Vickers gun. Two days later Collishaw had the same problem when he and his flight took off for an offensive patrol to the Ostend-Bruges area. The flight encountered a German two-seater at 12,000 feet so Collishaw closed in on a German two-seater at 12,000 feet and fired about forty rounds before his gun jammed. He broke off the attack to fix his gun, and then attacked once again, noticing that the observer was slumped over his gun, presumably hit. Collishaw followed the two-seater to 6,000 feet only for his gun to jam yet again, allowing the two-seater to escape during the delay. Later that same day, Collishaw had been dispatched to spot and circle a seaplane that had to make a forced landing off Nieuport. While the rescue vessel was on its way, four German fighters appeared on the scene. They weren't prepared for the Triplane's manoeuvrability, as Collishaw managed to get behind one of the HAs and fire a couple of bursts into him. The machine broke apart and plunged onto the beach below. Seeing this, the other three German machines headed for home. Even though at that moment Collishaw was out numbered three to one, the Germans were no match for the manoeuvrable Triplane.

No. 10 Naval Squadron, because of its location near the Belgian coast, had escaped what was to become known as "Bloody April" for the pilots flying further south on the Western Front. April 9, 1917 was the beginning of the battle of Arras and was meant to coincide with the Nivelle offensive of the French. Vimy Ridge was taken by the Canadians, and the British forces made several advances. The Nivelle offensive, however, which occurred later that month, was known in advance to the Germans and ended in disaster. During April, activity in the air was considerable. For the British, it meant supporting the ground offensive. For the Germans, their role was to prevent any air superiority during this time. By month's end, RFC losses were shocking.

> Nearly 250 British aircraft were shot down and over 400 men killed or wounded during April 1917. The achievements of the German scouts were staggering. Of the eight *Jasta* deployed on the Arras front there would be, on average, only seven aircraft flying a day — a total operational strength of just under fifty aircraft. Four men in particular stand out for their astonishing achievements during the month of April: Kurt Wolff with twenty-three victories, Manfred von Richthofen with twenty-two, Karl-Emil Schafer with twenty-one and Lothar von Richthofen with fifteen. Nevertheless, for all their success, it remains the case that day by day, through what became rather luridly known as "Bloody April", the men of the RFC had succeeded in performing their core function of providing photographs and artillery observation for the army.[5]

Collishaw and No. 10 Naval Squadron would need the very best flyers if they were to ever face Richthofen and his fellow pilots — and they did eventually meet. At the beginning of his time at No. 10 Naval Squadron Collishaw recognized that some of the pilots in his flight were not very dependable. They would leave him in the middle of combat with the enemy and return home. Collishaw complained to his commanding officer and Commanding Officer Bell agreed and sent them packing, replacing them with seasoned flyers from 3 Naval Wing.

No. 10 Naval Squadron continued in its role during the latter part of April and into early May, providing escorts for bomber squadrons like No. 5 Naval Squadron to targets at Zeebrugge and Ostend. They also went on numerous offensive patrols behind enemy lines, sometimes all the way to Bruges, or pursued hostile aircraft (HA) over Nieuport and Dixmude.

On May 1, 1917 Collishaw went up with two recent arrivals to No. 10 Naval Squadron, both Canadians — William Melville Alexander, from Toronto, and John Edward Sharman from Oak Lake, Manitoba. All three pilots all knew each other from flying together in 3 Naval Wing. The route for this afternoon patrol took them to Nieuport, then along the Belgium coast to Ostend, then due south to the German aerodrome at Ghistelles, west to Dixmude, and finally north to Nieuport. They were to repeat the rectangular circuit again upon reaching Nieuport. The first circuit was flown without incident. During the second round, however, W.M. Alexander was attacked from behind by an enemy Albatros two-seater near Thourout, east of Dixmude at 14,000 feet and flying into the sun.

William Melville Alexander, or "Alec," as he was referred to by his fellow flyers, recalled the encounter years later in a letter to R. Dodds, dated August 10, 1972.

It was the first time I had ever been fired on by an enemy and from that one episode, learned never to get careless when over enemy territory so far as vigilance was concerned. That particular action was the one which taught me more than any other, the necessity "to see" as much as possible in fact everything — and I believe was largely responsible for my being alive today.

We were out on a regular OP (offensive patrol) from Furnes aerodrome — about 4 miles behind the lines & 2 or 3 miles in from the coast — to patrol the area Nieuport — Ostend-Ghistelles — Dixmude. Whether there were 3 or 4 started out on the patrol I have forgotten — but when the action occurred there were just the three of us — Colly leading — myself on his left & the other man possibly Sharman on the right. My log and my recollection can't identify the third party. However the patrol time was nearly over and we were still over enemy lines flying westward for home in perfect formation just crusing speed and apparently not another machine in the sky when all of a sudden there was that terrifying rat-a-tat-tat of a machine behind us which automatically alerted all three of us & when I turned to see what it was all about, there not more than 100 yards behind was this enemy two-seater and I was the one he was shooting at. In other words, I was just a sitting duck and only the Almighty saved me. If I remember, there were 3 or 4 holes through my machine which meant 30 or 40 bullets were awfully close to my anatomy. I immediately made a fast climbing turn to get my gun on him to the tune of a few rounds but by that time he saw three triplanes coming in on him and being a smart individual just turned east & put his nose down & that was the last I saw of him.

To go back to Colly's report, I don't know what happened to the other two after I had turned to attack the enemy, once he put his nose down the tripe was no match for an enemy two-seater in a dive so I didn't follow for more than half a minute but in that short space of time got completely separated from the others & came back home.[6]

That incident made such a lasting impression on W.M. Alexander that he later taught new pilots the necessity of eternal vigilance.

The weather was good for flying in early May, so many pilots of No. 10 Naval Squadron were up on patrols behind enemy lines two, three, or even four times daily. Collishaw was up three times on May 1, 1917 and carried out four patrols on May 4. His Tripe often exhibited engine trouble, forcing Collishaw to turn back to base.

On May 10, while escorting Handley-Page bombers to Zeebrugge, Collishaw and his flight came upon three German scouts. Collishaw attacked one and after a few bursts of his machine gun the EA started to smoke and then caught fire as it spun down in a steep dive out of control.

This was Collishaw's first "flamer." Many pilots were very troubled to see a machine fall out of the sky on fire, and at times they were near enough to see the pilot in the stricken machine engulfed in flames. Pilots who observed such a horrific sight thanked heaven it was not them going to their death in such a fashion. Many had recurring nightmares of what they had witnessed long after the incident.

The German-held port of Zeebrugge on the Belgian coast was a particular thorn in the side of the British forces because it was the home of German submarines, destroyers, torpedo boats, and seaplanes — all of which could and did threaten English Channel shipping. The enemy forces were a constant threat to the vital cross-channel links and shipping routes to the Netherlands.[7] The British navy and air forces made numerous attempts to do damage to the harbour and port facilities at Zeebgugge, including the lock gates, with limited success. One attempt that took place on May 12, 1917 involved No. 10 Naval Squadron and Raymond Collishaw.

The operation of 12 May took three months of careful preparation. Weather conditions had to be absolutely right to ensure success. Bacon (Admiral Sir Reginald) needed the correct tidal direction along the coast, no low cloud to hamper the artillery observation aircraft, no mist over the target and no wind to disperse the smokescreen laid round the lumbering monitors.

Two cruisers, twelve destroyers borrowed from Tyrwhitt, three monitors each with a 15-inch gun, thirty-eight other ships and launches from the Dover Patrol duly arrived at the aiming point.

Early morning haze silenced the monitors until nearly 05.00 hours. By this time, the spotter aircraft were running low on fuel. Their task was made no easier by the arrival of the *Marine-fliegerabteilung Zeebrugge* in some considerable numbers. Their *Hansa-Brandenburg W12* fighters were very superior machines. In the fierce combat which followed, target observation became very much a secondary consideration for the pilots and observers of the Royal Naval Air Service. The monitors fired without correction. It was later proved that their range-finding was seriously amiss.

Bacon's force fired 200 shells from a range of thirteen miles. Forty of them were in the general area of the target. Fifteen landed within forty-five yards of the lock gates which remained serenely undamaged behind their concrete shelters.[8]

Wireless-equipped RNAS two-seaters were to have directed the fire of the monitors. Fighter cover was provided, including Collishaw's flight, for the spotting enemy aircraft and German naval vessels. That morning, seven Sopwith Pups from No. 4 Naval Squadron however, did manage to bring down three Albatros scouts near Zeebrugge. A little later in the day, Collishaw's flight encountered two German two-seater seaplanes. Any two-seater aircraft did not have the speed or flexibility of movement that a single-seater scout like the Tripe would have had. Collishaw immediately attacked one of the German two-seater reconnaissance machines at 8,000 feet and poured machine-gun fire into it until it crashed into the water.

One of the Triplanes flying with Raymond Collishaw that day was piloted by Flight Sub-Lieutenant M.W.W. Eppstein. He was shot down by enemy anti-aircraft fire. Maurice Eppstein, an Englishman, was No. 10 Naval Squadron's first casualty from enemy action. Collishaw and his flight continued to escort bombers such as Farmans, Caudrons, and Handley Pages over Zeebrugge and Dixmude on May 11 and May 12.

The last operational flight Collishaw made from Furnes was on the morning of May 14 where he had an indecisive scrap with a German machine over Zarren. That afternoon he and the rest of the squadron flew south to their new aerodrome at Droglandt in France, about 14 miles west of the town of Ypres. They became part of the RFC's 11th Army Wing, II Brigade. No. 10 Naval Squadronwas being transferred away from Dunkirk operations to be closer to the Ypres front in preparation for the Messines offensive. Many RFC squadrons were also moving north to the Ypres front from the area of the Somme to gain air superiority over the Germans in the coming battle.[9]

What the RNAS pilots were now facing on the Western Front bore no resemblance to what they faced at Dunkirk and other English Channel areas of operation. In fact, the demands of the Western Front were so intense it was causing a crisis in the morale of the pilots. S.F. Wise described it in the following manner.

> The best explanation for this crisis in morale seems to be a difference in service practice and experience. The RNAS squadrons lent to the RFC performed valiantly, but under conditions for which they were wholly unprepared. Raymond Collishaw, the most successful of all naval fighter pilots and one who rose superlatively to the challenges of the Western Front, put the matter in a nutshell when he spole of the "comparatively gentle" operations at Dunkirk. Conducted with relatively few casualties, these operations had permitted the building up of a body of pilots who had developed very considerable skills in the air, but the relentless psyshological pressures of the Western Front, with its incessant combats, proved a fearful shock to some of them…. Men who were physically or psychologically unable to measure up to the terrible demands of the air war were speedily winnowed out either by being returned to the depot within a few days of joining a squadron, or at the hands of German aviators. Neither RNAS leadership nor airmen had hitherto undergone this stern testing, and it is understandable that at both levels the resolution of some individuals wavered.[10]

The war in the air was a war of attrition and the loss of pilots were being felt in the RNAS just like they were in the RFC. Squadrons normally contained twenty pilots; however, with casualties and pilot shortages the establishment of a naval squadron was reduced to eighteen. By the time No. 10 Naval Squadron was sent to Droglandt, the decision was made to further decrease establishments to fifteen pilots. This meant that there would be three flights of five pilots each in No.

10 Naval Squadron. Thirteen of the fifteen pilots were Canadians and most had flown together in the former 3 Naval Wing. The squadron's pilot roster was as follows:

'A' Flight

F/S/L P.C. McNeil, Toronto (killed, June 3, 1917)

F/S/L C.E. Pattison, Winona, Ont. (wounded, May 20, 1917)

F/S/L L.H. Parker, Leeds Village, P.Q. (killed, June 14, 1917)

F/S/L K.G. Boyd, Toronto

F/S/L A.B. Holcroft, British (POW, June 24, 1917)

'B' Flight

F/S/L R. Collishaw, Nanaimo, B.C.

F/S/L E.V. Reid, Toronto (killed, July 28, 1917)

F/S/L J.E. Sharman, DSC, Oak Lake, Man. (killed, July 22, 1917)

F/S/L G.E. Nash, Stoney Creek, Ont. (POW, June 26, 1917)

F/S/L W.M. Alexander, Toronto

'C' Flight

F/S/L A.C. Dissette, Toronto (killed, June 2, 1917)

F/S/L J.A. Page, Brockville, Ontario (killed, July 22, 1917)

F/S/L J.H. Keens, Toronto (wounded, June 7, 1917)

F/S/L Q.S. Shirriff, Toronto

F/S/L D.F. FitzGibbon, British[11]

*P.Q. stands for "Province of Quebec"

Ellis Vair Reid was born in Belleville, Ontario, but had been raised in Toronto and was studying at the University of Toronto when he enlisted. He was the youngest of the Black Flight pilots. Reid was made a probationary Flight Sub-Lieutenant on January 10, 1916, then left for England a week later. He and Raymond Collishaw had sailed from New York to England on the same ship and had been at Redcar doing flight training together. Reid joined 3 Naval Wing on November 20, 1916 and then joined No. 10 Naval Squadron in early May of 1917.

John Edward Sharman, the oldest member of 'B' Flight, was born in September 1892, in Oak Lake, Manitoba. He was the son of a farmer — strong, with a robust physique. He was taking mining engineering at the University of Toronto when war broke out. Appointed a probationary Flight Sub-Lieutenant in Canada on February 3, 1916, he arrived in England a few weeks later. Sharman was at Redcar at the same time as Collishaw, though he arrived later. Like Collishaw, he had trained at Eastchurch before being posted to 3 Naval Wing at Manston. They were members of 3 Naval Wing together on the Oberndorf raid in October 1916.

William Melville Alexander, born and raised in Toronto, was attending the University of Toronto when he joined the RNAS. Alexander took his aviation training at his own expense and obtained his pilot certificate at the Stinson Flying School in San Antonio, Texas. He obtained his Aero Club of America pilot certificate on April 5, 1916, and then went to England in the spring of 1916 and trained at Portsmouth, Chingford, Eastchurch, and Cranwell before being posted to 3 Naval Wing late in 1916 to carry out strategic bombing raids. Alexander joined No. 10 Naval Squadron in May of 1917. He was described as an intelligent flyer with a good memory.

Gerald Ewart Nash was from Stoney Creek, Ontario where his father operated a fruit farm. He took his education in nearby Hamilton. Nash joined the RNAS in early 1916 and was trained in England during the year at Fisgard, White City, Redcar, and Cranwell. In January 1917 he was posted to the Dover Aerodrome and then for a brief stint with 3 Naval Wing. He joined No. 10 Naval Squadron in March of 1917.

All four members of Collishaw's flight were excellent pilots, keen to impress and earn the respect of their flight leader and work together as a team.

It was decided to designate each of the three flights of No. 10 Naval Squadron with a colour to distinguish one flight from the other. 'A' flight became the Red Flight, 'B' became the Black Flight, and 'C' flight was blue. The aircraft from each flight were painted in their respective colours. The Black Flight had the metal engine cowling painted black as well as the metal panels covering the top and sides of the fuselage, just behind the engine. Heavy canvas discs covered the wire-spoked undercarriage wheels. These were also black. Red Flight's machines had just the cowling painted red, as well as the wheel coverings and part of the tail. The same parts of the Triplane were blue in the case of Blue Flight.

> These markings enabled aircraft to be identified by flight when in the air and also allowed the mechanics to recognize, as the machines landed, which belonged to their specific flight. In any sort of breeze the Triplanes were quite unstable when taxying and it was the custom for the mechanics to run out after an aircraft from their flight had landed and grab the wing tips, helping the pilot to bring the machine in.[12]

Collishaw and the rest of the Black Flight continued with the black theme by giving names to their planes. Collishaw named his the *Black Maria*, after the name for the old English paddy wagon, which, during the Black Death period of English history, was used to move bodies during the London plague. Reid's plane was named *Black Roger*, Nash's was *Black Sheep*, Alexander's was *Black Prince*, and Sharman's was dubbed *Black Death*, referring to the London plague itself. The names of the planes were painted in white letters about 3 inches high on either side of the cockpit on the fuselage, just forward of the pilot's seat.

The rest of each Triplane of No. 10 Naval Squadron was doped a darkened khaki colour which gave it a dark green hue, almost black in colour, in order to blend in to the countryside. The underneath of the tail, fuselage, and wings were doped using a clear compound that gave it the colour of the original canvas used to cover the frames of the aircraft, or were a light blue colour to blend in with the sky. The doping of the fabric had the effect of stretching it over the frame. It was not paint but had a lacquer-like consistency. Some of the Triplanes of the squadron had their red, white, and blue roundels or cockades as they were also called, and rudders toned down in colour by using a lightly pigmented dope to make them less conspicuous. Other Triplanes had the standard insignia with no dark wash over the roundels.[13]

Collishaw and others had to deal with their Vickers machine gun jamming quite often in combat. No. 10 Naval Squadron had discovered that the reason for this was that the parts of the machine gun had been fashioned so that they fit too closely. When the parts got hot from the friction of firing the gun, the metal expanded and the gun jammed. The solution was to polish the parts using an abrasive so that they would fit more loosely. Once discovered, this method was copied by all other RNAS squadrons.[14]

During the month of May, in preparation for the battle of the Messines Ridge, many squadrons were employed for line patrol. Their purpose was to determine whether the earth taken out of the ground by the Canadian and Australian tunnelling companies working below the Messines Ridge could be seen from the air. If so, the Germans would be alerted to the tunnelling and would know an offensive was imminent. Luckily, the dirt was taken behind the lines and was camouflaged, and so no trace of the tunnelling operation was evident. Messines Ridge, occupied by the Germans, was the high point of the front lines just east of the town of Ypres and gave the enemy a strategic advantage. The Allies were determined to take the ridge and had built up a force of 100,000 troops ready for battle.

It was a couple of days after the transfer of No. 10 Naval Squadron to Droglandt that the first flying at the new aerodrome took place. On May 18, 1917, Collishaw, Reid, and Nash went up on a line patrol over the Ypres-Armentières area. No hostile aircraft were sighted during this flight or the following two evening patrols the same day. The next day the squadron practiced formation flying. On May 20, morning line patrol was conducted by two flights of two planes each. It was not often that all five planes in the flight went up together — flights of two or three planes, sometimes four planes at a time, were more common. Again, no enemy planes were sighted.[15]

May 21, however, proved to be different. Nash, flying Sopwith Triplane No. 5492, and Alexander took off on morning line patrol. Gerry Nash later filed a report of what happened next.

> I was out with F/S/L Alexander but lost him near Ypres
> in thick clouds. I circled, trying to get a landmark for
> position, and sighted five enemy machines. I dived into
> the midst of them, and in course of a side loop found one

right in front of my gun, and fired a burst of 50 rounds. The pilot fell back, apparently dead or severely injured, and the machine immediately side slipped and went down completely out of control. I then turned and saw the remaining four under my tail and coming after me, firing as they came. I climbed about 300 feet and finding them about 200 feet below me, I turned and dived again, when the four machines scattered in all directions away from me. I fired a few more rounds at one or two of them as opportunity offered. I then climbed and tried to recover my bearings in the thick cloud, eventually reaching Dunkerque.[16]

The combat report for this instance is marked "believed crashed." The EA was a single-seater, probably an Albatros. One upper plane (wing) was painted red and the other was brownish-green with red crosses outlined on a white ground. All the machines appeared to be painted a different colour.[17]

While at Droglandt, and even before, while at Furnes, there were a number of accidents with Sopwith Triplanes related to structural failure of the aircraft while in the air. These crashes may have been due to the fact that there were different types of Triplanes; two different types of Clerget engines, an English model, and a French model; and two different types of wires used to brace the struts and wings. Some of these wires were found to be defective.

Having heard rumours and grousing of structural failure in the Triplanes used by No. 10 Naval Squadron Commander Bell needed some way of reassuring the pilots that their Triplanes were safe and superior aircraft. He called Collishaw into his office and insisted that the pilots' faith in their planes be re-established. So Collishaw took one of the Tripes up to demonstrate to the pilots on the ground watching that there was nothing to worry about. Collishaw took the aircraft through its paces — diving, looping, rolling, and spinning the machine in as many ways he could. He ended his demonstration with a crash dive, pulling out of it as close to the ground as possible. Collishaw experienced no problems with the airplane, which subsequently satisfied the other pilots.

On May 24, 1917, a new Aldis sight was installed in Collishaw's Triplane. This new type of gun sight looked like a telescope but was an optical device for aiming at an enemy target. The major advantage of this type of sight was its tolerance for where the pilot's eye was when looking into the sight: he could be off-centre when looking into the sight, but still could see the centre circle of the sight to determine when to shoot his machine gun. Many pilots used an open ring sight that was mounted on top of the Aldis as a backup.

Between May 23 and May 31, 1917, the squadron flew a number of morning and evening patrols, most of which were inconsequential. Few, if any enemy aircraft were spotted. However, on an offensive patrol on May 30 to Menin, Collishaw and his flight came upon a number of enemy aircraft. In a brief encounter Collishaw managed to bring one of the Hun machines down. The next day the flight encountered two German aircraft doing artillery spotting. They got away and flew back behind their own lines. RNAS Operations Report No. 34 specifies that during the period of May 17 to May 31 No. 10 Naval Squadron carried out twelve patrols, sixteen flights after hostile aircraft, and two escorts (during a period of RFC attachment). One hostile machine had been brought down and four were driven down out of control.[18]

Things were only going to get hotter for Collishaw and the pilots of No. 10 Naval Squadron. As spring made way for summer, the intensity of combat and the number of aircraft involved in the battles of the air would increase. In June and July of 1917, Collishaw and the Black Flight would encounter Manfred von Richthofen and his Flying Circus, their most serious challenge to air supremacy so far.

⟱7⟱
THE BLACK FLIGHT
JUNE, 1917

Upon finishing a month's leave, Manfred von Richthofen had just returned to *Jasta* 11 in mid-June after being credited with fifty-two victories. He was the highest scoring fighter ace of all the belligerents and had attained twelve more victories than the legendary Oswald Boelcke. During the month of May, 1917, the Kaiser and the war planners and propagandists made the most of Richthofen's time off to exploit the hero of the Fatherland by having him attend numerous social events with royalty and the high and mighty of the Prussian elite who ruled Germany. Now with his leave over, Richthofen was well-rested and ready to raise the effectiveness of his squadron.[1] The German eagles were gathering.

> *Jasta* 11 was too far from the new battle lines and on 9 June, during Richthofen's absence, the unit moved from Roucourt to Harlebeke, north-east of Courtrai, on the

4. *Armee* Front. Between the move and the arrival of new Albatros D.V aircraft, however, *Jasta* 11 achieved no further victories until Richthofen's return.

By the time Manfred von Richthofen returned to *Jasta* 11, Ltn. Karl Allmenroder had become the fourth *Staffel* member to receive the *Pour le Merite*. Now Richthofen had to raise other new pilots to Allmenroder's level of effectiveness.

Jasta 11's new airfield was far enough behind the lines for Richthofen and his pilots to spend uninterrupted hours gaining familiarity with their new aircraft before going into battle.[2]

The Albatros fighter had become the mainstay of the German air forces. The Albatros had gone through numerous modifications from the D. I through to the D. V, "D" standing for *Doppledecker* or two-winger. The D. III was still heavily in use in 1917. Equipped with an in-line engine and armed with two Spandau machine guns, the Albatros was a formidable foe. The D. III was powered by an in-line 200-horsepower Mercedes engine. The fuselage had a rounded appearance and had an almost egg-shaped rudder and semicircular tail section that looked like two feathers of a dart joined together.

In May 1917 the first D. V's began arriving at the front, this aircraft being referred to as the "lightened D. III" by Albatros. Despite its reduced weight, the new fighter did not give the *Jasta* pilots much of a combat advantage over the vastly improving Allied fighters. Indeed, the high command realised that the D. V could not hope for the technical superiority its predecessors from Albatros had enjoyed over its foes from mid-1916 through to the spring of 1917. Instead, they hoped that improved construction techniques associated with the new fighter would allow an increased number of aircraft to be supplied to the *Jasta*s, who in turn would use these to numerically overwhelm the opposition.

The main recognition feature of the D. V was its rounded fuselage and rudder ... Despite these modifications, the D. V still had a propensity for breaking up when held in a prolonged dive, which created more than a little unease amongst its pilots.[3]

The summer of 1917 was to see a flurry of activity in the air. As each side struggled for air superiority, the number of aerial conflicts increased and a long series of combats between the fighter pilots took place. Many of the German *Jastas* were situated at aerodromes near the Ypres front.

Raymond Collishaw's first real test of his ability to deal with the enemy occurred on June 1. He and the other members of his flight — Nash, Reid, Alexander, and Sharman — took off on an offensive patrol to the area over Menin. In their two and a half hour flight they encountered enemy aircraft three times: the *Jastas* were out in full force. The first time, the flight spotted three Albatros D. IIIs below them. Having the advantage of height, Collishaw led the dive on the unsuspecting German machines. Unfortunately his gun jammed as he was preparing to fire. The rest of the flight attacked and a dogfight ensued. Collishaw cleared the jam and came up on an Albatros, which was painted in a mottled pattern and had a large "L" on the side of its fuselage. At less than 100 feet he fired. The aircraft burst into flame. Collishaw followed it down and saw it crash near Menin.

Nash, in the same scrap, fired his tracers into an Albatros and saw it go down in a spin. No one in the flight saw whether it crashed or recovered. Squadron record books described it as a "... possible out of control."[4] Three more enemy aircraft were encountered to the east of Armentières on the return, one of which was an Albatros two-seater. Collishaw dove on the enemy, but again had gun trouble. Reid, however, fired on the two-seater that had a cross on the top wing interlaced with black and white squares. The rest of the wings, the tail, and the fuselage were a mottled colour. Reid described his combat as follows.

When I got a clear sight I opened fire and about my third tracer shot the gunlayer through the head from about 100 yards. He fell over to one side, I continued my dive to within 30 yards and opened fire again, getting the pilot through the base of the neck. He fell forward and the machine went down vertically.[5]

Reid's combat report was marked as "believed crashed."

The term dogfight refers to a series of individual combats. After a flight of scouts dove on the enemy, the group of airplanes being attacked would normally break formation and engage individual enemy aircraft. The pair of planes would become waltzing partners going in circles after one another's tail, each manoeuvring to get in a clear shot on the enemy. This usually went to the pilot, whose machine had the tighter turning capability, assuming that they were more or less equally matched. Decisions were made in split seconds with pilots having a fraction of a second to fire upon the enemy aircraft when it came into his gun sights. As they circled, each of the other planes would lose altitude and in some cases could be seen by thousands of troops on the ground.[6]

Two or three times a day, each of the RFC and RNAS squadrons on the Ypres front would send a flight of planes to fly at maximum height on an offensive patrol, usually 10 miles over the enemy lines and lasting two hours or more. The Germans could easily count the number of Allied planes in their territory and send up a superior force to attack. Consequently, the British were often outnumbered in combat with the resulting heavy casualties. Many times it was the newest and least experienced pilots who fell prey to the German marksmen before they had learned the skills of aerial combat.

Out on offensive patrol (OP) experienced flight commanders, knowing the advantage lay with the formation at the higher altitude, tried to attain even higher elevations at the sight of an enemy formation. Once a height advantage was attained, however small, one formation would head straight for the other. The other formation then would turn to face their attackers and a head-on engagement would result.

As the two formations approached, the enemy's tracer bullets seemed to be aimed directly at one's eyes, and there was a temptation to lower one's head as much as possible, just peeping along the sight to aim the guns.

There was always the fear of collision. Each pilot would hold on until the last second, pouring fire at the enemy, and there was always a feeling of surprise that one's plane had not smashed into one of the enemy's.[7]

The following day, June 2, Collishaw, Reid, Alexander, and Nash went up on a morning HA patrol. They were to intercept a German two-seater that was spotted in the area. Flight leader Collishaw, flying at the front of the flight, attacked the two-seater by diving on it from behind. The unsuspecting German machine went down out of control. The flight returned to the Droglandt aerodrome only to go up again that afternoon, escorting FE2bs from No. 20 Squadron on a photo reconnaissance mission. Assisting Collishaw's flight was 'C' Flight led by Flight Sub-Lieutenant A.C. Dissette. A group of enemy aircraft tangoed with the two flights of escorts but was unsuccessful in breaking up the formation of FE2bs. Collishaw brought an EA down out of control. However, for Arthur Dissette, the war and his life ended that day as he was seen going down into a wood near Preven, northwest of Ypres.[8] Dissette was a University of Toronto graduate and had sailed with Collishaw on the *Niobe*. At thirty-one years of age he had displayed the maturity to lead, and was described by others as a good formation leader with the ability to command.

The same two flights flew another escort mission later that afternoon without incident.

Raymond Collishaw received his first promotion on June 3, 1917, being appointed Acting Flight Lieutenant. The promotion to Flight Lieutenant was confirmed by month's end. June 3 was a memorable one for Collishaw, not only because of the promotion, but due to the fact that his flight accounted for the destruction of two EAs. Collishaw, Reid, and Alexander went aloft on an offensive patrol over Roubaix. They were joined by another flight that was led by Nash. At about 4,000 feet they spotted five Albatros D. IIIs. Once again Collishaw was the first to dive on hostile aircraft. He had one in his sights and fired about fifty bullets into it. The Albatros turned over, burst into flames, and plummeted out of control toward the ground below. Comparing the Allies' war records to the Germans', it was most likely that Collishaw had shot down Ernst Fisher.[9]

All was not positive on the day, however. 'A' Flight leader Percy McNeil was killed in combat. His three aircraft encountered a force of twelve Albatros. Pilot Leslie Parker managed to shoot down one of the enemy but not in time to prevent McNeil from being shot down by Officer Klein of *Jasta* 27. Like Dissette, McNeil was also from Toronto and had four victories to his name. He was known as a steady and reliable flight commander. The loss of two flight commanders in the space of twenty-four hours must have had a devastating effect on Collishaw and the rest of No. 10 Naval Squadron. The loss of McNeil and Dissette left Collishaw as the only remaining original flight commander since the squadron transferred to RFC command.

The loss of McNeil as 'A' Flight leader necessitated the transfer of John Sharman to replace him as acting Flight Lieutenant. By the end of the month his promotion to Flight Lieutenant was confirmed. Sharman's spot on Collishaw's Black Flight was taken by FitzGibbon. Nick Carter took command of the blue-nosed 'C' Flight after the loss of Arthur Dissette. Alfred W. "Nick" Carter was from Fish Creek, Alberta, just south of Calgary and was an engineering student at Queen's University in Kingston, Ontario before the war. Carter and fellow Albertan T.R. Shearer took their flying training at St. Augustine, Florida.

When not in the air, the pilots would relax and take their meals at the Officer's Mess. At Droglandt the mess was one long large room, half of it taken up by a "U"-shaped table and fifteen wooden chairs where the officers would have their meals. The other half was a sitting or drawing room. Both halves could be separated by a rather ornate flowered curtain. In the sitting room were two large, high-backed, comfy chairs with high arm rests and a canvas collapsible chair that looked like it was more suited for a beach than an officer's mess. The ceiling was peaked and the wooden slats and beams were open, like one would find in a rustic cabin. The floors were covered with Persian rugs and the walls were wallpapered with a dark, heavy, large pattern to give the place a rich, warm feeling. A number of lights were hanging from the ceiling as well as the tail rudder of a German plane, with a big black Maltese cross on it — a souvenir one of the pilots had recovered after it had crashed.

The rigor of this time of battle is illustrated by the pilots' number of flights and time spent aloft during the month of June. On June 4, Collishaw went on four sorties lasting over eight hours in total. Sometimes he went up alone, sometimes with other members of his flight or plots from other flights. He must have had tremendous stamina and determination. On the fourth flight of the day, an evening flight, Collishaw went up with Reid, Alexander, Parker, and FitzGibbon, and managed to bring an enemy aircraft down in flames over Lille.

On June 5, 1917, flying with Reid, FitzGibbon, Nash and Boyd (from 'A' Flight), Collishaw and the rest of the flight took off on a morning patrol. It was a bright, clear day with few clouds. Flying at 16,000 feet northwest of Menin, the flight spotted an Albatros two-seater and in formation dove on it, with machine guns blazing. The German machine was seen to go down burning. The No. 10 Naval Squadron record book records this engagement as, "… Collishaw, assisted by other pilots, shot down one two-seater observation EA."[10]

The flight continued on in a northwesterly direction. Collishaw dove on an Albatros two-seater and manoeuvred under its tail so that he could fire on the EA without being observed. He fired about 100 rounds into the machine, which fell on its side and tumbled toward the earth. Both Reid and FitzGibbon had a crack at the crippled machine as it descended.

As a lead up to the Messines offensive, which began on June 7, 1917, No. 10 Naval Squadron was ordered to fly offensive patrols consisting of two full flights of aircraft, or ten planes. On June 6, Collishaw led his flight on such an offensive patrol, during which they spotted an Albatros two-seater escorted by about fifteen Albatros and Halberstadt scouts. Collishaw and the rest of his flight went in for the attack. Collishaw downed two Albatros scouts in short order, sending both down in flames. He attacked a third enemy machine, firing his machine gun into the cockpit of the Albatros. He saw the pilot slump down and then the aircraft fell from the sky out of control. Nash was able to get behind the two-seater and fired several times into it until it too crashed into the ground. Nash then concentrated his fire at an Albatros scout. Firing at close range, he pumped about twenty rounds into it and the German plane was seen going straight down towards the ground. Reid attacked one of the Halberstadts from behind. He was still firing his machine gun as the German machine fell out of control. John Page also got one of the Albatros fighters by firing his tracer bullets into the pilot's back. Sharman, Alexander, and Keens were each credited with sending an Albatros down out of control.

In all, ten enemy machines were sent down, five having been destroyed and five down out of control. No. 10 Naval Squadron suffered no losses in the attack. June 6 was a big day for the Black Flight, with Collishaw getting three victories, Nash responsible for two, and one each for Alexander and Reid. Collishaw led two more patrols that day, including one with two full flights, but no enemy aircraft were spotted.

The assault on the Messines Ridge had been planned for many months. It was part of British Commander-in-Chief Douglas Haig's wish to roll the German forces all the way to the Belgian coast.

It had long been an ambition of the British commanders of the Ypres salient to take possession of the Messines crest and during 1917 their tunnelling companies had driven forward nineteen galleries, culminating in mine chambers packed with a million pounds of explosives. Just before dawn on 7 June 1917, the mines were detonated, with a massive noise heard in England … Nearly three weeks of bombardment, during which three and a half million shells had been fired, had preceded the attack. When the assault waves arrived on the Messines crest, permanently altered by the devastation, they found such defenders as survived unable to offer resistance and took possession of what remained of the German trenches with negligible casualties. At a blow the British had driven the enemy from the southern wing of the Ypres salient. Haig's ambition to drive in the centre and thence advance to the Flemish coast was greatly enhanced thereby.[11]

In the months leading up to the battle, tunnelling companies had been digging underground shafts. At 3:10 a.m. the biggest man-made explosion in history killed approximately 10,000 German soldiers. The blast signalled the start of the battle. Allied infantry left their trenches and made it across no man's land to the German defences, meeting little opposition.

The air arm of the Second British Army, 11 Brigade, had been reinforced in preparation for the coming attack.

> Two corps squadrons of RE8s and BE2es were added along with ... 1 and 10 (Naval) with their Sopwith Triplanes. In addition, 23 (Spad) and 40 (Nieuport) Squadrons of 1 Brigade were detailed to extend their offensive patrols to cover the 11 Brigade area, while the fighter, bomber and reconnaissance squadrons of 9 (HQ) Wing were moved north at the end of May to the Second Army zone. By the beginning of June Trenchard had concentrated twenty squadrons (half of them equipped with single-seater fighters) mustering well over three hundred serviceable aircraft. German reinforcements for the entire Fourth Army front, from Messines to the sea, fell short of this number, and in the battle area further reinforcements did not arrive in time for the fight.... it seems likely that enemy aircraft on the Flanders Front were out-numbered two to one, and along the Messines Ridge by a much higher margin.[12]

The day of the attack was hectic for the RFC and RNAS squadrons as well, being employed on contact patrol work, directing the fire of the artillery on German positions and reporting on the progress of the attack. The role of some squadrons was to carry out low-level strafing of enemy positions behind the lines with their machine guns, while others went on bombing runs targeting rail junctions and German airfields. No. 10 Naval Squadron flew offensive patrols deep inside enemy territory attacking German fighters so the latter would not be able to attack the British observation aircraft over the battle area.

On June 7, 1917 Collishaw led two flights of five Triplanes beyond Ypres near Lille. They spotted a formation of six Albatros scouts flying above them. They tried to catch them but couldn't. Luckily the Germans hadn't spotted them. Later, they came upon more than a dozen Albatros scouts below and dove upon them. In the ensuing dog fight Collishaw shot down a German machine that was attacking Nash. Next it was Nash's turn to send an enemy aircraft to its final resting place, having closed to within a dozen or so feet of it before firing. The manoeuvrability of the Triplane was proving to be more than a match for the German Albatros scouts. Collishaw was credited with bringing one enemy aircraft down out of control.

Reid, meanwhile, having been separated from the double flight of planes, had to make his way back to Droglandt on his own. On his return flight he came upon a German two-seater, which he attacked. His fire must have hit the pilot because the plane immediately nosedived down, crashing as it hit the ground. Sharman, also separated from the group, met three Albatros scouts and fought them off successfully, but as he did, he lost altitude. Sharman hit one scout with his machine-gun fire and it quickly hit the ground, as it was only at an altitude of 500 feet. Sharman had to pull up hard in order to avoid crashing himself. He then attacked another Albatros and sent it out of control. The third German biplane fled the scene. Shortly after, Sharman was attacked by four more scouts but he was able to outrun them and got back to the aerodrome safely. The only casualty of the day was John Keens, a Canadian from Toronto who suffered a bullet in the lung, but still was able to land safely on the British side of the lines. Thankfully, he survived his injury.

Not only was there victory on the ground on June 7, but the RFC and RNAS squadrons had successfully prevented the enemy aircraft from disrupting the coordination of British air and ground operations. In spite of the gains made on the ground, the air war continued unabated. Collishaw and the Black Flight were airborne by 4:40 a.m. the next day on an operational patrol and then again just after lunch. They chased a couple of artillery observation aircraft but did not bring them down. The third time up that day for the Black Flight was a two-flight, ten-Triplane patrol over the Menin-Lille area. Pilots of the Black Flight flew over six hours that day.[13]

Collishaw's Triplane, Black Maria, was No. 5490 — the plane he had flown for most of the time since arriving at Droglandt. Each pilot was assigned his own numbered plane to use unless it was under repairs. Engine overhauls and aircraft repairs were conducted at night, thereby maximizing daytime flying. The Clerget rotary engines used in the

Triplanes were overhauled after every thirty hours, or about five days, of flying. This work was done by the mechanics of the headquarters, which meant the mechanics assigned to the Black Flight and other flights could concentrate on their respective planes to keep them in top flying shape. If a pilot's own machine was still being worked on at the time of a flight he was given another one. Though this was an exception rather than a rule.

On June 9, Collishaw led another early two-flight morning patrol east of Ypres. Just as the No. 10 Naval Squadron Triplanes had crossed the lines at about 17,000 feet they spotted a group of Albatros D. IIIs below them.

The Triplanes dived to the attack and Collishaw found himself on the tail of one of the enemy machines which sought to escape by a series of tight turns. The Triplane was able to turn more tightly and Collishaw, lining up the Albatros in his gun sight, was just about to fire when a fusillade of bullets smashed into his cockpit. They came from another Albatros, which had come up from out of the sun, and although Collishaw was untouched his controls were smashed. The Triplane fell off on one wing and went down in a series of wild swoops, cartwheels, and dives, with Collishaw quite unable to do anything to control it. The attack had come at 16,000 feet and it took the Triplane, with its engine cut off, 10 minutes or more to reach the ground. Instead of going into a straight dive the aircraft continued its fluttering course downward and just before reaching the ground took a final swoop upwards, thus much reducing the impact. Nevertheless, the Triplane hit with a shattering smash and folded into a mass of wreckage. Collishaw, though, was able to crawl out with no more than bruises and, as he later recalled, a determination never again to allow himself to be caught by an enemy machine coming from out of the sun. The Triplane had come down near a line of British trenches and its descent had been followed by the troops in the area. A group of them ran to the wreckage and were amazed to find the pilot alive, if bruised and shaken.[14]

This was the first time Collishaw had been shot down in 1917, but his third time since arriving in France in 1916 — how many lives did this cat Collishaw have? By June 9 he had eleven victories, seven destroyed enemy aircraft, and four designated as out of control.

The day after his crash, in spite of his bruises and sore limbs, Collishaw was in the air again. On the first patrol of the day, flying machine No. 5466, he had engine trouble and had to return to the Droglandt aerodrome. A midday patrol over Menin was uneventful. During the third and last patrol of the day, during the early evening and again over the Menin area, an enemy formation was spotted. The Triplanes engaged the German scouts — Collishaw attacking one, trying to get into position behind the foe. The German machine was weaving in and out of the clouds. Just as Collishaw was ready to fire on the EA he saw it escape into a dense cloud formation. He followed it but it had disappeared.

Three patrols occurred on June 11. On the first patrol there was a scrap with the enemy, but no enemy planes were destroyed. No hostile aircraft were observed on the second patrol. The third flight of the day around 7:00 p.m. proved to be more fruitful. Flying his new Triplane No. 5492, Collishaw, with the rest of his flight in formation, attacked an enemy two-seater over Menin, causing it to break apart in the air. No one pilot could be given credit for the kill. Previously flown by Gerry Nash, Triplane No. 5492 would be flown by Raymond Collishaw for the rest of his time with No. 10 Naval Squadron.

The Black Flight — Collishaw, Reid, Alexander, and FitzGibbon — took off on a dawn patrol on June 12. Over Courtrai they engaged a Halberstadt and sent it down out of control. The afternoon flight was uneventful. So too were the first two of three flights on June 13. On the last flight of the day they sent another Halberstadt down out of control but it went into a bank of clouds and disappeared. The Triplane pilots could not tell whether the enemy machine had been shot down or not.

Six Triplanes flew an early morning patrol on June 14: Collishaw, Reid, Alexander, and FitzGibbon of the Black Flight along with Sharman and Page. Over Menin they spotted three German planes — two Albatros scouts and a two-seater below them. The Germans were in the process of attacking several FEs. Collishaw picked out an Albatros and attacked. After firing a burst at the EA it fell, only to level out and head for home.

Sharman, Reid, and Alexander all engaged the enemy planes, but no decisive results followed. On the return flight, Sharman, Alexander, and Collishaw attacked a two-seater close to the lines north of Armentières, but due to their guns jamming the German plane got away. There was, however, a dark spot on the day. Les Parker from 'A' Flight failed to return and was thus presumed dead. It was later determined that Parker was probably brought down by German Fritz Krebs from *Jasta* 6.[15]

June 14 was a day to celebrate for Raymond Collishaw, after learning that he had been awarded the Distinguished Service Cross (DSC), his first British decoration. The message came through from headquarters of the 22nd Army Wing, to which No. 10 Naval Squadron had just been transferred — a re-organization in preparation for the upcoming battle of Ypres. The medal was confirmed on June 20, 1917 and the citation reads: "In recognition of his services on various occasions especially the following. On June 1st 1917 this Officer shot down an Albatros Scout in flames, on June 3rd, 1917 he shot down an Albatros Scout in flames, on June 5th, 1917 he shot down an Albatros Scout in flames, on June 6th he shot down two Albatros Scouts in flames and killed a pilot in a third. He has displayed great gallantry and skill in all his combats."[16]

The DSC was awarded to naval officers, whereas the Military Cross (MC) was given to army officers. Known as the Conspicuous Service Cross, it was renamed the Distinguished Service Cross in October 1914 and awarded to naval officers below the rank of Lieutenant Commander. The medal is a plain silver cross with rounded ends. In the centre of the obverse, within a circle, is the monarch's crowned Royal cipher. The reverse is plain. The ribbon is divided into three equal parts of dark blue, white, and dark blue.

The officers of No. 10 Naval Squadron organized a party that night to celebrate the news of Collishaw's award. It was a fairly low-key affair, not extending into the small hours of the next day.

The Navy did provide the pilots a weekly make and mend: a break of half a day off. Often pilots just relaxed and went to bed early on those half days off. Others would race through lunch, pile into whatever transportation was available, and head to the nearest town in search of entertainment, drink, and more fancy food than what they were used to. Invariably the pilots would roll back to Droglandt in a happy state and much the poorer. Regardless if they over-indulged or not, pilots would be wakened early the next morning for the dawn patrol. Barely able to keep their breakfast down, they put on their flying suits and headed out. The pilots, once in their open-air cockpits and aloft, could breathe in the crisp morning air, which seemed to have a sobering effect on them. To gain altitude the pilots flew back and forth just behind their own lines before venturing across the enemy lines.

Six Triplanes took off on the early patrol on June 15: Collishaw, Reid, Alexander, and FitzGibbon from the Black Flight, along with Holcroft and Taylor. Over Lille at 16,000 feet they saw a pair of two-seaters below them and dove after them. Collishaw's gun jammed, so other members of the flight continued to press the attack. The enemy dove away and escaped. The flight then turned north and less than a half an hour later they came upon five Halberstads north of St. Julien.

Toward the end of 1915 the Halberstadt Aeroplane Works produced a single engine scout named the Halberstadt D. I. This aircraft was powered by a 100-horsepower Mercedes engine. A later version, the D. II, came out in the summer of 1916 and had a more powerful 120-horsepower Mercedes engine. Both models had a single Spandau machine gun. The D. III model had a 120-horsepower Argus engine and like the previous versions of the Halberstadt was a sturdily built machine. It was probably the Halberstadt D. III that faced the Black Flight at this time of the war.

It was Collishaw's proven technique to get up close to an enemy aircraft before firing his gun. This is exactly what he did this time against the Halberstadt. He flew in behind the enemy and fired about fifty rounds into it. The Halberstadt spun down toward the ground as Collishaw kept firing into the machine. He was now the hunted, not the hunter, as a German aircraft was on his tail. The Triplane made a hard turn and turned the tables on the EA, with Collishaw ending up behind the foe. His gun jammed so he had to break off the fight. FitzGibbon, meanwhile, had shot down another Halberstadt. Both pilots watched it tumble earthward. At this point in the dogfight Alexander was under attack from behind by two Halberstadts. Both Collishaw and FitzGibbon came to his rescue. Having cleared his gun jam by this time, Collishaw drove off the two German scouts.

Later the same day the Black Flight joined Sharman's Flight for a patrol over Menin. They happened upon a formation of two-seater Aviatiks. Collishaw got close to one and fired on the German machine. His tracer bullets went right into the cockpit. The Aviatik slowly went into a near-vertical dive, side slipping and diving before falling completely out of control. The other enemy planes managed to escape. Sharman returned to the aerodrome because of engine failure, while the rest of the double flight carried on. Over Moorslede they encountered several two-seaters, escorted by about a dozen Halberstadt and Albatros scouts. The two flights of Triplanes attacked the enemy planes with the sun to their backs. Collishaw picked out an Albatros as his first victim. Only when he was close enough, not more than 100 feet, did he fire, causing the EA to falter before then falling into a dive and out of control. Reid had an enemy machine on his tail, but Collishaw rescued him by taking a shot at the German machine, which immediately broke off the attack. A Halberstadt scout was also following Alexander closely. Luckily for him, Collishaw noticed his friend in peril and attacked the Halberstadt at once. He fired off a number of bursts from his Vickers machine gun, causing the wings on the EA's right side to fold up and fall away in a tattered mess.

Collishaw witnessed Reid strike an Albatros, which fell over on its back and continued downward out of control. Reid then attacked one of the Halberstadts and sent it down too. John Page, one of the 'C' Flight pilots, sent another plane down out of control. On the day, Collishaw was credited with destroying one enemy aircraft and sending two down out of control. The rest of the squadron sent five machines down out of control. In the first half of June, No. 10 Naval Squadron accounted for fourteen enemy aircraft destroyed and eighteen driven out of control.[17] The reputation of the Black Flight and the other flights of No. 10 Naval Squadron was increasing, as was its effectiveness. This was, in part, due to the power and agility of the Sopwith Triplanes. With a competent pilot aboard, the combination was deadly.

The three patrols Collishaw led on June 16 were uneventful. So too was the early morning patrol on June 17. On the evening of June 17, however, Collishaw led Reid, Alexander, FitzGibbon, and 'A' Flight member Ken Boyd on a patrol near Armentières. They met up with five Spad scouts from No. 19 Squadron. Together they flew to the area around

Roulers, where they encountered eight Halberstadt scouts flying below them. The Triplanes dove first, followed by the Spads. Collishaw made three separate attacks on the enemy planes without result. He then dove on one that was attacking a Spad. After fifty rounds, the EA stalled and appeared to go down out of control — though sufficient observation was not obtained of the machine to make it absolutely certain.[18] Collishaw was given credit for this kill.

Meanwhile, Reid attacked another one of the enemy at close range, shooting the pilot in the shoulder. The enemy aircraft fell over and side-slipped, going down vertically out of control. This was observed and verified by Flight Lieutenant Collishaw.[19]

The Black Flight flew the usual morning and evening patrols from June 18 to June 23 with only indecisive results. The last week of June would be much different.

Soon after the return of Richthofen to his *Jasta* 11 on June 14, it moved from Douai northwards to the Ypres front and was based at Marcke, almost directly opposite Droglandt.

Crown Prince Rupprecht of Bavaria, nominally a senior German military commander on the Western Front, announced on 24 June 1917 the formation of *Jagdgeschwader* I (Fighter Wing 1), comprising the 4. *Armee* units *Jagdstaffeln* 4, 6, 10 and 11. The Geschwader was to be a self-contained unit, dedicated to achieving aerial supremacy over decisive battle sectors ... and to the greatest degree possible, was to be combined at one airfield. The formation of a single massive fighting unit, *JG I*, was largely a reaction to the deployment of Royal Flying Corps units in greater strength.[20]

Richthofen left his beloved *Jasta* 11 in the capable hands of Karl Allmenroder to head the newly-formed *JG1*.

The acting Staffel leader had watched out for the newer pilots as carefully as he had been looked after. He wrote to his sister: "There are always new men arriving at the Staffel and I am the only one of the old pupils who Richthofen still has around him. You may well think that he does not want to let me go and that at the moment I do not want to get away. [But] I will take my long leave later. The entire responsibility [of Staffel leadership] has been given to me by Richthofen. Hopefully I will remain in his Staffel a long time!"[21]

At this time, the machines of *Jasta* 11 were painted a dull blood-red colour, either the entire aircraft or parts of it. Other *Jastas* took on a wide variety of colour combinations for their planes. For example, *Jasta* 5 aircraft had either their tails or both tails and parts of the fuselage painted green. Most of *Jasta* 2's Albatros machines had white tails. In fact, most *Jastas* allowed their pilots to paint their machines however they wished. Some had them painted black and white, others a bright blue, and others were painted in a mottled motif. Most had large symbols or letters on the side of the fuselage like a flower or a death's head.

Naval Ten pilots were in constant combat with those of von Richthofen's Hunting Group and they came to recognize some of the group's aircraft through their distinctive individual markings. They were also familiar with the names of von Richthofen and some of his more successful flyers. At the time, however, they had no way of identifying the pilot of any enemy fighter with which they tangled although in some instances they were able to make a good guess as to his *Jasta*.[22]

On June 24, 1917, Collishaw's Black Flight, made up of Reid, Alexander, Nash, FitzGibbon, and Taylor left the Droglandt aerodrome early in the morning, along with John Sharman's 'C' Flight. Their mission was to escort two D.H.4s doing photographic work over Menin. When they were over Moorslede with the D.H.4s below, a formation of about fifteen Albatros D. IIIs appeared. They went for the D.H.4s and the Triplanes went for the Albatros, some of the German scouts sporting the red markings of *Jasta* 11. Collishaw managed to get behind one of the red machines and closed in to within less than 100 feet. He got off a burst of about forty rounds and saw the wings come off on one side of the plane before it went down and crashed. Collishaw had no time to dwell on his victory as four of the Albatros machines quickly ganged up on him. It took all of his skill and determination to take evasive action. As he fought to avoid being hit, he lost altitude drastically, almost hitting the ground. He managed to shake off the pursuers and got safely back to Droglandt flying at almost ground level. Collishaw's victim was most likely Erich Reiher of *Jasta 6*.[23]

Meanwhile, during his encounter, Flight Lieutenant Sharman noticed that some of the enemy machines were red and others were mottled green. He attacked one of the EA and fired about sixty rounds at close range, finishing his firing at a range of about 40 feet. Sharman saw his tracers enter the fuselage close to the pilot and the machine seemed to lose control. At this point Sharman's attention was interrupted by another enemy attacker, which he drove off. He then immediately saw the first machine 2,000 feet below falling out of control. As he watched, the tail plane, or fin, and one right wing came off and the machine fell in pieces. This was confirmed at the time by a pilot of No. 1 Naval Squadron who observed the fight, and a day or two later by a message from infantry in the neighbourhood.[24]

Two pilots from No. 10 Naval Squadron were lost that day, both from Sharman's 'C' Flight. They were Robert Saunders, who was killed, and Alan Holcroft, who had been shot down but survived as a prisoner of war. Saunders fell to one of *Jasta* 11's star performers, Karl Allmenroeder (his 28th victory), while Holcroft was brought down by another pilot from that unit, *Leutnant* Gisbert-Wilhelm Groos.[25]

Allmenroder was born on May 3, 1896, at Wald, near Solingen in the Rhineland, the son of a Pastor. He had wanted to be a doctor and had commenced his studies at Marburg when war broke out. He was sent with Field Artillery Regiment Nr. 62 to the Eastern Front, but contrived a transfer to the air service and was sent to the Halberstadt Flying School. On passing out of the school he was posted to *Fl. Abt.* 227, where he flew chiefly artillery co-operation missions. The career of Boelcke stirred his imagination and he once more sought a transfer, this time to fighters. In November 1916 he was posted to *Jasta* 11; on February 16, 1917, he scored his first victory. On April 2 he scored his sixth, and was appointed deputy squadron leader by von Richthofen and the two of them hunted well together.[26]

Richthofen appointed Allmenroder initially to be his right-hand wingman, but Allmenroder succeeded Richthofen as squadron leader of *Jasta* 11 when Richthofen left to command the entire *Jagdgeschwader.* Photos of Allmenroder in uniform show a serious looking young man with short, cropped hair. He had sharp, penetrating eyes that showed his determination, somewhat pointed ears, thin lips, and a smallish mouth, which gave a similar impression of determination and concentration. Karl had followed in the footsteps of his older brother Willy, who was also a fighter pilot.

Richthofen claims to have shot down one of the two D.H.4s in the same encounter of June 24.

.... however, there is no doubt that Manfred von Richthofen shot down a D.H.4 near Becelaere, just over 20 km west of his own airfield and still within German lines. He reported: 'With six machines of my *Staffel*, I attacked an enemy formation consisting of two reconnaissance aeroplanes and ten fighter aircraft. Unimpeded by the enemy aircraft, I managed to break one of the reconnaissance aeroplanes in my fire.'

The two-seater shot down on 24 June was logged as Richthofen's 55th victory. He was not distracted by the escorting Sopwith Triplanes of No. 10 Squadron, RNAS, as his comrades dealt with them.[27]

Despite their losses, General Plummer, commander of the British 11 Army sent No. 10 Naval Squadron the following note: "Officers Naval Squadron No. 10, — Collishaw and Sharman — did very good service and deserve great praise."[28]

The following day, June 25, 1917, 'B' Flight lost one of its original members, Flight Sub-Lieutenant Gerry Nash. The day started out in a rain storm during a mid-morning offensive patrol, again in the Menin area. Collishaw, Sharman, Reid, and Alexander met five Aviatiks and Collishaw managed to bring one down out of control. In the late afternoon, Collishaw led a flight of six Triplanes: Reid, Alexander, FitzGibbon, Nash, and Raymond Kent, a recent arrival to the squadron. Their task was to carry out a line patrol between Armentières and Dixmude, just behind the enemy lines. They flew at between 7,000 and 8,000 feet. Suddenly a formation of Albatros was right on top of them. The sky was full of twisting and turning planes as each one tried to line up an enemy aircraft in their sights. Each side squared off against the other. The Germans' element of surprise had sputtered out as Collishaw's 'B' Flight broke ranks and quickly recovered. Flight Sub-Lieutenant Nash went after the leader, an all-red Albatros D. III with a white spinner, engine cowl, and elevators. This machine was piloted by none other than Karl Allmenroder, the leader of *Jasta* 11, who quickly got the upper hand on Nash. The Black Sheep was last seen falling down behind the enemy lines. As Nash was falling, Allmenroder tipped his wings as a signal for the other Albatros to break off the dogfight. Nash nursed his damaged machine and made a forced landing. He then had the foresight to set the Black Sheep ablaze before being captured and made a prisoner of war. Nash was Allmenroder's twenty-ninth victim. Kent was also missing after the dogfight was over, but turned up safely later at Droglandt.

On June 26, Collishaw led an offensive patrol with FitzGibbon, Alexander, Reid, and Taylor over Zonnebeke and had three indecisive engagements with EA two-seaters. Flight Sub-Lieutenant Taylor had been compelled to change machines when starting, and owing to this delay, failed to pick up the formation. He crossed the lines under the impression that the four machines in front of him were those of his Flight, but the four two-seaters proved to be EA and turned on him in attack. Taylor picked out one of the EA and fired a good burst at him. The EA fell over on one side and went down apparently out of control. Taylor then managed to evade the rest of the enemy planes and landed at Berre, east of Hazebrouck, his machine badly shot with a number of bullet holes in the fuselage, close to the seat.[29]

On June 27 Allmenroder devised a trap for the Black Flight. He would split his *Jasta* in half with one formation of three Albatros, including himself, flying around as bait in full view at a moderate height. The other half would fly at a higher altitude, barely within sight of the others, and would be waiting to pounce on Collishaw's Tripe Hounds. As the *Jasta* was approaching the area over Lille, the Black Flight attacked the lower level of Albatros. The upper tier couldn't attack in time and the Black Flight cut through the lower tier of Albatros. Collishaw shot at one of the fleeing Albatros from a far distance, not his normal procedure. Once the dogfight was over, *Jasta* 11 reformed, but one of their own was missing. Their leader was seen descending in a slow glide. The nose started to dip, then the machine plunged into the ground.

The Squadron Record Book for No. 10 Naval Squadron describes what appears to be a fairly routine operational patrol for June 27, 1917:

> Collishaw led OP which took off at 5:20 p.m. and returned between 7:35 and 7:40 p.m. It included Reid, Alexander, Fitzgibbon and Kent. At 6:10 p.m. one EA two-seater observed and attacked with indecisive results, over lines north of Armentières. At 7:10 p.m. three Albatross scouts seen in storm over Fortuin and attacked, also indecisively, the enemy getting away in the mist…. Height 16,000 ft., until storms caused patrol to descend. Visibility bad at the end of patrol.[30]

The record of combats for Raymond Collishaw, extracted from the Air Historical Branch, Air Ministry, provides the following description of the same events:

> Collishaw and Flight Sub. Lieut. Alexander engaged a 2 seater aircraft north of Armentières. Although the 2 seater was observed to drive very steeply, it was probably under control.
>
> Collishaw led an offensive patrol and he led his formation down to assault a formation of three red coloured Albatross believed to belong to No. 11 Jasta.

Another hostile formation of three red Albatross had taken up a threatening attitude above and so Collishaw decided to open fire at long range on the target below. He did so, and while he was firing, the upper-most hostile Fighters assaulted him and his pilots. There was no time to see what happened to the lower targets, as Collishaw and his pilots had to take immediate avoiding action. Collishaw had six indecisive combats during this patrol.[31]

Some have suggested that the long-range shot by Collishaw at the red Albatros had killed Karl Allmenroder. However, Alan Bennett in his book *Captain Roy Brown — A True Story of the Great War, 1914–1918, Volume I,* researched the fact that Karl Allmenroder crashed in no man's land at 09:45 hours on June 27, 1917. So when Collishaw fired on the red Albatros D. V during his evening patrol, Allmenroder had been dead for over eight hours. Allmenroder, the twenty-one-year-old Rhinelander and leader of *Jasta* 11, had thirty victories when he was shot down, thirteen days after being awarded the *Pour le Merite.*

The pilots in Allmenroder's formation could scarcely believe that he had been shot down because the firing had been done from such long range. A German officer observer on the ground watched Allmenroder's fall. His aircraft went momentarily out of control and then proceeded to glide, what appeared to be normally, to the eastward; but after a brief interval, the Albatros went into an uncontrolled dive and crashed.[32]

Gerry Nash, lying in a hospital bed in Courtrai, upon hearing the church bells from St. Joseph's Church, inquired as to what was going on. He was then made aware that it was for the funeral of Karl Allmenroder. The funeral itself took place in Allmenroder's hometown of Solingen-Wald, with Baron von Richthofen in attendance.

The notoriety of No. 10 Naval Squadron was increasing. On June 28, 1917, Air Marshal Hugh Trenchard, the head of the RFC, visited the squadron to congratulate all the pilots on their good work. In the evening of the same day Collishaw took his Black Flight up to 16,000 feet over Armentières where they spotted an EA two-seater, but the engagement was inconclusive. Again, that evening they conducted another patrol, this time over Fortuin. An enemy Albatros was sighted but, because of bad weather, it escaped into the mist.[33]

During the period from June 16 to June 30, No. 10 Naval Squadron carried out thirty offensive patrols. Many engagements with enemy machines had taken place, five of which were decisive.[34] The squadron's total count for the month of June was nineteen enemy machines destroyed and eighteen driven out of control. These successes did not come without a price, however.

> Notwithstanding the fact that they were rated as generally superior in performance to the Albatros and Halberstadt scouts, the Sopwith Triplanes by no means had it all their own way. Between 15 May and 30 June the squadron lost six of its Canadian members, three killed and three wounded or missing. In addition, at least two other members of the squadron were lost, one being killed and the other taken prisoner.[35]

The war in the air was a war of attrition, with both sides suffering casualties. July would test the Black Flight to the maximum. They would also encounter the Red Baron.

THE BLACK FLIGHT
JULY, 1917

MUCH HAS BEEN WRITTEN ABOUT THE SO-CALLED "KNIGHTS OF THE Air," those chivalrous airmen who waved at one another when their guns jammed. Yes, it is true the pilots from both sides had a certain professional respect for one another. For example, if a pilot was shot down behind enemy lines, the opposing side often dropped a note at his or another airfield saying he was alive and had been taken prisoner. The death of a famous pilot resulted in wreaths or messages of condolence dropped at his aerodrome. Flyers downed behind enemy lines and not seriously hurt were often given food and drink by the enemy pilots in the squadron mess, before being sent to a prisoner of war camp.

Normally, however, air combat in the First World War was a deadly and ruthless business. It was about gaining an advantage over your opponent. The advantage came with height — being able to dive on him from above, or attacking from a blind spot, such as from below, or approaching from out of the sun. If an enemy had a gun jam, the advantage was yours and you attacked knowing he could not shoot back. Often, if there were only two combatants, each would circle the other at the same altitude trying to get behind the other's machine. This waltzing in a circle might last for a full five minutes while each pilot looked for an advantage over the other. The aircraft with the smallest turning circle would be able to get behind. At any time one aircraft could attempt to escape by diving quickly away, hoping the enemy would not be able to catch up. The machine with the faster diving speed would either be able to pull away from the other and escape, or pull in behind the machine trying to escape and shoot it down.

Pilots used and perfected a number of offensive and defensive tactics in order to get the advantage over the enemy plane. For example, when an enemy machine was behind them, pilots could employ the Immelmann turn, named after the inventor Max Immelmann — an early German ace of the First World War. This strategic move involved pulling up into a half loop, then rolling the aircraft to the right and completing the loop, ending up behind the enemy, ready to fire and destroy them.[1] Another variation of the same move is to pull up as if going into a loop, then point the nose of the plane down and dive on the opposing plane.

Pilots learned climbing turns called *chandelles*, and how to turn in the opposite direction of their opponent when behind and below him. If they turned in the same direction as their opponent, he could easily dive on them from above. If he turned first in the opposite direction and then rolled toward the enemy plane, he could pick up speed and find himself coming in under the enemy tail, ready to shoot.

Those pilots who had great success shooting down the opposition were those who could manoeuvre close enough to the target plane. Gun accuracy increased the closer pilots got to the enemy, thus eliminating problems with the gun sight, performance of the machine, having to use deflecting fire, and loss of elevation issues. For most, the only certain way of downing an enemy was to achieve a position immediately behind and fewer than 150 feet away.[2]

On top of strategic considerations, air combat also took its toll on the pilots' nerves, as William Alexander explains.

When you came over the lines, your nerves were just taut from the time you entered the danger zone until you got back, and you'd be three-quarters of an hour over the lines. Even if you didn't get into a fight, you had to watch like a hawk. I've gotten out of a machine and lifted the goggles to let the air get at my eyes. I'd be physically tired for no other reason than nervous stress. I just was scared to death.[3]

July would be just as exhausting and taxing for No. 10 Naval Squadron and Collishaw's Black Flight as was June. On July 2, 1917, General Gough, the head of the British Fifth Army paid the squadron a visit, and like Trenchard a few days prior, congratulated the squadron on its good work and many victories.

That same day, Collishaw, with Reid, Alexander, FitzGibbon, and a new arrival, John Allen, together with Sharman's flight, went up on a morning patrol over Poelcapelle, northeast of Ypres. They spotted a pair of German Aviatiks just below them. Collishaw dove and was followed by the rest of his flight. He nearly collided with the enemy machine, which, after it realized it was under attack, tore away and escaped. Turning his attention on the other Aviatik, Collishaw fired a burst that hit the pilot. The two-seater slowly turned to one side and tumbled out of control. Other members of the flight witnessed it crash, but Collishaw didn't see it fall because the rear gunner of the Aviatik hit his engine and he had to break off the engagement and head back to the aerodrome at Droglandt. He was rewarded for all his efforts to date by being promoted to Acting Flight Commander.

July 3 saw the Black Flight run into heavy opposition. Leading his flight on an offensive patrol over Menin, Collishaw and his pilots tangled with several enemy fighters. The whole patrol observed one plane falling and breaking up in the air, but no one in the flight could take credit for the kill. Later that day, Collishaw, along with Reid, Alexander, FitzGibbon, and John Allen, encountered twenty-one enemy fighters over Courtrai, but nothing decisive resulted. July 4 saw the Black Flight, with the help of Sharman's flight, meet eighteen enemy aircraft but with no definitive results.[4]

The death of *Jasta* 11 leader Allmenroder in late June meant that a replacement was to be named. Manfred von Richthofen called on his old friend and *Jasta* 29 leader Lieutenant Kurt Wolff to transfer back to his former *Jasta* 11 — this time to lead the squadron and to provide the same strong leadership that Allmenroder had exemplified.

Wolff, a year older than Allmenroder, was born in 1895 in the small town of Greifswald. Wolff was an officer in a railroad transportation regiment before becoming a pilot. He had a slim build and a graceful air about him. Wolff had dark eyebrows and hollow eyes. He always seemed to have a happy expression. This graceful manner changed, however, once he was airborne. Then he was a serious, capable, and precise combatant.

The *Geschwader* or *JG1* as it was referred to, with Richthofen in command, was assembled in early July at Marcke on the southwest edge of Courtrai. This central location was now the home of *Jastas* 11, 10, 6, and 4. The estate of Baron Jean de Bethune was converted for military purposes. The sprawling green lawns, the adjacent castle, and the other buildings of the area called Marckebeke were ideal for the centralized location needed for *JG1*.[5]

Flying his trusted Sopwith Triplane No. 5492, Collishaw and the Black Flight, made up of Reid, Alexander, and FitzGibbon took off from the Droglandt aerodrome at 10:00 on the morning of July 6. Near Deulemont, some 6 miles northeast of Armentières, they spotted a half a dozen British FE2ds being attacked by an overwhelming number of German Albatros fighters. There were thirty or more including some of the new Albatros D. Vs. It turned out the FEs (from No. 20 Squadron) had been first attacked by Richthofen, who continued to fly with his old unit even though he commanded the new *JD1*, and six or seven red Albatros from *Jasta* 11. Then planes from other *Jastas* joined in. Under attack, the FEs would take up the defensive position of forming a circle with their gunlayers blazing away at the enemy. Each time an Albatros would attack to break up the circle, the rear gunners would drive them off. Collishaw and the rest of 'B' flight dove to their rescue. A wild dogfight erupted. Planes were twisting and turning, trying to get an enemy plane in their sights for just a second or two, long enough to get in a burst of fire. They also had to be aware of any machines on their tail trying to apply the same strategy to them. Because they were so outnumbered, Collishaw and his pilots had no time to follow up an attack to ensure they had destroyed an enemy plane. Collishaw got behind a red Albatros and fired a quick burst at the aircraft, which went down like a stone. It was each man for himself as each of the Triplanes twisted and turned to avoid being shot at and to try to get into a position of advantage in order to fire on the enemy. In the melee Collishaw shot down five more enemy aircraft. Alexander closed in on a machine that was on Collishaw's tail and fired a burst right into the German pilot's back. Alexander turned and fired at another Albatros, which fell out of control. Ellis Reid also managed to shoot an EA down out of control.

Meanwhile, the FEs were putting up a tremendous show. These slow and cumbersome pusher aircraft managed to hold off the attackers as best they could.

It was Woodbridge who fired at Richthofen's red Albatros, from long-range. Kurt Wolff led the attack on the FEs.

> In the tight formation, Wolff was a few yards ahead and below the Rittmeister as Richthofen singled out the leader and plunged down. The F.E. pusher biplane carried the observer-gunner in front and the pilot in the rear cockpit. Except for the engine it had no rear protection.... As the distance narrowed, Richthofen was vaguely aware of Wolff's opening burst on the lead plane and of Woodbridge's quick return fire.... as Wolff flashed past the outmoded two-seater, the Captain turned to meet the red Albatros, giving Woodbridge a clear target. Woodbridge ... singled out the attacker behind Wolff and tensed for the head-on attack. He swung his gun, aligned the sights on the looking biplane and began firing in steady bursts ...[6]

Richthofen later wrote:

> I had not yet cocked [my machine guns], there was still so much time until I got into combat with my

opponent. Then I watched as the observer, in great excitement, fired at me. I calmly let him shoot, for even the best sharpshooter's marksmanship could not help at a distance of 300 metres. One just does not hit!

Then he turned completely toward me and I hoped to get behind him in the next turn and burn his hide. Suddenly there was a blow to my head! I was hit! For a moment I was completely paralyzed … My hands dropped to the side, my legs dangled inside the fuselage. The worst part was that the blow on the head had affected my optic nerve and I was completely blinded. The machine dived down.[7]

Woodbridge later gave this account of the attack.

Then something happened. We could hardly have been 20 yards apart when the Albatros pointed her nose down suddenly. Zip, and she passed under us. Cunnell banked and turned. We saw the all-red plane slip into a spin. It turned over and over and round and round. It was no maneuver. [sic] He was completely out of control. His motor was going full on, so I figured I had at least wounded him. As his head was the only part of him that was not protected from my fire by his motor, I figured that's where he was hit.[8]

One of Woodbridge's bullets had indeed hit Richthofen in the head, scoring along the skull and splintering bone without penetrating. He initially had blacked out.

Richthofen regained enough mobility to switch off the engine and then, as his body began to respond, his vision returned. He looked at the altimeter. It showed 800m. He restarted the engine and headed eastward. As the world came into focus for him, Richthofen looked around and saw that two comrades, Ltns. Otto Brauneck and Alfred Niederhoff had come down with him. They stayed with their commander as he set down in a field of high grass near Wervicq, Belgium.[9]

Richthofen, who was taken to hospital, would not return to action until mid-August. In all, the Black Flight accounted for nine enemy planes destroyed or brought down out of control on that fateful July 6, 1917.

The RNAS summary of the fight reported that Collishaw had brought six of the enemy down out of control while the RFC communiqué credited him with one out of control and five more "probably out of control". Alexander received credit for destroying two of the enemy fighters and Reid was credited with one destroyed.[10]

General Plummer, commander of the Second Army, sent his congratulations to No. 10 Naval Squadron saying, "An excellent day's fighting — results remarkable. Lieutenant Collishaw Naval Squadron No. 10 did splendidly, as he always does."[11]

Much has been written about the Red Baron. To some he was a ruthless, cold-blooded killer, a hunter who perfected his trade in the air. To the men of his "Flying Circus" he was an effective leader, a mentor, and a strict disciplinarian.

Growing up near the woods of the Weistritz Valley in present-day Poland, the young Manfred loved to hunt game on horseback. He was a good shot and enjoyed the chase. Starting his military training in 1903, von Richthofen was commissioned as a *Leutnant* in 1912 and entered an Uhlan cavalry unit. The unit was on the Eastern Front at the beginning of the war, but was soon transferred west to the German border town of Metz, just west of Verdun, France. In the ensuing months, Manfred became bored with static trench warfare. Both sides had dug in, forcing a stalemate. Here, the cavalry was useless as neither side could outflank the other. Bogged down in the mud and mire of the trenches, Manfred looked for a way out of his situation. In May of 1915 he enrolled in the German Air Service and started out as an observer in two-seater aircraft.

Flight Sub-Lieutenant G.L. Trapp of No. 10 Naval Squadron, killed November 12, 1917.

During the summer of 1915, Manfred flew reconnaissance missions on the eastern front, supporting Austro-Hungarian troops near Brest-Litovsk. By mid-September his unit had been transferred to the French front near the town of Champagne. He quickly honed his skills in the air, and by early 1916, had completed training as a fighter pilot, in charge of his own single-seater scout. The legendary Oswald

Boelcke, who was the highest-scoring ace at the time, personally chose Manfred to join his *Jasta* 2.

Boelcke gave his pilots precise instructions on how to behave in the air and in combat. His word was gospel. Richthofen's first kill came on September 17, 1916. Just over a month later, his hero and mentor, Oswald Boelcke, perished in a mid-air collision with one of his own flyers. By January 1917, Richthofen had become a name to be reckoned with, scoring sixteen victories and earning Germany's highest decoration, the Orden Pour Le Merite. He commanded *Jasta* 11. It was at that time that Richthofen came up with the idea to have his new Albatros D. III painted all-red, mostly as a dare to the Allied pilots to come and get him. Manfred wanted to be noticed. Richthofen had attracted skilled flyers around him, pilots like *Leutnant* Karl Allmenroder and *Leutnant* Kurt Wolff, just like Boelcke had done in the past.

Richthofen was all work, rarely drinking or smoking. He did not partake in parties and *Jasta* celebrations and was often to bed early, ensuring he got enough rest for the next day's flying.

He would lecture his pilots on proper flying techniques and manoeuvres for combat, and taught them the finer points of attack and defence in the air. He was a serious commander, yet cordial to officer and ground crew member alike. Richthofen was dedicated to the Fatherland, his Kaiser, and his family, including his *Jasta* family. He set a strong example for others to follow. By April 1917, Richthofen had shot down forty-four enemy machines.

On July 7, 1917, the day following the big scrap with Richthofen, Collishaw, along with John Sharman, Reid, FitzGibbon, Page, and George Trapp, a new arrival to the squadron from New Westminster, British Columbia, went up on an early morning patrol. Trapp was one of three brothers in the flying services. None of them survived the war. Collishaw would go on to marry Trapp's sister Neita. The flight took off at 5:00 a.m. Near St. Julien they encountered a dozen Albatros fighters. The fight that followed was indecisive and the German fighters ended it by breaking off the engagement. Upon re-forming his flight, Collishaw noticed Sharman, Page, and Reid were missing. He continued on with FitzGibbon and Trapp. The three remaining planes ran into more Albatros scouts, one of which got on the tail of FitzGibbon's plane. Collishaw quickly got behind the German and at a range of 30 feet, opened fire. The Albatros went down in a spin and did not recover.

On his way home, John Page met up with a French Spad and together they attacked three Albatros. Page ended up shooting one down, but the other two escaped. John Sharman and Charles Pegler each destroyed a two-seater on a separate flight that day.

On the ground, the British Fifth Army, which No. 10 Naval Squadron supported, were preparing for a big offensive that was to become known as the Third Battle of Ypres. The air offensive that was to go into effect on July 8 had to be postponed until July 11 due to inclement weather. Despite being grounded for a couple of days, Collishaw received encouraging news on the July 8 that he had been awarded the Distinguished Service Order (DSO).

The citation for the award, published later, reads:

> For conspicuous bravery and skill in successfully leading attacks against hostile aircraft. Since the 10th June, 1917, Flt. Lt. Collishaw has himself brought down four machines completely out of control and driven down two others with their planes shot away. Whilst on an offensive patrol on the morning of the 15th June, 1917, he forced down a hostile scout in a nose dive. Later, on the same day, he drove one hostile two-seater machine completely out of control, one hostile scout in a spin, and a third machine with two of its planes shot away. On the 24th June, 1917, he engaged four enemy scouts, driving one down in a spin and another with two of its planes shot away; the latter machine was seen to crash.[12]

The DSO is similar in shape to the DSC. It is also a cross with curved ends, yet it is overlaid with white enamel. On the obverse, in the middle of the cross is a green enamel laurel wreath, which encloses the imperial crown. The reverse is the royal monogram within a similar wreath. It is suspended from its ribbon, which is crimson with dark blue edges, by a swivel ring and a straight bar decorated with laurel leaves.

At the time Collishaw received notice of his award, Sharman received notice he had received a bar to his DSC, signifying he had received the decoration twice. He had previously received the DSC while he was with 3 Naval Wing. A bar to a decoration is a silver bar, about a quarter of an inch high, and is attached to the ribbon above the medal itself. Its length covers the width of the ribbon.

Ellis Reid also received notification that he had been awarded a DSC. His citation read:

In recognition of his service on the following occasions: On the 6th June, 1917, he attacked and drove down one of four hostile scouts. This machine dived nose first into the ground and was destroyed. On the afternoon of June 15th, 1917, he was leading a patrol of three scouts and encountered a formation of ten enemy machines. During the combat which ensued he forced one machine down completely out of control. Next he attacked at a range of about 30 yards another hostile scout. The pilot of this machine was killed, and it went down completely out of control. This officer has at all times shown the greatest bravery and determination.[13]

On July 11, Collishaw and the Black Flight were up flying again on both a morning and an evening offensive patrol. The evening patrol was made up of Collishaw, Alexander, Reid, and FitzGibbon. Over Wervicq they encountered a couple of Aviatiks, but the pair of enemy planes managed to escape. Later in the flight they came across a number of Albatros fighters over Polygon Wood. Collishaw managed to shoot one down and so too did Alexander. Collishaw saw Alexander's victim fall from the sky in a spin from which it couldn't recover. Unfortunately No. 10 Naval Squadron lost one of its pilots that day. Raymond Kent was shot down by *Leutnant* Walter Blume of *Jasta* 26. Kent managed to land his aircraft safely but did so behind enemy lines, and so was made a prisoner of war.

The lead up to the attack on Ypres created ever-increasing activity in the air. On July 12 the RFC communiqué stated that there was more fighting in the air on that day than any other time since the start of the war. No. 10 Naval Squadron's 'C' Flight was on dawn patrol by 4:22 a.m. led by Nick Carter, formerly from 3 Naval Wing. Because of the number of casualties experienced by No. 10 Naval Squadron, Nick Carter was transferred into the squadron on July 2, to take over a flight. Alfred Williams "Nick" Carter was born on April 29, 1894 and grew up in Calgary, Alberta. He transferred from the Canadian Expeditionary Force (CEF) in 1916 and flew with 3 Naval Wing as well as No. 3 and 10 Naval Squadrons. Carter would end the war with the rank of a Captain and with a score of fourteen victories.

Carter's flight of Triplanes took the inner route, flying close to the lines, whereas Collishaw's and Sharman's flights took the distant patrol deep into enemy territory. Reid and Alexander flew with Collishaw while Sharman had Page, Charles Pegler, and Cecil Lowther, a new replacement pilot. At 16,000 feet over Polygon Wood east of Ypres they spotted three Albatros machines below them. Diving on them in formation, Collishaw fired on a red Albatros and witnessed the pilot slump down, apparently hit. The enemy plane then tumbled down in an uncontrolled spin. The initial attack on the three enemy planes caused other Albatros to come to the rescue of their comrades. Soon, Collishaw's and Sharman's flights were surrounded by some thirty Hun aircraft, some painted red, others green, and still others painted brown and yellow. These German aircraft were probably from *Jastas*, 11, 5, and 4.

Sharman dove on one of the Albatros, putting over fifty rounds into it and forcing it down. He had no time to follow it down, as he was too busy getting into position to attack another EA. After a brief skirmish it too went down out of control. Reid had lined up a German aircraft and fired an accurate burst, causing its wings to fold back. The pilot of the stricken machine had no control over it, and it did a number of cartwheels and spins as it plummeted toward the ground. Reid then managed to get behind another Albatros and fired his machine gun at close range. The Albatros went straight down until it crashed. Collishaw was attacked by six red Albatros but managed to out-manoeuvre them, escaping the fight and heading for home.

Two No. 10 Naval Squadron pilots were casualties that day. John Allan was wounded but managed to bring his plane back to Droglandt. He then was hospitalized. Charles Pegler was shot down and killed behind enemy lines, probably by German pilot Guttler of *Jasta* 24.[14][15]

The month before, while still at 3 Naval Wing, Carter was involved in an incident that, in hindsight could be seen as humourous, but at the time was close to being a deadly experience. On a return flight from north of Cambrai, "Nick" Carter, Jimmy Glen, and Aubrey Ellwood, once they had crossed the lines, were engaging in their usual sport of "contour-chasing," flying their aircraft close to the ground. Carter's Pup suddenly came to a halt in mid-air. He was upside down, swinging back and forth. He had flown into a cable, which was attached to an Allied observation balloon. The cable had wrapped itself around the propeller of Carter's machine. The weight of the Pup forced it to gradually descend down the cable until it gently touched the ground.

The air war had turned into a war of attrition with the goal being how many planes each side could destroy of the other. No. 10 Naval Squadron soon became known as the Suicide Squadron, because of the casualties inflicted upon it by von Richthofen's *JG1*. The Germans always had the advantage because they stayed in their territory and let the enemy come to them. Secondly, the westerly winds made it difficult for the Allied planes to return to base if they had engine trouble, or if they were at all shot up. Collishaw at one point wondered if the squadron was at the end of its rope. He was starting to feel the stress of combat as No. 10 Naval Squadron's casualties were mounting. With the number of combat missions he and his fellow pilots were flying they were at the point of exhaustion. It might have served as some consolation for No. 10 Naval Squadron to receive, on July 13, 1917, a note of congratulations from the head of all the British forces, Douglas Haig himself. However, it might also have been Collishaw's physical state at the time that accounted for what happened to him on July 14.

On July 13, a number of patrols took place over the Menin, Cambrai, and Polygon Wood area. There were a number of encounters with the enemy, but the results were indecisive. No enemy machines were shot down. On July 14, however, Collishaw got the scare of his life. Over Polygon Wood he and his flight met up with a number of enemy scouts. A dogfight ensued and the usual waltz occurred with the planes circling each another. Each was trying to get behind the other in order to get a good shot off, and all the while glancing behind to make sure they weren't attacked from the rear. Collishaw's Triplane could make tighter turns than the enemy machine. Just as he had the German plane in his sights, a third

HA appeared and it was going straight for Collishaw. At the last moment, the Triplane zoomed underneath the oncoming airplane. The force of the move was so great that Collishaw's safety harness broke. He now was out of the cockpit of his machine and holding on to the two centre struts of the Triplane for dear life. Since no one was at the controls, the Triplane continued in its downward direction, spiralling out of control. It would then tilt its nose up, only to commence a descent once again. All this time Collishaw was hanging on as best he could. He could not keep this up forever. The strength in his arms was ebbing quickly. The other members of Collishaw's flight looked on in horror, powerless to do anything. Suddenly, the Triplane pulled up sharply on its own, forcing Collishaw back into the cockpit. He struggled back into his seat, grasped the control column, and righted the Triplane. Collishaw had fallen almost 10,000 feet. He headed home as quickly as possible, exhausted after such a scare.

This incident profoundly shook Raymand Collishaw. It was his fourth narrow escape from death in two and a half years. It should be remembered that pilots were not issued parachutes in the First World War. The primary justifications the British used against the use of this life-saving device were:

1. That pilots, given a means of escape, would be tempted, when under threat, to abandon their machines prematurely.
2. That although it was right for crews of kite balloons to be offered a means of escape because they were vulnerable and couldn't hit back, aeroplane crews were equipped to defend themselves.
3. That the parachutes available were altogether too bulky for stowage in the tiny cockpits of the time, and too complex and cumbersome for external fitting; that their weight (28 lbs.) would have detracted from aircraft performance; that they would have become entangled with the tailplane or some other obstruction on release; and that they were unreliable anyway.
4. That most fatal crashes occurred on take-off and landing or when stunting at low level, when height was insufficient for a parachute to open.[16]

In spite of the harrowing experience Collishaw had the previous day, he was back up leading his flight on the morning of July 15, and again on an evening patrol over Polygon Wood. During this latter patrol the flight encountered thick anti-aircraft fire, or "Archie" as it was referred to, at 12,000 feet.[17] Shells were exploding all around Collishaw's flight. One of them hit his machine, breaking one of the wire cables attached to the engine cowling. Pieces of metal flew off, one piece lodging itself in one of the lower wings causing his Triplane to go into a spin. Through a combination of throttling his engine on and off, Collishaw was able to maintain control over the machine and attempted to fly west toward his own lines. German infantry shot at him as he crossed the lines, but he was able to crash safely in his own territory, breaking the undercarriage of his Triplane in the process.

This was the fourth time Collishaw had been shot down and the fifth time he came close to either being killed or taken prisoner. Twice in two days he was forced to do incredible things with his body and his machine in order to fly another day. It is unimaginable how resilient he must have been to get right back up in his Triplane day after day, to do his duty to his country and to the Allied cause.

On July 16, Collishaw led his flight on a morning and a late evening patrol. This latter patrol was a twelve-aircraft affair of 'A', 'B', and 'C' Flights led by Carter, Collishaw, and Sharman, respectively. Flight Sub-Lieutenant H. W. Taylor, of 'A' Flight, had difficulty keeping up and ended up joining a flight of six French machines. North of Polygon Wood they met four EA scouts and Taylor managed to get fifty rounds into an enemy machine, which fell out of control and then broke up in the air.[18]

During the period of July 1 to July 16, 1917, No. 10 Naval Squadron carried out thirty-five offensive patrols for a total of 338 hours and five minutes flying time. Twelve enemy aircraft were driven down out of control: four by Collishaw, three by Alexander, three by Reid, and one each from Page and Taylor.[19]

On July 17, Collishaw led a patrol consisting of Trapp and Sharman over Polygon Wood. An engagement took place with three hostile scouts and Collishaw managed to bring one of the Hun planes down. Sharman and Trapp damaged two others.[20] Meanwhile, southeast of Polygon Wood, Flight Sub-Lieutenant Lowther attacked one of five Albatros scouts engaged by his flight and hit the pilot, who fell forward while the machine went nose-diving before going completely out of control. During a general engagement near Roulers, planes from a number of British squadrons had a running air battle with thirty to thirty-five enemy scouts. Flight Lieutenant Carter of No. 10 Naval Squadron got to within 150 feet of one of the EA and fired about twenty rounds into it, causing it to go down completely out of control.[21]

Further patrols took place over the next two days, but with no decisive results. However, on July 20, Flight Commander Collishaw led Reid, FitzGibbon, and Alexander of the Black Flight while John Sharman led 'C' Flight consisting of George Trapp, John Page, and Charles Weir. Weir was from Medicine Hat, Alberta, and had joined the squadron earlier in the month. Over the Menin-Messines sector near Lichteryelder, they encountered about twenty enemy scouts, most of them of the older Albatros variety. Alexander scored first by pumping about fifty rounds into one of them from about 200 feet away. Collishaw, flying close to Alex, saw the machine burst into flames and go down. Collishaw then went on the attack, shooting at an Albatros that had positioned itself behind one of the Triplanes. Collishaw could see his tracer bullets go right into the pilot. He slumped down and the machine went over into a dive. Being engaged immediately in another combat, Collishaw couldn't follow his victim down to confirm the kill. In the meantime, Ellis Reid fired on an enemy at less than 100 feet. As the enemy turned steeply to get away, Reid fired again, hitting the pilot this time and sending the enemy machine down.[22] Howard W. Taylor was wounded in action this day.

July 21 was another busy day for No. 10 Naval Squadron. Flights 'C' and 'B' went up with the same pilots and machines as the day before. Morning patrols amounted to little. During the evening patrol over Passchendaele, the two flights spotted twenty enemy aircraft below. A system of signalling had been devised to alert other Allied planes in the area to join the fray. John Sharman used it for the first time this day by firing a red Verey cartridge from his plane. This signal flare was a call to action for other planes in the area. A number of SE5s and Nieuports joined in as Collishaw and Sharman's flights dove on the enemy formation. Collishaw was able to come in close behind one of the enemy machines and fired a quick burst of machine-gun fire. He did not see it fall as other German machines came into his sights. He fired at one, hitting the pilot and causing it to go into a spin. He fired on a third aircraft and it too was seen going down out of control. Collishaw was credited with driving three enemy airplanes out of control.[23] It is believed they were Fritz von Brosart, Oswin Kirmse, and Ludwig Meyer.[24]

July 22, 1917 was a sad day for No. 10 Naval Squadron, for they lost both John Sharman and John Page. Early morning at 6:00 a.m., Collishaw, Alexander, Reid, and FitzGibbon took off along with Sharman's flight of Page, Weir, and Trapp. Carter's 'A' Flight took off later and patrolled another area. 'B' and 'C' flights spotted two German two-seaters crossing over the lines several thousand feet above them doing observation work. The Triplanes rose to intercept them, but could not climb fast enough to catch them as the two-seaters turned for home. Between Ypres and Messines the two flights encountered two formations of Albatros. Normally, No. 10 Naval Squadron's flights flew in a loose "V" formation with one flight being 2,000–3,000 feet above the other. This time the Black Flight was at 16,000 feet with Sharman's flight much higher and off to the one side. One of the enemy formations engaged Sharman's 'C' Flight while the other dove for Collishaw and his flight. During the dogfight, Collishaw noticed Ellis Reid shoot down one of the enemy machines. Suddenly, Alexander and a couple of the others noticed John Sharman's machine disintegrate and fall in pieces. Whether he had been hit by anti-aircraft fire, or by an artillery shell meant for a target on the ground, remained a mystery. In later life, Mel Alexander dispelled this theory, stating he had seen the wings of Sharman's Triplane fold back as he dove on an enemy machine. The cause of Sharman's demise, according to Alexander, was due to the stress on the stranded steel cables attached to the Triplane's wings. The force of the dive caused the cables to snap.

Collishaw saw George Trapp attack and shoot down an enemy Albatros. Then the fight was over as quickly as it started. All the hostile aircraft had disengaged and flew for home. The two flights re-formed with all of the Black Flight present, but only two Triplanes represented 'C' Flight. John Page was missing as well as Sharman. It later came to light that Page had been shot down and killed, but not before shooting down two of the enemy planes first. Page was possibly the victim of *Jasta* 11 pilot *Leutnant* Otto Brauneck, who claimed he had shot down a Triplane from No. 10 Naval Squadron that day. It was his tenth victory.[25]

The loss of these two pilots was a heavy one for the squadron. Sharman, who was made acting flight commander just days before his death, was an excellent fighter pilot. He showed great promise as a future leader and could have been a high-scoring ace. In May, 1917 Sharman had been awarded the DSC, and in July, a bar to that decoration. At the time of his death he had accounted for nine enemy machines shot down.

A number of flights took place on July 23. On the evening patrol, Collishaw went up with Alexander and Reid, while Nick Carter led 'A' Flight, made up of George Trapp, Charles Weir, and Ted Glasgow, a Canadian from Toronto who had recently joined the squadron. Over Houthulst Wood, the two flights encountered several formations of enemy fighters. Carter and his flight, flying above Collishaw's flight, took on some of the enemy while more of the hostile aircraft attacked Collishaw and his flight. More machines from both sides joined the melee, including SE5s and Nieuport 17s from No. 29 Squadron. Collishaw closed in on two Albatros D. IIIs, but his attack was nullified by his machine gun jamming. Then, Collishaw and Reid both dove on two of the enemy and again Collishaw's gun jammed. Reid, however, managed to fire on a grey Albatros. It went down in a spin. A Nieuport flown by Second Lieutenant W. B. Wood came up under an enemy Albatros and fired into the German plane's belly. It went down out of control.

In a report dated July 23, 1917, General Plummer, Second Army Commander, commented on the day by saying: "A very successful day's fighting. Collishaw did splendidly, as usual."[26]

At this time, the preparation for the third battle of Ypres was now well underway and the artillery were trying to soften up the enemy in advance of the infantry attack. Between July 17 and 30, the British blasted the German defences with over four million shells of various sizes. In addition, the artillery fired an average of two million shells per week during the balance of the campaign. Field Marshal Haig's objective was to take Passchendaele Ridge and roll up the German front north all the way to the English Channel — a very ambitious plan indeed. The British Fifth Army launched its attack on the morning of July 31, 1917 after an incredible artillery barrage. The Third Battle of Ypres would last into the fall of 1917 with General Currie and the Canadian Corps finally taking the town of Passchendaele on November 11 after suffering over 15,000 casualties.

During the latter part of July, Collishaw was given a new Triplane, No. 533. This machine was fitted with twin machine guns. Half a dozen of these experimental machines were produced and No. 10 Naval Squadron had acquired one. As the senior Flight Commander, Collishaw was given the chance to fly it. He eagerly agreed. Due to the extra weight of a second gun, the performance of the machine suffered above 10,000 feet but Collishaw felt that the extra firepower more than made up for this deficiency.[27] Now he had the same firepower as the enemy machines that were firing at him.

Collishaw was flying his new Triplane No. 533 on July 24 when he went on a patrol with Ellis, Alexander, Des FitzGibbon, and a new nineteen-year-old pilot from Toronto named Ted May. They were on their way back to the Droglandt aerodrome when one of May's wings folded up and he went down in a spin. No enemy aircraft were in sight. May died on impact. He had only been with the squadron a matter of days. Carter's 'A' flight was on an inner patrol near Langemarck at the time. Carter attacked four enemy aircraft in succession, which were in the process of attacking a British observation machine, and obtained decisive results against the second one by firing thirty rounds at close range. The EA went down out of control and the remainder of the German machines dispersed and escaped.[28]

The squadron was visited the next day by Brigadier-General Trenchard, who passed along his congratulations and the following letter, which read:

> The Aerial Offensive has been carried out during the last 10 days with considerable energy and vigour, and there is little doubt that the German Air Service on this front is being really hard pressed and is gradually being worn down.
>
> The number of decisive combats has considerably decreased during the last few days which is a sure sign that the German morale is breaking down.

It is of the greatest importance to complete this wearing down process during the next few days and to completely shatter the morale of the Germans in the air.

It is fully realised that this fine weather is throwing a great strain on pilots in both Corps and Army Squadrons, but they must realise that the success of the forthcoming operations is dependent on our absolute supremacy in the air.

Corps machines must carry out their work well over the targets that they are observing on. Fighting patrols must work well out in front of the Corps machines and must miss no opportunity of engaging and destroying enemy formations.[29]

Many of the pilots scoffed at this sort of directive from HQ, knowing that they were doing their best and doubting whether the German morale was in fact at low ebb.

Carter and Collishaw both led patrols on July 25 and 26 but without any decisive results.[30] During the flight on July 26 Collishaw tested his two guns before encountering the enemy and they were both jammed. He had to break off formation with the rest of the flights carrying on without him. Now on his own, Collishaw spotted an RE8 under attack by two Albatros scouts, which were all white with black crosses. Collishaw opened fire on one of the enemy machines and observed his tracer bullets going all around the cockpit. The Albatros quickly dove away so Collishaw tried to fire on the other one. His guns jammed again, so there was nothing he could do but return to the aerodrome.

The last flight Collishaw flew with No. 10 Naval Squadron was on July 27, 1917. It was also one of its most successful. The morning flight had to be cut short due to low clouds. The aircraft could get no higher than 500 feet. After he landed, Collishaw was called in to the Squadron Commander's office. Commander Bell handed Collishaw a message from RNAS Headquarters at Dunkirk, informing him he had been granted three months leave in Canada. Before he could go on leave though, the rest of the day's flying had to be completed. All three flights of No. 10 Naval Squadron took off in the early evening, under clear skies. Carter led 'A' flight composed of Glasgow, Weir, and Lowther. Collishaw led the Black Flight with Reid, FitzGibbon, and Gerald Roach, a young British pilot who had joined the squadron just that morning. Mel Alexander was the new acting flight commander of 'C' flight, having taken over from Sharman. With him were Howard Saint and two recent arrivals, John Cole and Harold Day.

This was a special mission, one that had been in the works for some time. The idea was to send out a patrol of FE2ds far behind enemy lines, attract the attention of the German fighters, and lure them westward to where dozens of Allied fighters would be ready to pounce on the unsuspecting enemy. It was hoped that numerous German aircraft would be shot down and thereby achieve air superiority for the upcoming battle of Ypres that would commence on July 31, 1917.

Eight FE2ds from No. 20 Squadron, the one that shot down Righthofen earlier in the month, took off at 6:15 p.m. Their destination was Menin, about 20 miles behind enemy lines. They flew at 12,000 feet when they reached Menin, and there to greet them were about twenty-four enemy Albatros machines. Half the Albatros scouts tried to cut off their retreat while the other half attacked them from behind. The FE2ds turned to the northwest, trying to defend themselves as best they could, but still trying to fly to the rendezvous point over Polygon Wood. They finally reached Polygon Wood and met up with fifty-nine allied fighters, including RFC squadrons, French scouts, and the twelve Triplanes from No. 10 Naval Squadron. However, more enemy machines arrived as well. Some of the enemy aircraft remained above the FE2ds. The Allied fighters were flying in layered formation, at different altitudes, some as high as 16,000 feet.

Carter's flight attacked a formation of Albatros scouts, with Carter getting close in behind one and firing machine-gun rounds which went right into the pilot. The Albatros fell to earth. Collishaw's flight dove on some German fighters who were aided in the ensuing fray by some Albatros D. Vs. Collishaw attacked one of them and let loose with his dual machine guns. His tracers went right into the cockpit of the aircraft, killing the pilot immediately. The Albatros's wings crumpled from the firepower of Collishaw's Triplane, and as it fell, pieces of the machine flew off.

Ellis Reid had his hands full during this melee. He was able to manoeuvre into a position to get off a burst of fire at an Albatros Scout. The enemy machine broke up in the air and was seen going down in pieces. He immediately turned his attention to another Hun machine. This time he fired right at the pilot of one of the older versions of the Albatros (probably a D. II), whose machine went down completely out of control. Moments later, Reid was waltzing with an enemy Albatros. Around in circles they went, down to 4,000 feet. The superb turning ability of the Triplane enabled Reid to eventually get behind the EA. He fired and the Albatros nosedived and crashed into the ground.

The air battle lasted for about an hour. Number 56 Squadron downed three enemy aircraft and No. 10 Naval Squadron destroyed or sent six of the German machines down out of control, three by Reid, two by Collishaw, and one by Carter. The FEs were given credit for six German fighters, two sent down in flames, one which broke up in the air, and three which were seen to crash. The Allied losses were an SE5 from No. 56 Squadron and Gerald Roach from No. 10 Naval Squadron. Alexander had seen an enemy fighter get behind and above Roach's Triplane and had tried to drive off the enemy Albatros from Roach's tail with a few shots from long-range, but was unsuccessful. The German opened fire on Roach, who went down, mortally wounded.[31] In all likelihood, it was *Jasta* 11 pilot *Leutnant* Carl-August von Schonebeck who had shot down the young Gerald Roach.[32]

The next day, July 28, 1917, Collishaw did not fly. That day Carter had received a delivery of Sopwith Triplane No. 536, equipped with two machine guns. However, the action in the air continued with morning and evening offensive patrols led by Alexander and Carter. With Alexander were Reid, Cole, Saint, Day, and FitzGibbon. Over Dadizeele at about 7:50 p.m., the flight encountered about a dozen EAs. During the fight, Alexander drove one of the enemy machines down out of control. Reid was also believed to have shot down an EA, but was last seen around 8:00 p.m. and failed to return or to report.[33]

There was speculation that Reid, like Sharman before him, had been brought down by anti-aircraft fire. The loss of Reid was a great blow to the squadron. The day he was brought down he was recommended for the DSO. He had also previously been recommended for the DSC.

The recommendation from Squadron Commander Bell to the Officer Commanding the 22 Wing, RFC on July 28, 1917, reads as follows:

Reference my 306 of 23rd inst. I have the honour to recommend Flight Sub-Lieut. Ellis V. Reid, D.S.C. as a suitable recipient of the D.S.O. During the five days that have elapsed since writing that letter, Flight Sub-Lieut. Reid has added five more enemy machines to his account.

23rd July: Near Polygon Wood, he shot down one machine out of control, pilot apparently being hit.

27th July: In a general engagement with a number of enemy aircraft, north of Courtrai and Menin, this pilot first drove two E.A. off one of our machines; was then attacked by two more, one of which he drove down, broken in pieces; then fought another two, shooting the pilot of the second one, whose machine went down out of control; and finally attacked another, fighting it down to 4,000 feet and seeing it crash on the ground as a result of his attack.

28th July: During an engagement over Dadizeele, Flight Sub-Lieut. Reid was observed in combat with one of several E.A. which went down out of control and broke in pieces as it fell. This was noted by Flight-Lieut. Alexander. Flight Sub-Lieut. Reid was seen flying between Dadizeele and Roulers after this engagement was finished and the sky clear of E.A. but he did not return from the patrol.

Flight Sub-Lieut. Reid is a pilot of very exceptional skill and possesses all the necessary coolness and daring to enable him to use it consistently to good purpose.[34]

Reid was later awarded the DSC posthumously. The recommendation for the DSO was not approved.

At the same time, Commander Bell recommended Collishaw be awarded a bar to his DSO. This recommendation, also dated 28 July, reads as follows:

> I have the honour to submit the name of Acting Flight-Commander R. Collishaw, D.S.O., D.S.C. as a suitable recipient of a Bar to the former Decoration. Since receiving the D.S.O., less than three weeks ago, Flight Commdr. Collishaw has added seven more enemy machines to his long list of decisive combats.
>
> 11th July: Near Mooreslede, he drove down an enemy scout machine completely out of control.
>
> 12th July: Over the Polygon wood, in a fight with a large number of E.A., he attacked a red Albatros Scout, and shot the pilot, when machine went down completely out of control.
>
> 20th July: With his flight, he attacked 15 to 20 enemy scout machines, between Menin and Messines. During the engagement which followed, he shot the pilot of one machine, which went down entirely out of control.
>
> 21st July: During a general engagement near Passchendaele, he drove down two E.A. out of control, shooting the pilot on the second instance.
>
> 27th July: In another general engagement, north of Courtrai and Menin, he shot down one Albatros Scout, which fell to pieces in the air, and shot the pilot of another, which fell completely out of control.
>
> He has given a splendid example to all officers in this

Squadron, never lacking in courage, discipline or any of
the qualities necessary to make a splendid fighting pilot,
and he is an exceptional officer.[35]

During the period July 17 to July 31, 1917, No. 10 Naval Squadron
carried out thirty offensive patrols and one special mission in pursuit of
enemy aircraft, for a total of 215 hours and forty-nine minutes flown.
One hundred and twelve combats took place, of which nineteen were
decisive. Four hostile machines were destroyed and fifteen were driven
down out of control.[36]

No. 10 Naval Squadron had a tremendous impact in the war in the
air over the Ypres front between May and the end of July, 1917. Seventy-
nine enemy machines had been shot down by the squadron.

In this period of time, Collishaw accounted for twenty-seven
and Reid was credited with seventeen of these machines — over half
of the total! Raymond Collishaw and the Black Flight were a force to
be reckoned with and had proven their flying and fighting prowess to
their commanders and to the German flyers who faced them. These and
other victories did not come without loss, however. From mid-May to
the end of July, No. 10 Naval Squadron suffered seventeen casualties. Of
the fifteen original pilots who started at Droglandt, only three were left:
Collishaw, Alexander, and FitzGibbon. Of the others, two were posted
from the squadron, two had been wounded, two were prisoners of war,
and six had been killed. So, in two and a half months the squadron of
fifteen had more than 100 per cent turnover.

Raymond Collishaw left No. 10 Naval Squadron on August 3, 1917
for a three-month leave in Canada. He had twenty-seven victories, and
including enemy machines possibly shot down, his total was thirty-eight.
Both the British and German high command made a point of sending
their top aces off on leave at around the forty-victory mark. Richthofen
was ordered home after forty-one victories. By the time he actually went
on leave, his score was fifty-two. When top scorer Bishop reached the
level of forty-seven victories (August 1917), he was ordered to his native
Canada to serve as part of a recruiting campaign.... Collishaw, after
thirty-eight victories (July 1917) ... was also ordered off to Canada, not
returning to action until year's end.[37]

Collishaw on leave to Canada, summer 1917.

After Collishaw left No. 10 Naval Squadron, there were some notable victories amongst his former colleagues. For example, Melville Alexander was recognized for his achievements, especially on August 22, 1917.

> .... a patrol of Naval Ten led by 'Mel' Alexander, intercepted a number of Albatros scouts which were attacking a formation of DH4s. In the dogfight that followed Flight Sub-Lieutenant J.G. Manuel of Edmonton, who had joined the squadron on his first operational posting only nine days earlier, destroyed one enemy machine and drove another down out of control, while Alexander and Flight Sub-Lieutenant G.L. Trapp were each credited with one out of control. This marked Alexander's third victory in five days, a feat which won him the DSC.[38]

The impact of the six naval squadrons, including No. 10 Naval Squadron, which was attached to the RFC, has not been fully appreciated in the annals of history. Their role in the spring, summer, and early fall of 1917 on the Western Front was pivotal, and they helped gain the upper hand in the war in the air over Ypres at that time. They had met and battled Richthofen and his forces, and had conducted themselves with vigour and determination.

SEAPLANE DEFENCE
SQUADRON

Collishaw left No. 10 Naval Squadron on August 3, 1917, making his way to England via Dunkirk and Boulogne. He spent several days in England before leaving for Canada. Collishaw arrived in Montreal mid-August. On his way to visit his parents in Nanaimo, Collishaw was asked to speak to numerous Men's Canadian Clubs and other audiences in the major cities along the way. The story of Raymond Collishaw appeared in many newspapers across Canada at this time, as his reputation as a war hero had preceded him. Many wanted to honour and recognize him for his many exploits in the air. Collishaw was a sign of hope for many who were continually hearing about the mud, the blood, and the suffering in the trenches of the Western Front.

Because of the distance between the war in Europe and Canada, Collishaw saw little real evidence of the effect the war was having in his home country. Life went on as usual. He did notice a number of young men in RFC cadet uniforms in the streets, evidence of the British flying training program, which had firmly established itself earlier in the year. Newspaper articles had glorified the war in the air, giving fanciful accounts of pilots' exploits. These were due to letters home from pilots, in which they had embellished the truth, or from editors at the newspapers who had vivid imaginations. Collishaw also encountered a lot of ignorance about flying in wartime. He recalled meeting one elderly lady who had a grandson in the RFC who thought all pilots flew in hot air balloons.

Collishaw showed his concern for the pilots he had known during his journey westward by visiting the families of those pilots who had been killed. It must have been a difficult set of meetings for both Collishaw and for the families. Invariably they would ask Raymond how their son had perished. He had to choose just the right words to help them understand the circumstances of the demise of their son and yet leave them feeling proud of his contribution to the war effort.

One such family was the Trapp family who lived in New Westminister, British Columbia, near Vancouver. George Trapp had flown with Collishaw in No. 10 Naval Squadron and perished while Collishaw was on leave in Canada. Stanley, who had also joined the RNAS, was killed in December 1916 while flying with No. 8 Naval Squadron. The third brother, Donovan, was to die in 1918 while flying with No. 85 RFC Squadron. During his visit with the Trapp family Raymond met the sisters of the Trapp pilots and fell in love with Neita. They became engaged and would marry some six years after their first meeting.

On his return trip from Nanaimo, Raymond Collishaw stopped in Toronto to visit friends. The visit was captured in a news story in one of the Toronto papers, which appeared some time in late October or November. The story referred to him being credited with thirty-seven victories and the fact he commanded the celebrated Black Flight. What is important to note is the press the Black Flight was receiving at home — it was quickly gaining an international reputation.[1]

Collishaw returned to Dunkirk at the beginning of the third week of November 1917. Expecting to return to No. 10 Naval Squadron, he was posted to the Seaplane Defence Squadron on November 24, stationed out of St. Pol near Dunkirk. The squadron, formed on July 1, 1917 under the name Seaplane Defence Flight, had originally flown seaplanes, but by the time Collishaw arrived its name had changed to Seaplane Defence

Author's Collection.

Sopwith Camel 2F.1, National Aviation Museum, Ottawa.

Squadron and was equipped with the 130-horsepower Clerget-powered Sopwith Camel. It was under the command of Squadron Commander Ronald Graham, and one of his Flight Commanders was Leonard Slatter. Other Canadians in the squadron included Philip Fisher and J. E. Potvin. Collishaw was made Flight Commander of 'A' Flight. The Seaplane Defence Squadron's major tasks were: the aerial protection of Royal Navy vessels operating off the French and Belgian coasts; flying escort patrols for RNAS bombers hitting Zeebrugge, Bruges, and other targets; or carrying out reconnaissance missions over these points and doing offensive patrols over the coastal area of Belgium.

Wing Captain C.L. Lambe, in charge of RNAS operations out of Dunkirk, was facing a crisis in morale. Pilot losses were heavy in the squadrons, which were assisting the RFC on the Western Front, and so too was the stress of relentless flying. In a five-week period prior to the end of October, casualties, illness, and transfer saw the loss of sixty-one pilots; only nineteen replacements were sent out.[2]

The best explanation for this crisis in morale seems to be a difference in service practice and experience. The RNAS squadrons lent to the RFC performed valiantly, but under conditions for which they were wholly unprepared. Raymond Collishaw, the most successful of all naval fighter pilots and one who rose superlatively to the challenges of the Western Front, put the matter in a nutshell when he spoke of the "comparatively gentle" operations at Dunkirk. Conducted with relatively few casualties, these operations had permitted the building up of a body of pilots who had developed very considerable skills in the air, but the relentless psychological pressures of the Western Front, with its incessant combats, proved a fearful shock to some of them.[3]

William Melville Alexander, in a letter to S.F. Wise, author of the seminal work, *Canadian Airmen and the First World War*, spoke of the state of morale.

To answer the morale question, one must take a hard look at the number that left the unit. In most cases the strain was just too much for them which I personally observed. Replacements were not keeping up with casualties and the R.N.A.S. was forced to disband No. 6 squadron and their pilots went to those units required … To sum up, I would agree with both F/M Haig and Gen. Trenchard there was good reason for apprehension over morale but not much was done about it until Nature stepped in and brought the winter, thus curtailing operations.[4]

The nature of the work at the Seaplane Defence Squadron and the demands of air combat there bore no resemblance to the stress and strain found near Ypres with No. 10 Naval Squadron. Being on the Channel was more like a rest period for pilots, with far fewer sorties than on the Western Front — just one a day compared to three or four with No. 10 Naval Squadron. In addition, the weather was so bad as to curtail flying for days at a time.

Department of National Defence, 20080040-012

Cockpit of a Sopwith Camel. Notice the long Aldis sight between the two machine guns.

The Seaplane Defence Squadron was equipped, however, with the latest in fighting machines. The Sopwith Camel replaced the Sopwith Triplane in the fall of 1917 and became the mainstay of the British air forces for the rest of the war.

The Camel, a design by Herbert Smith of Sopwiths, came together through the efforts of a team of Sopwith men. Designed specifically to house two guns up-front, firing through the propeller, the scout bore some resemblance to the Pup, although the design team decided to have the main mass weight positioned right up front, with the engine, guns/ammunition, pilot, fuel, and oil tanks all housed within the first third of the fuselage. This gave it a rather squat, bullish appearance.

Another identifying feature was the wings. The upper-wing, to assist production, was made in one piece, perfectly straight with no dihedral, while the lower wings had increased dihedral. Ailerons were fitted to upper and lower wings, making the whole structure very manoeuvrable, especially with a 130-hp Clerget engine as its powerplant. This large rotary engine (that is to say the whole engine went round with the propeller), which rotated clockwise when viewed from the cockpit, together with the mass frontal weight gave the Camel a massive right-hand turn capability.

This in itself was fine for pilots once they had gained experience on the type, but in the beginning it came as a shock, especially to pilots coming off docile training types, or service machines like the Pup. The Camel's nose tended to drop during a steep turn to starboard (with the rotating engine), and for it to rise with a port climbing turn (against the rotating engine). In both cases the pilot had to put on left rudder.[5]

Nearly 5500 of these aircraft were built, and between July 1917 and the armistice Camel pilots scored 1,300 victories.[6] The Sopwith Camel was heavier than its predecessor, the Pup, and more powerful and thereby faster, too. It was, however, just as manoeuverable as the Pup. Because of its powerful rotary engine, the Camel tended to drop on right-hand turns and rise on left-hand turns. It was the first British fighter to have two Vickers machine guns as standard equipment. By all accounts it was a magnificent fighting machine and became the mainstay of the RNAS and RFC squadrons for the duration of the war. S.F. Wise compared the Camel to the SE5a.

... the Sopwith Camel, a stubby little machine that was to become the most famous of all British fighters. The Camel did not have the speed of the SE5a, but the concentration of weight in the forward section of its short fuselage and the pronounced torque of its engine, which made it unstable and somewhat hazardous to fly, also meant that in the right hands it had quite startling agility. The Camel mounted a pair of belt-fed Vickers firing through the propeller arc, giving it even greater fire power than the SE5. In 1917 the Germans had no real answer to these aircraft, the Albatros D-V and D-Va, introduced in mid summer, not being appreciably better than the D-III.[7]

On November 26, Collishaw had his first flight in a Camel, but it wasn't until November 30 that he got his first taste of action with the Seaplane Defence Squadron. He was leading 'A' Flight on a high offensive patrol over Bruges. The flight had two indecisive combats with four enemy seaplanes over the Zeebrugge pier.[8]

The next day the flight was on offensive patrol over Zeebrugge. They attacked three German seaplanes and chased them down to 4,000 feet. Collishaw got on the tail of one of them and fired off a burst, sending it down. He didn't see the enemy machine crash into the sea or on land, so he could not be credited with the victory.

Part of the Fleet protection role the squadron played involved flying out to sea, sometimes as far as 50 miles, to protect ships and vessels they were designated to cover. When they did arrive over the designated ships they were often greeted with friendly fire from the ship's anti-aircraft guns. This occurred even when the ships knew they were coming, their estimated time of arrival, and how many planes would be providing the protection. Despite the protests and complaints from the pilots of this situation to higher authorities, nothing seemed to be done to correct it. The other major disadvantage to the pilots of the distant Fleet patrol was the monotony of flights over water. Very few enemy machines were encountered far from shore. Navigation, too, was challenging in these circumstances as there were no landmarks to go by, unlike flying over land. Precise flying was the order of the day, with little room for error.

The Seaplane Defence Squadron was outfitted with D.H.4 bombers. Built by the British aircraft manufacturing company de Havilland, the D.H.4 was widely used in the First World War and saw service in every theatre of the war. It could carry 460 pounds of bombs and had either one or two fixed forward-firing Vickers machine guns for use by the pilot and one or two free-ranging .303-inch Vickers machine guns for the observer/gunlayer. Powered either by a BHP or a Rolls-Royce Eagle III engine (230–375 horsepower) the D.H.4 could attain a top speed of 119 miles per hour at 3,000 feet and could climb to 10,000 feet in sixteen minutes, twenty-five seconds. It had a ceiling of 16,000 feet and could stay airborne for three and a half hours. The D.H.4 had a wingspan of a little over 42 feet, 4 inches and was 29 feet, 8 inches long. The biggest disadvantage in the design of the D.H.4 was the great distance between pilot and observer, making communication between the two difficult.[9]

When flying escort duty with the D.H.4s, Collishaw noticed their pilots had the same trait as the pilots of the 1 1/2 Strutters in 3 Naval Wing — namely, once they unleashed their bomb loads they raced back straight for home base. The Sopwith Camel escorts were left circling the bombing targets wondering where they all went. On returning home in formation they faced all the enemy anti-aircraft fire alone.

Collishaw's flight was escorting the Fleet to Ostend on December 4 when they encountered five EA scouts. They attacked them without decisive results, chasing them down to the shore near Ostend.[10]

On December 5, 1917, Flight Commander Collishaw was leading a patrol at 18,500 feet, a few miles north of La Panne, a few miles inside Belgium. He spotted a hostile Albatros two-seater and closed in to about 150 feet before opening fire. The observer of the enemy aircraft did not see his attackers. Both Collishaw's guns jammed after a few shots so he was forced to turn away, at which time the EA's observer fired on Collishaw. Flight Sub-Lieutenant Moyle, who was also attacking the Albatros, had to break off the engagement due to engine trouble.[11] Four days later Collishaw's flight was on patrol at 19,500 feet over Nieuport when they ran into an enemy two-seater. Collishaw led the attack and the hostile machine fell out of control and crashed near Middelkerke. No one pilot was able to take credit for the kill, as it was a joint effort of the whole flight.[12] On December 10, Collishaw had another scrap with an enemy fighter only to have his guns jam again, forcing him to break off the action.

It wasn't until December 19 that Collishaw was able to knock anything down out of the sky on his own. He and two other Camel pilots were escorting D.H.4s, carrying out spotting for naval fire onto shore targets. Between Ostend and Zeebrugge they spotted two Albatros two-seaters. Fellow flight member Flight Sub-Lieutenant Mackay, from Sunderland, Ontario, dove at one of the two-seaters as it tried to turn and escape. He fired two bursts into it, during which time the observer stood up in the rear cockpit, held up his arms as if to surrender, and then fell completely out of the machine as it fell to the ground. The other two-seater got away. Collishaw's flight then met up with a formation of four enemy Albatros fighters. Collishaw pounced on one, sending it down out of control.

During the latter half of December Collishaw's flight was called on to provide escort for spotting machines, which assisted naval units used for bombarding shore targets like Ostend and other locations. On one occasion, near Ostend, Collishaw was leading the entire squadron. At 20,000 feet they saw a formation of enemy aircraft coming up to meet them. Collishaw and company dove and fired on the German aircraft but it was so cold Collishaw's guns jammed. The squadron continued pressing the attack nonetheless. The German machines took evasive action and Collishaw's squadron chased them away. On landing, each pilot in the squadron confirmed their guns had frozen up as well. Years later, Collishaw met the German squadron leader who had opposed them that cold December day, only to be told his machine and the rest of his squadron had experienced the same difficulty! No shot had been fired during the entire episode.

Raymond Collishaw was appointed acting squadron commander due to a flying accident involving Squadron Commander Ronnie Graham on December 29, 1917. Graham was stunting to impress his fiancée, a nursing sister who was stationed in a nearby hospital. He crashed into the hospital and was seriously injured. Collishaw got his first taste of official bureaucracy as the new Squadron Commander shortly after his appointment. The top brass were planning a naval bombardment of Zeebrugge in another attempt to smash the locks at the base of the canal that led to the submarine and destroyer docks at Bruges. The operation was on the books for several weeks and could not begin due to inclement weather. The bad weather, consisting of low clouds, high winds, and snow storms, continued from the end of December into January 1918, making flying impossible.

Operations at Dunkirk were very crowded. Four RNAS wings were operating out of the same location with all of the squadrons almost interwoven. Captain C.L. Lambe, in command of the RNAS at Dunkirk, explained to Collishaw the necessity of moving his squadron out of Dunkirk to reduce the congestion, to an aerodrome some 10 miles away. On January 10, they moved to Burgues, 7 miles inland from the coast. At this point in his flying career Collishaw had flown a total of more than 559 hours.

Collishaw planned to use the squadron officers and the ratings to help with the construction and painting of their new aerodrome. The officers disliked this work intensely but they moved all their belongings with them, including the huts they used for accommodations. By the following day, in record time, they were ready to resume normal flying operations.

Further reductions in activity were made in Dunkirk when the seaplane station was turned over to the Americans and the Curtiss "Large America" flying-boats sent back to Felixtowe, England. Anti-submarine patrols were now to be handled by a new squadron, No. 17 Naval, flying D.H.4s, while the fighter pilots of the former Seaplane Defence Squadron became the nucleus of fighter squadron, No. 13 Naval Squadron, under the temporary command of Raymond Collishaw.[13]

On January 14, Collishaw led the squadron on an offensive patrol over Zeebrugge. On this flight they had seven indecisive combats with enemy machines. Then they encountered German seaplane bombers who were escorted with their own fighter escorts. Collishaw managed to destroy one of the seaplanes with the squadron accounting for two more of the enemy machines. This was Collishaw's last victory with No. 13 Naval Squadron. The name of the squadron had been changed on January 15, 1918 from Seaplane Defence Squadron to No. 13 Naval Squadron. He flew four more patrols with the squadron, the last being on January 21, 1918.[14]

By that time, Squadron Commander Graham had recovered from his injuries and was ready to resume command of No. 13 Naval Squadron. Collishaw was therefore appointed on January 23 to command one of his old units, No. 3 Naval Squadron, flying out of Bray Dunes in between Dunkirk and Nieuport.

NO. 3 NAVAL SQUADRON

1918

RAYMOND COLLISHAW, AS THE NEW SQUADRON COMMANDER, WAS well aware of No. 3 Naval Squadron's reputation and whose shoes he would be filling. Previous commanders included Red Mulock and Lloyd Breadner. Collishaw had served under Squadron Commander Red Mulock when he was previously attached to 3 Naval Wing and would now be replacing Squadron Commander Lloyd Breadner, from Ottawa. Breadner and Collishaw had sailed together to England in early 1916.

During Bloody April 1917, No. 3 Naval Squadron had shot down forty-five enemy aircraft. During its four and a half months with the RFC on the Somme front it had destroyed eighty German machines, losing only nine of its own aircraft.

The squadron had moved to Bray Dunes on the channel coast about 7 miles northeast of Dunkirk in early January 1918, and came under 4 Naval Wing. No. 3 Naval Squadron was still at Bray Dunes when

Collishaw took it over. He would do all he could to ensure the squadron had the same strong leadership as had been exhibited by Mulock and Breadner. No. 3 Naval Squadron had a high Canadian content when Collishaw arrived, with ten of its eighteen pilots being Canadian.[1]

The role and duties of No. 3 Naval Squadron were the same as No. 13 Naval Squadron — namely, protective patrols over British naval vessels off the coast, providing escort for D.H.4 bombing raids, and offensive patrols behind the German lines into Belgium.

Collishaw was fortunate to have a group of very talented pilots under his command. Through a friend at the Admiralty, he was able to ensure he received only very good calibre replacement pilots. Many of the pilots Collishaw had flown with the year before were still flying in No. 3 Naval Squadron, including Tich Rochford, Harold Beamish, and Fred Armstrong, who were his flight commanders, and George Anderson, Jimmy Glen and Art Whealy.

The pilot establishment of the naval fighting squadrons had been raised to eighteen to match that of the RFC's squadrons.[2] 'A' Flight was led by Flight Commander Harold Beamish, DSC, 'B' Flight by Flight Commander L.H. "Tich" Rochford, and 'C' Flight was under the command of Flight Commander Fred Armstrong, DSC.

As Squadron Commander, much of Raymond Collishaw's time was taken up with administrative matters related to the pilots, their machines, and the ratings (the ground crew). Opportunities to fly were drastically reduced for Collishaw as he learned his new role. Most of his time in January and February of 1918 was on the ground. Collishaw was in charge of the accommodations, squadron reporting, intelligence, feeding the squadron members, and their pay and general well-being. Every Commanding Officer should have an appropriate office, so one of his staff, Lieutenant Dudley Taylor, in charge of the squadron's records, set out to obtain one for Collishaw.

Dudley Taylor … had his attention drawn to an empty French camp at Adinkerke only a mile or so from Bray Dunes. He noticed that inside this camp was a very nice wooden hut, eminently suitable for our CO's office. So one night he took a lorry and a gang of ratings to the entrance of the French camp where a sentry was on guard. Dudley spoke to him and perhaps slipped him a few francs and the lorry with the ratings was allowed to pass into the camp while Dudley remained and conversed with him in his fluent French. The gang of ratings soon dismantled the hut, loaded it on the lorry, picked up Dudley at the gate and returned to Bray Dunes, the French sentry being quite unaware of the lorry's contents.[3]

Although Collishaw spent most of January and February occupied with running the squadron, Leonard "Tich" Rochford, in his book *I Chose the Sky*, describes a number of encounters with the enemy during that period of time.

During the morning patrol of 28th January when leading 'B' Flight and accompanied by three Camels of 'A' Flight, I observed below us two DFW two-seaters at about 10,000 feet above the Houthulst Forest. With Glen and Devereux I attached one of them, firing at point-blank range. The observer was either killed or wounded and the engine hit as the propeller ceased to revolve. Flight Lieutenant Hayne reported seeing this EA going down in a spin. Other EA were also encountered on this OP near Roulers. MacLeod attacked one and after he had fired a burst of 100 rounds it slipped into a spin and was still spinning at about 2,000 feet, though MacLeod was unable to see the final result. I attacked another DFW but without any decisive results.[4]

... on 17th February 'C' Flight, while on an OP, encountered a formation of eight Albatros Scouts near Roulers and a number of combats took place. Art Whealy attacked one of the EA, diving on it and firing a burst at about 100 yard range after which the EA went down out of control.[5]

DFW stood for *Deutsche Flugzeug Werke Gesellschaft*. In fact, No. 3 Naval Squadron captured a DWF the previous September and Tich Rochford was chosen to fly it to England, where it was put on display.

At the beginning of 1918, the number of American forces in France was increasing by the thousands. Their entry into the war the previous April held the promise to their French and British Allies of much-needed reinforcements. Even by the estimation of General Pershing, commander of the United States forces, the numbers were less than planned.

> By the end of January approximately 120,000 combat troops, 34,000 engineer troops, and 61,000 for other services were in France. Although promising that was, of course, only a beginning, as we were still far behind our schedule, and the shipment of men and material from home remained haphazard and not in the proportions needed. We were rapidly approaching the time when we were expected to be of some help to the Allied cause and it was necessary that our forces should be balanced to make them as independent as possible.[6]

Russia had dropped out of the war in December 1917 when an armistice was signed at Brest-Litovsk. By March 1918 a peace treaty between the Germans and the Bolsheviks had been agreed to. The collapse of the Eastern Front allowed the Germans to transfer its divisions located there to the Western Front for one last-ditch effort to win the war. The offensive had to take place before the Americans amassed sufficient troops to make victory impossible. The Allies were anticipating a German offensive some time in March, but they did not know exactly where or when.

General Ludendorff, commander of the German armies, knew that German strength sufficed for only one great blow against the Allies, "before America can throw strong forces into the scale," which would mean the end of February or beginning of March. The object must be to "beat the British." By attacking the old Somme battlefield of 1916, Ludendorff suggested, the assault divisions, in an operation code named Michael, could drive up the line of the Somme River towards the sea and "roll up" the British front. It was decided the Michael attack would come on March 21, 1918.[7]

Collishaw and No. 3 Naval Squadron, in anticipation of a possible German assault, were ordered to move from Bray Dunes at the end of February. On March 1, 1918, the squadron moved to Mont St. Eloi, 50 miles to the south and a few miles northwest of the city of Arras.[8] They came under the command of the RFC's 10th Army Wing of I Brigade and were one of the squadrons assigned to the British First Army.

No. 3 Naval Squadron was just one of several units transferred out of Dunkirk. The headquarters of 4 and 5 Naval Wings and No. 3 to 9 Naval Squadrons, inclusive, were removed from Dunkirk and were placed directly under the Commander-in-Chief, BEF, Douglas Haig. All that remained for naval duties of Dunkirk's once-sizeable organization was a reconnaissance squadron, the D.H.4 anti-submarine squadron, and three squadrons of Camels.[9]

When No. 3 Naval Squadron arrived at Mont St. Eloi, they took over from No. 8 Naval Squadron, who were to be sent back to England for a rest. One of Collishaw's first decisions upon arriving there did not make him very popular with the No. 8 Naval Squadron pilots, including its squadron leader Chris Draper. Collishaw kept for his squadron Draper's 150-horsepower Bentley-powered Camels, trading his less powerful 130-horsepower Clerget-powered Camels in return. Draper would not go along with the idea so Collishaw went to Dunkirk to ask his superior Captain Lambe about it. Lambe agreed, leaving Draper no choice but to give up his 150-horsepower machines to Collishaw's squadron.

Mont St. Eloi was situated a few miles northwest of Arras and about 10 miles west of Vimy Ridge. The aerodrome was situated on the summit of a ridge and on the opposite side of the valley, below which were the ruins of an old church.[10] This airfield was unique in that it was home only to RNAS squadrons. It was a spacious and comfortable aerodrome with a good landing surface and excellent approaches for the aircraft. There were two hangars for the machines. The accommodation for the officers and men consisted of canvas tents that were placed behind the hangars. Various huts and sheds for the stores, engine shop, and offices had been placed at a right angle to the hangars, all buildings forming the shape of an "L."

In preparation for the expected battle, the RFC's artillery co-operation squadrons were kept busy registering British artillery on German targets; bombing raids hit rail junctions, depot and supply areas, and enemy aerodromes, while reconnaissance aircraft ceaselessly took photographs of the enemy's lines and supply routes up to the trenches. No. 3 Naval Squadron's role was to escort the reconnaissance machines and carry out their own offensive patrols. In the first twenty days at Mont St. Eloi the squadron shot down fourteen enemy machines. Art Whealy, Aubrey Ellwood, Harry Chisam, and Tich Rochford destroyed two EAs each.

The size of the fighting forces had changed from when Collishaw had flown with No. 10 Naval Squadron in 1917 to when he arrived to command No. 3 Naval Squadron in the spring of 1918. In 1917, full squadron strength usually meant ten to fifteen machines, while patrols of individual flights numbered between three and six machines. By early 1918, squadron strength had risen to eighteen, and later, in the last year of the war, was brought up to twenty-four aircraft, with the full squadron partaking in offensive patrols as was normal procedure. However, the basic unit of attack was a flight of between four and six machines. The four flights of a squadron, when out on patrol together, would fly in stages or a stacked formation with one flight flying at about 15,000 feet and the other flights each about 500 feet above and to the side of the flight below it. The top flight would provide the protective cover for the rest of the squadron in case of attack by the enemy.

In early March, the Squadron was involved in offensive patrols (OP). Leonard "Tich" Rochford described his preferred tactics when on OP as follows:

Immediately after take-off we formed up and headed towards the line at our best rate of climb. Whilst still climbing along the line, all pilots maintained a thorough search of the sky, especially above and below to the east so as to spot any EA as soon as possible. If these were sighted I made certain that we were above and, ideally, up-sun to them. Clouds, too, were used as cover from which to stalk the enemy. This positioning was important before initiating an attack which was made by a steep dive by the whole flight.

I always tried to avoid prolonged involvement in "dog fights" there being no sense in relinquishing the advantage of superior height. Nor did I favour headlong charges by my formation into that of the enemy — particularly if they were in greater numbers.[11]

The German air services also had their own expansion plans, doubling the number of *Jastas* from forty to eighty by the time Operation Michael was launched.

They had concentrated their air units in preparation for the big offensive and when it commenced on March 21 they held a numerical advantage in the battle area, confronting 579 serviceable British machines of which 261 were fighters with 730 aircraft, 326 of them being fighters, including the Albatros D-V and D-Va, the Pfalz D-III and the new Fokker Triplane.[12]

The Fokker Dr.I, "Dr" standing for Dreidecker or "three wings," was designed by Anthony Fokker. It had a 110-horsepower Oberursel rotary engine, produced at the Motorenfabrik Oberursel, A. G., a company that Fokker owned.[13] The Fokker Triplane was patterned after the Sopwith Triplane, which had appeared on the Western Front in 1917. A few of these aircraft had fallen into enemy hands when forced to land in German-held territory. Fokker and his design team took a great interest in the Sopwith Triplane and eventually produced the Fokker Triplane.

The Dr I, even with three wings, had far less wing area than its biplane contemporaries — 200 square feet, as compared to 229 for the Albatros D V, 238 for the Pfalz D III, or 227 for the Spad 13. Its design balanced this reduction of supporting surface with a thick aerofoil section which gave relatively greater lift (and drag too, but the goal was manoeuvrability, not speed). Its wings were short and narrow, giving little lateral resistance, and its fuselage was short — 18 feet, even shorter than that of the Camel. The Dr I, moreover, was of the standard Fokker steel-tube construction with hollow box-spar wings, and was therefore light, a featherweight, in fact. Its weight was 1200 pounds, while the Spad, S.E.5, Albatros and Pfalz all weighed in at about a ton.[14]

The Dr.I was armed with standard dual machine guns. Manfred von Richthofen adopted the Dr.I as his aircraft of choice and scored the last twenty-one of his eighty victories flying an all-red Fokker Triplane.

On March 21, the German offensive, also known as the Ludendorff Offensive, began. A heavy mist shrouded the land, hiding the enemy's attack forces. German artillery bombarded the British lines and an area behind the front line trenches in the early hours of the morning. The British Third and Fifth Armies were hit hardest.

A compact mass of seventy-six first class German divisions fell upon twenty-eight British divisions, of unequal quality, the Germans advancing behind a surprise artillery bombardment across a front of fifty miles, on a morning of mist thickened by the use of gas, chlorine and phosgene and lachrymatory shell.…

As evening fell on 21 March, the BEF had suffered its first true defeat since trench warfare had begun three and a half years earlier. Along a front of nineteen miles, the whole forward position had been lost, except in two places … Guns had been lost in numbers, whole units had surrendered or fled to the rear and heavy casualties had been suffered by those that did stand and fight. In all, over 7,000 British infantrymen had been killed but 21,000 soldiers had been taken prisoner.[15]

Collishaw's squadron was ordered on offensive patrols behind the enemy lines, but were prevented, due to the mist, from taking off. They were not airborne until around noon. Their patrol took them opposite the British Third Army. Tich Rochford described what happened that day with his flight.

> The fog had cleared and it was a sunny day but visibility was poor and it was difficult to see the ground through the haze. After flying for about an hour I saw below us a large number of EA, among them a red triplane, near Douai. We attacked them and picking out an Albatros Scout I opened fire at close range and he went down out of control. I then had two more combats with Albatros Scouts, both with indecisive results. Jimmy Glen had helped me to shoot down this Albatros Scout out of control and Armstrong, with 'C' Flight, got another one down in the same category. The presence of the red triplane among those EA seemed to indicate that it was von Richtophen out with his Circus.[16]

In that same altercation, Jimmy Glen was shot in the nose and mouth by the pilot or gunner of an Albatros two-seater. Although wounded, Glen managed to bring his machine down on the British side of the lines, crashing just east of Bapaume.

For the next three days they patrolled in the same area and shot down no fewer than thirteen enemy aircraft. Only two of their own planes were lost due to a mid-air collision. Both pilots were Canadian: Lloyd A. Sands from Moncton, New Brunswick, and William Moyle from Paris, Ontario. The pilots apparently collided with one another during an attack against enemy aircraft at 15,000 feet over the skies at St. Quentin. The two Camels tumbled together into no man's land. Their bodies were not recovered. Both pilots were just twenty-three years old. Flight Lieutenant Sands had been with Collishaw in 3 Naval Wing in Luxeuil.

On March 25, No. 3 Naval Squadron was diverted to low-level bombing and strafing attacks on the advancing German divisions. These were desperate measures and the British high command was using all possible means of quelling the German attack. It was a hectic and hair-raising time for RFC and RNAS squadrons, as the pilots flew many missions each day and subjected themselves to ground fire from enemy infantry in the form of rifle and machine-gun fire, flying at no more than 25 to 50 feet above the ground.

No. 3 Naval Squadron, like most squadrons at the time, would look for anything that moved, including troops or convoys of trucks. Each Camel was loaded with four 25-pound bombs, which they would drop at low level on the target, then circle around and come in again on them with both machine guns blazing. Having exhausted all their ammunition, they would return to the aerodrome to re-fuel, re-arm, and go out again in search of targets. Flight Commander Fred Armstrong was killed on March 25, 1918, performing such a mission. The following day, William Chisam, from Edmonton, was injured in the hand in a low-level attack, but managed to return to the aerodrome. His injury was such that he was no longer able to fly for the duration of the war.

Flight Commander Frederick Carr "Army" Armstrong had shot down an enemy aircraft in each of the first four days of the Ludendorff Offensive, bringing his total to thirteen victories. The tall, fair-haired Canadian was known as a fearless flight leader and a very daring pilot. Flight Sub-Lieutenant Arthur Whealy would take over as acting Flight Commander.

The low-level attacks by Collishaw's squadron and other squadrons continued during the ensuing days. Skills in aerial combat did not matter when bombing or strafing ground targets and the likelihood of being shot down was the same for a rookie pilot as a veteran. A.T. Whealy, for example, would fire some 13,000 rounds into the enemy during strafing missions against enemy forces during their offensive.

On 27 March, as the Germans drove to within 15 miles of Amiens, the RFC continued to press its assault against their ground forces. This day saw the culmination of the British effort at close ground support. The III, V, and IX Brigades were reinforced by ninety-seven machines of I Brigade, and thirty of II Brigade, and along the length of the British front the RFC discharged 313,000 rounds of machine-gun fire and about 100,000 pounds of bombs at the enemy. Using pilots of locally-based squadrons as patrol leaders because of their knowledge of the front, even I and II Brigade's fighters made an average of four flights each and some machines of Raymond Collishaw's No. 3 Naval Squadron made as many as six sorties during the day.[17]

March 27 was an eventful day for Richthofen and his *JD1*, for it marked one of the most successful days in the *Jagstaffel's* history. The Red Baron and his pilots carried out 118 sorties, thirty-nine inconclusive air combats, and thirteen successful combats, including Manfred von Richthofen's seventy-first, seventy-second, and seventy-third victories.[18]

The German advance continued unabated to the extent that Collishaw's No. 3 Naval Squadron had to abandon its aerodrome at Mont St. Eloi on March 28, 1918. They packed up what they could and moved to Treizennes, near Aire, and about 22 miles northwest of Mont St. Eloi. By month's end, the German attack was blunted, but they had advanced more than 20 miles on a front of 50 miles, and stood not more than 5 miles from Amiens.[19]

The enemy offensive led the Allied forces to name French Marshal Ferdinand Foch as Commander-in-Chief to coordinate all troops on the Western Front. The British air forces were to be consolidated as well. The RFC and RNAS merged to become the Royal Air Force (RAF). This merger was a long time in the making.

> South African lawyer, politician and soldier Jan Smuts, one-time enemy of the British, had been invited by Prime Minister David Lloyd George to join his War Cabinet, and in 1917 he was asked to produce a report into the direction of air operations. Specifically, Smuts was directed to consider the reorganization of the air services, and the best means of implementing bombing operations. In his report, Smuts noted the "competition, friction, and waste" that arose from the existence of rival air services.... he concluded that the Royal Flying Corps and the Royal Naval Air Service should be amalgamated into a new air service ... Smuts' recommendations were accepted by the War Cabinet

and a bill was duly presented to the House of Commons, proposing the formation of the new service.[20]

On November 29, the Air Force Bill received Royal Assent and an Air Ministry was formed on January 2, 1918, which was on par with the Admiralty and the War Office. The new service, the RAF, came into being later on April 1, 1918.[21] Reaction to the merger ranged from disappointment to hostile opposition.

Jealousies and friction in Whitehall had sometimes been reflected at squadron level, and distaste for the merger was general. The RNAS, having been part of the senior service, felt superior, "and they acted it", according to Lieutenant H. R. Puncher, who flew alongside them on what had been a naval squadron. The RFC, in the front line of the ground fighting for so long, could not accept inferiority. Both services were proud of their origins and achievements and had developed loyalties almost as fierce as those of a regiment. They were lukewarm, if not hostile, to the change, which, as typically understated by Bryan Sharwood-Smith, was "greeted with no great enthusiasm". Tommy Trail wrote more frankly: "We were proud of the RFC and of ourselves, and we wanted none of this new thing." Yet the ugliness was often in the eye of the beholder. "I can only say that as a squadron officer," wrote Lieutenant-Commander R.M. Bailey, RN, of the alleged animosity, "I never experienced it at all in France."[22]

The demise of the RNAS was regretted by the aircrew rank and file, to whom the Canadians belonged, but principally for sentimental reasons. "It was a sad moment," wrote Raymond Collishaw, "... when my squadron had to strike the Royal Naval ensign ... which we had proudly flown even when we were serving with the army on all its fronts." By the time the RAF was incorporated, it had grown to a force of 55,066 personnel with 2,949 airplanes and seaplanes.[23]

In spite of the merger, some of the RNAS pilots continued to wear the uniforms of the Royal Navy. Collishaw was one of them. He can be seen in photos wearing the distinctive dark blue uniform of the Royal Navy and white-peaked cap with the emblem of the RNAS in the centre. Others wore the RFC maternity jacket with a high collar while others switched to the new Royal Air Force kit.

NO. 203 SQUADRON (RAF)

The merger of the RFC with the RNAS meant that No. 3 Naval Squadron became No. 203 Squadron, and Collishaw became a Major (the RAF having adopted army ranks). The newly named squadron was to see more ground strafing and bombing because the Germans, on April 9, 1918, launched an offensive in the area of the Lys River on the fronts held by the British First and Second Armies.

> The Battle of Lys was, on a smaller scale, virtually a replica of the March offensive. Even the weather conformed; as the Germans launched their initial assault against the northern flank of the First Army on 9 April they moved forward through a thick fog which blanketed the battlefield and reduced visibility to forty yards. The Portuguese division which held part of XI Corps' front broke almost immediately and disappeared

from the battlefield. The Germans quickly began to exploit this gap, swinging north on the flank of the British 40th Division towards the Lys at Bac St Maur. By evening German troops were across both the Lys and the La Lawe rivers and in the suburbs of Estaires, having penetrated more than four miles into the British line on a front of ten miles.[1]

The speed of the German advance and the accompanying bombardment resulted in chaos. The aerodrome at La Gorgue, some 3 1/2 miles behind the lines, was the home of former No. 8 Naval Squadron. Now renamed No. 208 Squadron, it was under the command of Chris Draper. The last thing Draper wanted was to see his squadron captured by the enemy. Having lost contact with headquarters and in the confusion of battle an erroneous report was received that the Germans were nearing the airfield. Rather than see his squadron captured, Draper ordered his seventeen machines be burned in one gigantic bonfire. The squadron made their way through the fog by ground transport to Serny. Within forty-eight hours the unit was fully re-equipped and shooting down enemy aircraft.[2] Collishaw felt the burning of the machines was unnecessary and joked with Draper later that his squadron pilots had offered to fly them away from danger if he did not want his pilots to do so. Draper apparently was not amused by the comment and was probably still resentful toward Collishaw for taking his planes from under his nose back in early March.

Collishaw's squadron moved airfields the same day, not because Treizennes was under attack but to make room for other squadrons who were moving in. Both No. 203 and No. 210 Squadron (formerly No. 10 Naval Squadron) moved from Treizennes to the Liettres (also known as Estree Blanche) aerodrome, a few miles away. By 2:00 in the afternoon the fog had cleared sufficiently to allow twenty Camels of Collishaw's No. 203 Squadron, five from No. 40 Squadron and fifteen from No. 210 Squadron, to bomb and machine-gun German infantry in the neighbourhood of Bac St Maur, Estaires, and Festubert with persistence and accuracy.[3]

By April 10 the Germans had widened their attacking front to include part of the British Second Army's sector. Wings of the First and Second Armies were used exclusively for close ground support.

On the 11th the Germans took Merville in the north and Nieppe in the centre, pushing the First Army back into Messines on the southern flank, but their gains were far short of those of the first day. The British retirement was orderly, unlike the confused retreat of the First Army three weeks earlier. With clear weather in the afternoon, the squadrons of 1 Brigade were able to drop four hundred 25-lb bombs and fire fifty thousand rounds at ground targets. More significantly, they were reinforced during the day by 22 (Bristol Fighter) and 41, 46, and 64 (single-seater fighter) Squadrons.[4]

Rochford described one of the missions flown on April 11 in the following manner.

> … while on a low-flying mission, Little (Flight Commander Robert A. Little) encountered three EA two-seaters and with his flight attacked them. They were in turn immediately attacked by six Albartos Scouts, one of which Little engaged and sent down in a spin. He followed it and finally saw it crash near Neuve Eglise. On the same day Whealy despatched an LVG two-seater close to the canal near Sailly-sur-Lys and Glen destroyed an Albatros two-seater in flames near Givenchy.[5]

The work of No. 203 Squadron was recognized in April with the award of the DSC to Tich Rochford on April 1, and on April 10 it was announced that Flight Lieutenant A. T. Wealy had been awarded the DSC as well. Collishaw's pilots were getting the recognition they well deserved.

The fight on the ground, however, was having a frightening effect on General Douglas Haig, so much so that he issued his famous "Backs to the Wall" order on the morning of April 12, asking everyone to fight on to the end.

April 12 was a splendid day for flying. The sky was clear and visibility was excellent. On this day the RAF flew more hours, dropped more bombs, and took more photographs than on any day since the war began.

Setting an example closely followed by many of the other squadrons involved, the sixteen available pilots of 201 Squadron, at least five of them Canadians, logged a total of eighty-nine hours of operational flying during the course of "a very hot day's work." The phrase was S.W. Rosevar's, the Port Arthur man who was one of the Squadron's three Canadian flight commanders. He reported catching German infantry "on the march along a road and swept them three times leaving many of them lying on the road. The others jumped into ditches and I gave them some more." Another Camel squadron with a sizeable Canadian complement, Collishaw's 203 Squadron dropped 196 bombs and fired 23,000 rounds during the day.[6]

The weather became worse. From April 12 to 15 it was wet and misty. Although Bailleul fell to the Germans on April 15, they failed to take Kemmel Hill on April 17. By the latter half of April, the German attack had dwindled and then ground to a halt.[7] The bad weather had grounded flights on both sides of the line. Richthofen's *JD1* had recently moved to a more suitable airfield south of Cappy, less than 2 miles from the front.

The new airfield was only a fresh, grass-covered open spot along the road to Bray. Barracks had to be brought in from Rosieres and erected, while the landing and take-off area was prepared by British prisoners of war and members of a German machine-gun company. Captured British tents provided protection from the rain for personnel and aircraft.[8]

On April 20, Raymond Collishaw visited his friend Arthur Roy Brown. Brown was from Carleton Place, Ontario. Both were former RNAS pilots and Brown was now a flight leader of No. 209 Squadron. Brown and Collishaw's squadrons were stationed close to one another, so Collishaw decided to pay Brown a visit.

He remembered a handsome, black-haired, square-jawed pilot full of joy for flying. The man he found that afternoon was utterly different. There were grey hairs in his head, he had lost twenty-five pounds and his once-sparkling eyes were now blood-shot and sunken in his face. Brown admitted he'd been living for more than a month on a diet of milk and brandy. He said he had already had a nervous breakdown and that he was suffering from a severe ulcer. Collishaw was shocked and begged his friend not to fly any further missions. But both men knew that was impossible.[9]

The next day, April 21, 1918, Captain Brown and his flight of No. 209 Squadron pilots were on patrol over the Somme River. Rookie pilot Wop May had been told by his flight commander Roy Brown not to engage the enemy, but to remain above any combats. May entered the fray when enemy machines were spotted, and attacked. Manfred von Richthofen ended up on May's tail and followed him down to low altitude, as May tried to escape his pursuer. Brown, noticing that his young pilot had got himself into trouble, came to his rescue, diving on the red Fokker triplane. Brown fired his machine guns and the red triplane crashed near a group of Australian infantry.

The credit for killing Manfred von Richthofen has been the source of long and no doubt endless debate. Capt. A. Roy Brown, DSC, leader of No. 209 Squadron's 'A' Flight, filed a combat report in which he recounted: "Dived on large formation of 15–20 Albatros Scouts D5's and Fokker triplanes, two of which got on my tail and [then] I came out. Went back again and dived on pure red triplane which was firing on Lieut. May. I got a long burst into him and he went down vertical and was observed to crash by Lieut. [later Sir Francis] Mellersh and Lieut. May. I fired on two more but did not get them."[10]

Historian Alan Bennett, in his two-volume biography of Roy Brown, which was painstakingly researched, concluded beyond a doubt that it was Roy Brown who shot down Richthofen and not Australian infantry fire. The loss of Richthofen was a significant blow to the German air forces. He had single-handedly accounted for eighty British and Allied machines. A more serious problem, however, was the effect of the British naval blockade on Germany and the shrinking supply of oil and fuel for the German aircraft.

> The naval blockade had long prevented any significant seaborne importation of oil into Germany, and the dislocation in their Balkan supply brought about by Romania's entry into the war against the Central Powers in 1916 and her subsequent defeat in 1917 was now making itself felt directly.... At the beginning of June (1918) the monthly fuel quantity (of the German air force) was reduced to 7,000 tons.... Fighter squadrons were rationed to 14,000 litres (3080 gallons) per month.... From June on, the fighter squadrons were virtually limited to less than ten individual flights per day.[11]

Collishaw's No. 203 Squadron continued its ground attacks to the end of April and into the month of May 1918, but not without casualties. From the start of the German offensive on March 21 to the end of April, the Squadron suffered eight pilots killed and two wounded.[12] These special ground support missions were taking their toll on the remaining pilots, as Rochford described.

> These Special Missions — sometimes four or more in a day — imposed a much greater strain on one than did the Offensive Patrols. At the same time we lost more pilots, some, shortly after joining us, others being old friends who had served in the squadron for a year or more. The element of doubt as to the outcome of the German advance was also a cause of tension not to mention the unsettling, tedious and frequent moves to new aerodromes.[13]

Library and Archives Canada, PA-002789.

Major Raymond Collishaw with Captain A.T. Whealy in the cockpit of his Sopwith Camel F.1, No. 203 Squadron at Izel-le-Hameau (Filescamp Farm), France, July 12, 1918.

On May 19, (Rochford says the move took place on May 16) the squadron moved to Izel-le-Hameau, south of Liettres and about 10 miles from Arras. The squadron returned to its normal operational duties by mid-May, resulting in the shooting down of twenty-nine enemy aircraft, as opposed to only ten during the month of April when they were primarily flying ground support missions. On the very day the squadron moved to its new location, EA were shot down by Beamish, Breakey, Britnell, Le Boutillier, and Whealy. The following day, Rochford downed an EA, which crashed near Beaupré, and Beamish got one near Merville. Hayne attacked a DFW two-seater from behind letting off two good bursts of fire. The EA dove to escape, with Hayne following closely. The EA was seen to stall, side slip, and finally crash near Steenwerke. The squadron claimed four victories on May 18, two on May 19, and one each on May 21 and 22.

During late May 1918, the Germans carried out night raids behind the British lines using twin-engine bombers. Although No. 203

Squadron's pilots were not trained in night fighting, Flight Commander Little decided to attack these bombers on his own on the night of May 27. Hours passed and there was no sign of Little or his Camel. Later, a report came into the squadron of a downed Camel with the body of a dead pilot lying beside it. Rochford described the fate of Robert Little in his book *I Chose the Sky*, as follows:

> From the wrecked condition of his machine it seems probable that Little was either dead or unconscious at the moment of impact. At some time prior to this he had been wounded in the thigh by a single bullet. He was officially reported to have died from his wounds and shock. The full story of Little's tragic last flight that night will never be known, but he must have been wounded by the return fire of a gunner when attacking an EA. Many years later Raymond Collishaw told me that he had made a thorough research of the activities of the German twin-engined bombers on that particular night in May 1918. None of these claimed to have encountered a British aircraft, but a German two-seater did in fact claim to have shot down a British aircraft at the appropriate time and place. Maybe that unknown two-seater's observer fired the fatal shots which so abruptly cut short the magnificent fighting career of this outstanding pilot.[14]

At the time of Little's death he had forty-seven victories, ten of which he had scored in the last two months with No. 203 Squadron.

With the administrative duties under control, Raymond Collishaw himself was able to get into the air using Rochford's Camel D3417, as Rochford was on leave in London. His flying was a little rusty after such a long absence from aerial combat and the two engagements he had on June 9, 1918, with the enemy were not decisive. The next day, however, he fared better, killing or badly wounding the observer of an LVG two-seater that he attacked. On June 11, Collishaw was leading the squadron on an evening offensive patrol when they spotted a formation of Pfalz D.IIIs

Library and Archives Canada, PA-178408.

Officers of No. 203 Squadron, RAF, visiting the grave of Captain R.A. Little, DSO, DSC, who was killed on May 28, 1918. Left to right: Captains L.D. Bawlf, A.T. Whealy, H.F. Beamish, Major Raymond Collishaw, Captain L.H. Rochford.

below them and to the west of Armentières. Collishaw and the rest of the squadron dove onto the formation. Collishaw, having chosen his target, fired on it and watched it disintegrate before his eyes. He then turned to another EA and gave it a couple of bursts from his dual Vickers. The Pfalz D.III tumbled out of control.

Any rust he felt left Collishaw by June 15, when he led his squadron on an escort mission, protecting a number of RE8s. They ran into a formation of Fokker D.VIIs — the newest German machine to arrive at the front. The D.VII was considered by many to be the best all-round fighter of the war.

This machine, which had been adopted as the standard German production fighter for 1918 ... has often been described as the outstanding fighter aircraft of the First World War. The Allies thought it so good that the Armistice terms specifically ordered the surrender of all D.VII's. Three versions were produced, but the most effective was the 185-hp BMW-engined version. This aircraft had a better rate of climb and higher operational ceiling than either the Sopwith Camel, SE5a, or the Sopwith 5F1 Dolphin which was just beginning to come into service with the RAF. It was not quite so fast and the British machines but exceptionally manoeuvrable above ten thousand feet and gave its pilots a significant edge in high-level combat, other things being equal.[15]

Collishaw pounced on one of the new Fokkers, got away 150 rounds into it and it went down, being observed to crash. Moments later he sent another one down but did not see whether it went out of control or whether the pilot had taken evasive action. Collishaw had his third victory that day sending a Pfalz Scout down out of control. Raymond Collishaw felt wonderful in the cockpit, flying again after so many months away. In the ensuing weeks he was able to fly three or four times a week. On June 26, Collishaw shot down another Fokker D.VII and on June 30 he was victorious over a Pfalz scout. July 2 saw Collishaw shoot down a Halberstadt over Merville.

Rochford describes an example of Collishaw's hospitality, friendship to others, and caring for his fellow officers when he tells the story of Collishaw inviting several American and Canadian officers to the mess for drinks on July 4, American Independence Day.

> When the time arrived for them to leave us, many were in such a state that few of them could remember from where they came. So Collishaw put them all in a Crossley tender and he himself sat in front with the driver; he ordered the driver to stop at various camps, fetched out the Officer of the Guard and asked him whether any of these drunken officers belonged to his unit. Eventually all were safely delivered to their respective units.[16]

Library and Archives Canada, PA-002826.

Commanding Officer Raymond Collishaw and the Officers of No. 203 Squadron, RAF at Izel-le-Hameau, France, July 12, 1918. Front row (left to right): Lieutenants W. Sidebottom, W.A. Carter, I.W. Hunter, Bingham, Townsend, Dixey, Gordon E. Duke. Centre row (left to right): Captains Louis D. Bawlf, Art T. Whealy, Harold F. Beamish, Major Raymond Collishaw, Captains L.H. Rochford, E.T. Haynes, D.A. Haig. Rear row (left to right): Lieutenants F.T.S. Sehl, Fitzpatrick, F.G. Black, R. Stone, Nelson, Adams, Cecil H. Lick, Captain J.D. Breakey, Rudge.

This incident shows how Collishaw gained and kept the respect of his pilots and ground crew. He would go out of his way to help others. He cared deeply for the men of his squadron and they returned those feelings by working hard and willingly following Collishaw's instructions. The pilots of No. 203 Squadron followed Collishaw into battle knowing they were led by someone who was an expert flyer and was someone they held in the highest regard.

Collishaw's victories were adding up in the month of July. He started by bagging a DFW over Roye on the 14th. Then, on July 16, Major Collishaw led an early evening special patrol over Ypres and beyond. At 9:00 they attacked a flight of six Fokker D.VIIs. Collishaw closed to within 100 feet of one of the enemy Fokkers and opened fire. He could see his tracers going right into the cockpit of the machine, which subsequently went into what looked like a controlled dive.

Collishaw had no time to follow the plane down, as he was attacked himself by three Fokkers. He tried to out-manoeuvre them. Collishaw was forced down to 2,000 feet before he finally disengaged from his deadly pursuers. About a half an hour later the patrol spotted a pair of DFW two-seaters above them. Collishaw and his pilots from No. 203 Squadron climbed to meet them, with squadron commander Collishaw pouring over one hundred rounds into the cockpit of one of the enemy machines as he approached it. The DFW fell from the sky and as it did it crashed on the other machine, taking it down with it as they locked in a deadly embrace.

When he returned to the Le Hameau aerodrome with his squadron he discovered that he had been awarded the Distinguish Flying Cross. The citation to this medal reads:

> This officer is an exceptionally capable and efficient squadron commander, under whose leadership the squadron has maintained a high place in the Army Wing. He has carried out numerous solo patrols and led many offensive patrols, on all occasions engaging the enemy with great bravery and fearlessness. Up to date he has accounted for forty-seven enemy machines, twenty-two in the last twelve months.[17]

The Distinguished Flying Cross (DFC) was established in June of 1918 and awarded to officers of the RAF for acts of courage, valour, and devotion to duty. The DFC is a silver cross, which on the obverse displays the cross arms. An airplane propeller appears on the vertical axis and feathered wings are on the horizontal axis. A central laurel wreath encircles the entwined letters "RAF." The reverse is the Royal cypher above the date "1918." The ribbon is violet and white alternating horizontal stripes. After July 1919 the stripes were diagonal.

For some time Collishaw and Captain Rochford, who was becoming one of the squadron's more successful pilots, had been hatching a plan to raid an enemy aerodrome early one morning. The two chose Dorignies, about a mile from Douai and approximately 25 miles from their base at Le Hameau.

The two of them took off at 3:40 in the morning on July 22, 1918. Unfortunately, Tich had been visiting friends in No. 64 Squadron the night before, and when Collishaw went to his quarters to rouse him, it was obvious Tich just wanted to sleep. Tich was loyal to his commander and managed to get dressed, have some tea and biscuits in the mess, and then scramble into his flying gear and take off with Collishaw into a cloudless sky with all the stars out in their finest glory. Each of their Camels had been serviced and armed with full ammunition belts and four 25-pound bombs. Rochford managed to arrive at Dorignies first and flew down to about 200 feet and let loose with his machine guns, spraying the hangars and other buildings. He then dropped three of his four bombs on the German living quarters and the fourth on a hangar, which immediately caught fire. With all his ammunition gone, Rochford headed home.

By then dawn was beginning to break, and as Collishaw flew in he could see three planes being wheeled out of a hangar. He made several strafing runs at them and dropped his bombs on some of the aerodrome's buildings. As he turned away from his bombing run he noticed a German two-seater about to land from a night patrol. The pilot and observer must have wondered what was going on. Collishaw attacked the EA when it was at 800 feet from the ground. It nosedived and crashed onto the airfield near a row of hangars and burst into flames. Collishaw then flew back to Le Hameau, arriving shortly after Rochford.

Anxious to see what damage the two pilots caused, Collishaw had his Camel refuelled and re-armed, and by 5:30 a.m. he had returned to Dorignies. The Germans were ready for him and, not wanting to succumb to further indignities, three Albatros D.Vs jumped on Collishaw as he approached the aerodrome. Raymond Collishaw turned back toward his own lines and out-manoeuvred them, but not before getting off several machine-gun bursts at one of the Albatros scouts. It fell out of control and crashed near the Scarpe River.

Later that morning, Tich led his 'B' Flight, consisting of five machines in all, on an offensive patrol. They soon saw a two-seater Armstrong-Whitworth below them being attacked by a couple of Fokker D.VIIs. Diving to the aid of the "Big Ack," as the Armstrong-Whitworth was nicknamed, Rochford's flight attacked and shot one of the Fokkers down out of control. The other Fokker was destroyed by the observer in the Armstrong-Whitworth, who showed great skill with his rear-facing machine gun. They then spotted five Fokker D.VIIs at 9,000 feet. Rochford's Flight climbed to 17,000 feet to gain the advantage of height and then dove on the Fokkers. Rochford describes what happened next.

> Over Carvin I decided to attack the EA and dived steeply onto them. Picking my Fokker, I held my fire until I was almost colliding with him. I got off one short burst and he fell out of control. Sidebottom shot down a second which was seen to crash, and a third one fell out of control after being attached by Stone. I saw Rudge attack a fourth, which went down in flames. We lost sight of the remaining Fokker, after he had broken off the fight and dived away eastwards. When we resumed formation to return home, I noticed one Camel was missing and after landing at Izel-le-Hameau discovered the missing pilot was Rudge. None of us had seen him go, but later the Germans reported he had been shot down and killed.[18]

On the same day, Captain Louis Bawlf, a Canadian from Winnipeg, shot down a DFW two-seater bringing the day's tally to eight enemy machines destroyed. By the end of July, Collishaw's Squadron No. 203 had shot down twenty-nine enemy aircraft; eight downed in June, and 21 in July.

The news of Collishaw and Rochford's exploits that morning travelled fast. Congratulations started to flow in, including one from Major-General J. M. Salmond, commander of the RAF in the field. Slamond had recently taken over from General Trenchard. Canadian Corps Commander Lieutenant-General A.W. Currie also offered up his congratulations. Collishaw was recommended for the Victoria Cross and Rochford for the DSO. However, by the time the awards were approved, they were downgraded to a Bar to Colishaw's DSO and a DFC for Rochford.[19] A similar but unsubstantiated daring attack on a German aerodrome by William Bishop on June 2, 1917 resulted in the award of a Victoria Cross. Such was not to be the result for Raymond Collishaw. The citation to Collishaw's award reads as follows:

A brilliant squadron leader of exceptional daring, who has destroyed fifty-one enemy machines. Early one morning he, with another pilot, attacked an enemy aerodrome. Seeing three machines brought out of a burning hangar he dived five times, firing bursts at these from a very low altitude, and dropped bombs on the living quarters. He then saw an enemy aeroplane descending over the aerodrome; he attacked it and drove it down in flames. Later, when returning from a reconnaissance of the damaged hangars he was attacked by three Albatross scouts, who pursued him to our lines, when he turned and attacked one, which fell out of control and crashed.[20]

On July 28, 1918, on a special mission over La Bassée with Flight Lieutenant A.T. Whealy, Collishaw attacked a DFW two-seater. Although his tracer fire was seen to enter the fuselage of the enemy machine, it got away in a nosedive. A few days later Collishaw was more successful. He shot down a DFW, which crashed into a canal over Merville. This victory was confirmed by Allied anti-aircraft observers.[21]

The life of a squadron commander was not all honours and decorations, though. The job had its darker and sadder moments as well. Collishaw found writing home to the parents of fallen comrades a most difficult and painful task. He could not tell the parents the awful details of how their son actually died, but rather stuck to pointing out that the pilot died instantly. Collishaw flew with these men and got to know them personally. Each one was looked upon as a friend, and when they were gone it took its toll on everyone, especially Major Collishaw. As the Commanding Officer, he could not delegate the task of writing home to the parents of the lost pilot.

Collishaw also had to consider the morale of his men and had to provide them with all the support possible. He always seemed to have a smile on his face and always appeared to be in a cheerful frame of mind. By his own actions in the air he inspired each and every pilot, from the seasoned veterans to the newcomers on the squadron. Collishaw made sure no pilot kept to himself, brooding over what his fate might be.

Instead, he made sure everyone was busy when not in the air by playing games of cards or participating in a sing-along by the piano. Everyone was part of the team and had to partake in the social events of the squadron. Collishaw did not put up with those who did not pull their weight and do their fair share. He shipped them out as soon as it became evident they could not act at the standard expected.

Of his own thoughts and feelings, Collishaw kept those to himself. Outwardly, he exuded cheerfulness and confidence, but underneath the surface he too had periods of sadness and anxiety. The war took its toll on everyone, regardless of rank. Being in charge of the squadron and the men in it was a heavy burden. Raymond Collishaw was responsible for their future. He had to ensure newcomers were trained on the proven techniques and tactics in the air so they could survive and gain confidence. He trusted his experienced flight commanders to do their jobs, as he knew they would.

The evening of July 31 was a notable one for the squadron, noted not for victories but for the partial destruction of the aerodrome of Izel-le-Hameau. Halfway through a concert party the squadron was having, German bombers attacked the base. The first pass did little damage, but after the concert was over and the party had moved into the mess with the officers drinking and singing around the piano, a second flight of bombers attacked with better accuracy. Bombs straddled the mess, shaking the building, knocking pictures off the walls, and breaking the glasses in the bar. Pieces of shrapnel wounded a number of the officers. The wounded were sent away in an ambulance to hospital. Rochford tells of his role and that of Collishaw after the raid.

> Having dealt with the wounded, Collishaw and two or three of us walked up towards the aerodrome to make a further check-up. Lying dead in the roadway behind the hangers we found the body of one of the concert party with a gaping wound in his back, a bomb having landed only a few yards from him. Later, Collishaw, Whealy and I proceeded to one of the machine-gun posts on the aerodrome where we remained in case more bombers should attack the camp.

Soon afterwards a bomber flew over the eastern boundary of the aerodrome and dropped bombs among the buildings of No. 13 Squadron. One bomb scored a direct hit on a hut in which airmen were sleeping. Collishaw left Wheatly and myself in the machine-gun pit and walked across the aerodrome to 13 Squadron where he found nearly all the men in the bombed hit had been killed or badly wounded. He stayed to organize the transfer of the wounded to hospital.[22]

The Allies continued to prepare into early August 1918, for what was to become known as the Amiens offensive. The Canadian and Australian Corps would provide the major thrust into the German-held territory, with British and French forces on their flanks providing support. Twenty-nine infantry divisions would be involved. The largest concentration of tanks ever used in battle, over 400 of them, would rumble across the lines and assist the infantry to take out points of enemy strength such as pill boxes and machine-gun nests.

For the attack General Rawlinson deployed the Canadian Corps on the right between the Roye-Amiens road and the Villers-Chaulnes rail line, the Australian Corps in the centre between the railway and the Somme, and III British Corps on the left between the Somme and the Ancre. Three Canadian, two Australian, and three British divisions were to mount the assault, supported by the massive fire power of almost 1400 field guns, 684 heavy artillery pieces, 324 heavy tanks, and 96 Whippet tanks.[23]

Plans for the RAF were also under consideration.

On 1 August General Salmond submitted proposals to Haig for the employment of the air force. In the preparatory phase the RAF's principal task was to help maintain security for the forthcoming operation. This meant preventing German reconnaissance of the allied positions, as well as patrolling behind the Fourth Army front in order to report on any abnormal movement which might also be visible to the enemy.[24]

Bad flying weather during the first week of August severely restricted the activities of both the Allied and German air reconnaissance. During the evening of August 7, before the battle was to begin, two Handley-Page bombers patrolled for three hours over the lines at the point where the battle was to be launched, flying back and forth at moderate altitudes. This tactic was used to drown out the sound of British tanks being assembled just behind the lines, in readiness for the attack the next day.

On August 8, at 4:20 a.m., a deafening artillery barrage commenced. The Allied troops and tanks moved forward through the heavy morning mist. The Germans were completely taken by surprise. Some 800 British aircraft supported the Allied advance. Collishaw and his squadron managed to get airborne around 5:00 a.m. Throughout the day, his and many other squadrons flew continuously on low-level bombing and strafing attacks on the Fourth Army front against enemy infantry, vehicles, and any other targets they could find. The RAF squadrons were a welcome sight for the infantry. The aircraft would roar down just feet from the troop's heads as they fired on the retreating German troops. By noon that day, all roads leading from the battlefield were clogged with enemy infantry. In the words of German General Ludendorff, it was a "black day" for the German army.

Collishaw led four patrols that day, over the Roye Road, amounting to over eleven hours of flying, with every attack at less than 100 feet. Strafing the enemy positions on the ground was not a popular activity for any squadron, since the risk of being shot down was great. At 100 feet the pilot had nowhere to go but up, which would expose the belly of the aircraft to enemy fire and create an even bigger target to shoot at. So the pilots flew straight at their targets hoping the ground fire would not get them.

Over a 25-mile front where the offensive was launched, the RAF and the French air service had amassed more than 1,900 machines, over 1,000 of which were fighters. The Germans could only muster 365 airplanes, 140 of them being fighters.

Library and Archives Canada, PA-002792.

Major Raymond Collishaw (standing sixth from the left) and the pilots of No. 203 Squadron, RAF, in front of their Sopwith Camels on the occasion of an inspection by King George V, Izel-le-Hameau, France, August 8, 1918.

On that same day, August 8, 1918, No. 203 Squadron was paid a visit by King George V. The Camels were lined up in a long row, with each of the pilots standing at attention in front of his machine waiting for inspection. Rochford gives us his impression of the visit.

The King walked down the line with Brigadier General Pitcher, our Brigade Commander, immediately behind them were General Sir Henry Horne, Commander of the British First Army, with our CO, Major Raymond Collishaw, and the remainder of the entourage following them. The King stopped in front of me, said a few words, cracked a joke, at which we both smiled, and then continued on. Later, having completed the inspection he left with Sir Henry Horne in a staff-car to the cheers of all our squadron personnel who lined the road along which he passed. Peter, our brindle bulldog, gave his own special farewell by chasing the car and barking loudly all the time.[25]

Later that day an urgent request was received from Wing Headquarters for four of the squadron's pilots to be transferred to Squadron 201, to make up for the loss of pilots who had been making low-flying attacks all that day during the battle in front of Amiens. With Collishaw absent because of the King's visit, the remaining three Flight Commanders chose four pilots new to the squadron. This did not go well with the Wing Colonel, who ended up picking Lieutenants Stone, Sehl, Carter, and Sykes. They left at midnight in a lorry that took them to the aerodrome at Bertangles.

It was at this time that Collishaw received notification he had been awarded a bar to his DSO. By this time Collishaw had logged over 600 hours of flying time since coming to France, and a total flying time of almost 680 hours.

By August 11, the Allied forces had penetrated German-held territory some 10 miles. That day Collishaw, leading a patrol of his squadron's flyers, came upon a scrap between six Fokker D.VIIs and a flight of Sopwith Dolphins near Bray, 30 miles east of Amiens. Collishaw attacked and destroyed one of the D.VIIs that had just shot down one of the Dolphins. He then assaulted a second hostile scout, which started to fall out of control, but he was unable to watch its ultimate fate because he was himself attacked, his engine having been hit. He managed to get over the lines and landed at Bertangles.

Collishaw's victories that day were confirmed by No. 22 Squadron.[26] Two of the squadron's pilots were lost over the Roye Road the next day, and a third No. 203 Squadron pilot was lost over the same road on August 13. Notwithstanding these losses, Collishaw managed to shoot down a Fokker east of the Roye Road on August 13.

By August 14, in the battle of Amiens, the Allies had advanced more than 10 miles They had captured over 300,000 prisoners, and the German Kaiser was calling for the end of the war.

August 15 saw No. 203 Squadron move from Le Hameau, where they had been for nearly three months, south to their new aerodrome at Allonville near Amiens. It was surrounded by a horseshoe-shaped wood,

Library and Archives Canada, PA-165399.

Inspection by King George V of senior RAF officers, France. Major Raymond Collishaw, Commanding Officer, No. 203 Squadron, RAF, is visible behind and to the left of his majesty.

and the officers and personnel of the squadron lived under canvas tents. The hangars were of a portable type, small but functional. The mess was a large marquee and the sleeping quarters consisted of bell tents. On the opposite side of the aerodrome, at the edge of the wood, No. 80 Squadron was stationed in permanent hangars and hutted living quarters in the form of huts. This move brought the squadron closer to the Fourth Army's front line and under the command of the 22 Wing of V Brigade.

Collishaw's next victory came on August 15, when on an early evening patrol he came across a French Spad tangling with a pair of Fokker D.VIIs. He closed in on the dogfight and fired into one of the Fokkers, which fell from 8,000 feet and crashed. The Spad pilot managed to out-manoeuvre the other Fokker and sent it too to its final resting place.

Most of No. 203 Squadron's work during the middle of August was made up of ground strafing enemy infantry columns. The German army continued to fall back in disarray. Collishaw and his squadron also targeted anti-tank guns near Bray. The squadron also flew escort patrols, escorting D.H.4s from 205 Squadron on bombing raids. On such patrols the Camels were restricted in their movement, having to remain in close range of the machines being escorted. Rochford describes such formation flying:

> Normally we escorted two-seater bomber or photograph-reconnaissance formations which we met over a rendezvous point behind our lines where we formated on them, close behind, before setting course for the target.
>
> This type of formation made it very difficult for EA to get past the escorting fighters from astern and any that did were assured of a hot reception from the rear machine-guns of the two-seaters. Attacks made by the enemy on either flank of the formation were baulked by the outside members of the escort whose efforts were augmented, when necessary, by gunners of the escorted force.
>
> The most vulnerable positions were the rearmost members of the escort but the tighter they maintained their formation the safer they were as EA usually disliked tackling those which were well closed-up.
>
> When a whole squadron carried out an escort one flight kept close formation on the bomber/reconnaissance machines and the other two flew stepped up and positioned to prevent any high attacks which the enemy might develop at some distance from the main formation.[27]

It was on one such patrol that Rochford spied a new form of EA fighter, the Fokker D.VIII monoplane. This late entrant into the war in the air, unlike the normal biplanes, had only one plane, or wing, as we now call them. It was a sleek machine and very manoeuvrable. It had a speed of 127 1/2 miles per hour, a ceiling of 19,680 feet, and was powered by a 110-horsepower rotary engine. Its wingspan was a little over 27 feet and had a length of slightly over 19 feet.[28]

On August 22, the Allied ground forces resumed their attacks. On the morning of August 23, the Fourth Army had joined the offensive. The battlefront had now been stretched from Neuville to Lihons, south of the Somme.

On the Fourth Army front the bulk of the low strafing work fell to 203 Squadron, still commanded by Raymond Collishaw, who now had fifty-four victories to his credit. His skills in air combat honed to a fine edge, Collishaw disliked the chancy nature of close ground-support work, recognizing that a stray bullet was as likely to bring down a veteran ace as the rawest novice. His skill and experience counted for little when he flew against ground targets at fifty feet. Nevertheless, he was leading his squadron when one of his flight commanders, Lieutenant J. P. Hales of Guelph, Ont., was shot down near Villera-Bretonneux. Collishaw reported that he had seen the body lifted from the crashed Camel: from the ground the view was very different and an enemy war diarist plaintively reported "Low flying enemy aircraft overhead. No German planes in sight, no 'flak' guns firing."[29]

Rochford recalls he and Collishaw went by car to try to find Jack's crashed Camel, but the search was in vain.

A typical day for the squadron is described in V Brigade's summary for August 29, 1918.

Patrols of No. 203 Squadron dropped 20 bombs on a convoy of lorries on Peronne-Rancourt Road and fired 2500 rounds into objectives in this vicinity. 20 bombs were also dropped on convoy of lorries on Grand Prix Road east of the Somme and 2500 rounds fired. Capt. Whealy's patrol dropped 20 bombs on parties of men in the vicinity of Bussu east of Peronne. The bombs were seen to explode amongst these troops. 2800 rounds were fired into about 200 lorries on different main roads eastward of Peronne. Eight bombs were dropped on enemy huts and transport at Aizecourt, causing a large fire. 600 rounds were fired from a low altitude. 25 bombs were dropped into a battalion of infantry. The bombs were seen to fall amongst the troops who disappeared in shrubbery and were dispersed. About 100 lorries were also attacked, 3200 rounds being fired at them. 32 bombs were dropped and 4400 rounds fired at various ground targets.[30]

Collishaw's No. 203 Squadron returned to Izel-le-Hameau on September 3, 1918, and rejoined I Brigade, part of the 10th Wing. The low-level attacks on the retreating German army continued into September as the Allied infantry continued its advance. Air support of the ground forces was becoming more sophisticated as low-level air strikes were being carried out against specific targets identified by the British forces, such as a certain road junction, a village containing a congested group of enemy transports, or an anti-tank gun that was holding up the progress of the Allied attack.

On September 3, Collishaw led his squadron in low-level attacks over the Canal du Nord. On September 5, while over Bourlon Wood, Collishaw spotted a Fokker biplane about to attack a British Kite (observation) Balloon. He dived on the EA and fired a burst of his machine guns at close range. The enemy machine crashed in the British-held lines near Inchy En Artois and burned. The low-level flying over the Canal du Nord continued on September 7. Collishaw claims he got another Fokker D.VII on September 12, while leading his squadron on an offensive patrol over Cambrai. The German machine broke up in the air after Collishaw attacked it.

On September 20 the whole squadron went out on an OP and encountered fourteen Fokker D.VIIs. In the ensuing dog fight a number of Fokkers were downed. In one case a German pilot was seen to jump out of his aircraft with a parachute. This was one of the first times on the Western Front where pilots had seen an attempt to land by parachute. Unfortunately, the parachute failed to open properly and the German pilot fell to his death. Allied troops buried the pilot with his parachute.

When it was learned later at Brigade HQ that the German pilot had been buried in his parachute, Collishaw received orders to recover it. A party was sent out to open the grave, retrieve the parachute and then rebury the pilot. The parachute was brought back to Izel-le-Hameau where it was hung up on a tree in the orchard for at least a week in order to clear the stench from it which was horrible.[31]

Victories for Major Collishaw continued to mount up during the latter half of September. On September 24, while leading his squadron on a special mission over Epinoy, four enemy Fokker D.VII biplanes were attacked. Collishaw and his fellow pilots attacked from out of the sun. Collishaw picked out one of the Fokkers and fired at it without any results, and then turned to another one, fired a few bursts of his machine guns, and saw the enemy machine fall out of control. This victory was confirmed by another pilot and an anti-aircraft battery.

September 26 saw a combined effort on the part of Collishaw's No. 203 Squadron of fourteen Camels; No. 40 Squadron, made up of eleven SE5as; and No. 22 Squadron, equipped with eleven Bristol Fighters. Their objective was the German aerodrome at Lieu-Saint-Amand, some 9 miles northeast of Cambrai. The Bristols flew as escort. The SE5as went in first, dropping their bombs on the aerodrome's hangars and other buildings. Collishaw and his Camels went in next. Their bombs hit the hangars, which started on fire. Both the Camels and the SE5as then strafed the field destroying a DFW two-seater and numerous Fokkers parked in front of the buildings.

Some of the Fokker D.VIIs managed to take off and went after the enemy squadrons. Collishaw and two other Camels attacked them. Collishaw was able to send two down and saw them burst into flames as they hit the ground. It was quite a successful raid. Collishaw's No. 203 Squadron shot down or destroyed five enemy aircraft on the ground, while the SE5as of No. 22 Squadron destroyed two more. One Camel was shot down from ground fire but the pilot managed to land the aircraft safely and was made a prisoner of war.

The British and Allied forces pressed the attack and by the end of September were assaulting the Hindenburg Line. The 3rd and 4th Canadian Divisions were approaching the outskirts of Cambrai by September 30. The British First Army, which No. 203 Squadron was supporting, was moving toward the Saint-Quentin-Cambrai front.

On the First Army front there were now five squadrons allocated exclusively to the ground support function under Major Smythies, 40 Squadron having been added to the old hands of 54, 64 and 209 Squadrons, and No. 203 having replaced 208. Their main objectives were the crossings over the Sensee and L'Escaut canals, and "in many cases large numbers of troops, mechanical and horse transport, were seen on the bridges and heavily engaged with machine gun fire and 25-lb bombs. Many direct hits were made and numerous casualties observed." Seven hundred bombs were dropped and 26,000 rounds fired by the five squadrons during the day.[32]

No. 203 Squadron was also called on to attack enemy balloons (also called kite balloons) and Collishaw, in early October 1918, led two of his pilots on such an attack. As Collishaw dove in to attack the balloon he was in turn attacked from behind by a number of Fokker D.VIIs. He managed to evade them, but Flight Lieutenant Skinner was not so lucky. He was shot down by one of the Fokkers.

By early October, the British First Army, which included the Canadian Corps led by General Currie, was pushing toward Cambrai. By October 9 they held Cambrai firmly in place. On October 17, 1918, the Canadians entered Douai, and by October 24 No. 203 Squadron had moved to a nearby field some 6 to 7 miles to the east. It was the former home of a German *Jasta*. At this point in the war the enemy was in full retreat. However, Raymond Collishaw was not able to be with his beloved squadron to the end. He had received orders on October 21 to report to the Air Ministry in London. It was Tich Rochford who travelled with him in the squadron staff car to the aerodrome at Marquise, along with Peter, the squadron's bulldog, which Collishaw wanted to take with him but couldn't due to regulations. Rochford said farewell to "Collie" and wished him good luck. Collishaw turned over command of the squadron to Major T.F. Hazell. While Collishaw had been command of No. 203 Squadron it had accounted for 125 enemy aircraft, while fewer than thirty of its own pilots were killed or made prisoners of war.

Upon arriving in England, Collishaw learned he was to be posted back to Canada to assist with Canadian pilot training. At the beginning of 1917, the RFC had established a rather large and extensive flying training scheme.

The scheme was under the leadership of Brigadier-General C.G. Hoare, originally a pre-war cavalry officer from India, who had learned to fly early in the war. Collishaw had been selected as Hoare's senior staff officer, and as such, began a tour of the RAF training establishments in Britain to learn the latest pilot training methods and procedures. The posting was cut short with the signing of the armistice on November 11, 1918.

Collishaw was jubilant the war had finally come to an end and that he had survived the ordeal, but was also saddened by the loss of many friends who had not lived to see this joyous occasion.

There has been considerable debate, during the years following the war, of the number of victories the top-scoring aces actually accomplished. For example, many have questioned the number of kills Billy Bishop claimed.

> There was widespread scepticism within the RAF … over the seventy-two victories claimed by Major William Bishop. It is now generally believed that these doubts were the motivation for posthumously raising (Edward) Mannock's claimed score of around sixty-one victories right up to a frankly dubious seventy-three, "coincidently" just one more than Bishop had claimed. It was Mannock's occasional practice of giving or sharing his kills with his wingmen that provided a cover for this artificial post-war increase. And there he would remain, lauded in the history books as the highest scoring British ace of the Great War.[33]

Raymond Collishaw was third with, depending on what source is used, between fifty-nine and sixty-one victories. Most of these were when he was a Flight Commander in No. 10 Naval Squadron and the final twenty victories, between June and October 1918, were with No. 203 Squadron.

> In reply to an official Canadian request, not long after the armistice, for the number of aircraft that Collishaw had shot down, the British Air Ministry replied that so far as

the RAF Headquarters could determine it was 59, and that squadron records gave it as 61. The 59 figure resulted from a totting up of reports in RFC and RAF communiqués and RNAS operations summaries rather than from reference to any officially-maintained list of victories.[34]

S.F. Wise, in his book *Canadian Airmen in the First World War*, speaks of the relative ease, at the beginning of the war, of discerning whether a pilot had shot down the enemy since aircraft were much slower, less manoeuvrable, and the pilot could follow his victim down until he saw it crash. By 1917 and into 1918 fighter planes were faster, more numerous, and the dogfights were not the solitary combat of two machines, rather they were a melee of ten to twenty aircraft. You could not keep your sight on one aircraft for too long, otherwise you would be shot down. After such an encounter with the enemy, who could really confirm whether a pilot had administered the fatal blow on any particular aircraft?[35]

> Despite their inflated claims and credits, the "aces" of the war — the Vosses, von Richthofens, Bishops, Barkers and Collishaws — were anything but fakes. They earned and held the respect of their peers as well as that of the public by their flying, shooting, and tactical skills rather than by self-advertisement or the assiduous labours of public relations staffs. But the compilation of lists of scores and the many rankings of allied and German pilots so plentiful in the romantic and sensational literature which has been built up since the First World War often rest upon assumptions which will not bear critical scrutiny. At least as far as 1918 is concerned, claims of air victories by either side should be reduced by at least one-third.[36]

Despite the apparent lack of complete accuracy of the final victories of the aces like Collishaw, he stands out as one of the most pre-eminent flyers and leaders of the First World War. His courage and fortitude were unquestionable, his leadership skills, exemplary.

THE RUSSIAN ADVENTURE

RAYMOND COLLISHAW REMAINED IN ENGLAND INTO 1919 AND IT WAS at that time that he was offered and accepted a permanent commission in the RAF. He was now a career RAF officer and, considering his record during the war, was granted an extended leave in Canada.

The ship in which he sailed back to Canada contained many returning soldiers of the Newfoundland Regiment. This unit had almost been wiped out on July 1, 1916, the first day of the Battle of the Somme. Collishaw could not help but get wrapped up in the celebrations held for the returning soldiers when the ship landed in St. John's harbour. He rejoined the ship in the small hours of the following morning and continued his voyage to the Canadian mainland.

On his way to the West Coast by rail, Collishaw stopped in the major cities along the way, as he had done while on leave during the war, to visit the families of officers he knew who had been killed. He was impressed with how bravely these families bore their losses. Upon reaching New

Westminster, Raymond Collishaw visited his fiancée, Neita Trapp, and her parents, who also had to bear the loss of their three sons who had been killed while serving in the flying corps.

Not knowing where his next posting would be, the couple decided not to get married. That turned out to be a wise decision because Collishaw was asked to take command of an RAF squadron that was headed to south Russia to support the White Russian forces in their counter-revolution against the Bolsheviks. He accepted.

The Russian Revolution of November 1917 had toppled the Czarist regime and had taken Russia out of the First World War. The signing of the Treaty of Brest-Litovsk in early March 1918 between Germany and the Bolsheviks allowed the Russian revolutionaries the opportunity to consolidate their hold over the country. However, the White Russians had mounted a significant counter-revolution. Of the Allied forces in the Great War, the primary backer of the White Russian forces was Britain. She had sent considerable arms, supplies, and forces to North Russia, at Murmansk and Archangel, Vladivostok, at the eastern end of the Trans-Siberian Railway, and in the Caucasus in Southern Russia. Britain feared the spread of Communism and was prepared to do all it could to see the White Russian forces come to power in Russia. France was reluctant to get involved in the conflict and withdrew its army and naval forces from the Black Sea area.

By the spring of 1919, the commander of the White Russian forces in the Caucasus, General Anton Denikin, with the aid of the Don, Kuban, and Terek Cossacks, had moved into South Russia. Admiral Kolchak's forces, which were formed in Siberia, began to move westward towards Moscow. General Yudenitch's forces had formed in Estonia, and along with some international troops had begun to move on Petrograd from the west.

General Anton Denikin had been one of the most gifted officers on the Russian general staff during the First World War, and by August 1917 was made commander-in-chief of the Russian army on the southwestern front. It should be pointed out that around the time of the signing of the Treaty of Brest-Litovsk between the Germans and the Bolsheviks, and into the summer of 1918, the Bolsheviks did not have the support of the majority of the Russian population. For example, in Siberia there were no Bolsheviks in power. The Don and Kuban

Library and Archives Canada, PA-023553.

One of the homes in which Collishaw may have stayed while in Russia.

Cossacks were commencing hostilities against the Bolsheviks and in the south a volunteer army had been recruited through the joint efforts of Generals Denikin and Alekseyev.

Admiral Kolchak, an outstanding sailor and one of the most competent admirals in the Russian Navy, shortly before the collapse of the Tsar's monarchy, had been appointed commander-in-chief of the Black Sea's Fleet. Like many senior officers in the Russian forces, he favoured the formation of a government in opposition to the Bolsheviks, and was preparing a coup d'état. By the summer of 1918, Kolchak's army of resistance had formed at the far eastern end of Russia at Vladivostok and was moving westward toward Omsk.

A "reformed" government called the Directorate was created, made up of a number of political parties that had not supported the Brest-Litovsk Treaty, such as the Cadet Party and a number of socialist parties with the support of Generals Alekseyev and Boldyrrev of the Siberian Regional Government. By the autumn of 1918, the British and French governments were preparing to recognize the Directorate as the legal government of Russia. Alexander Kerensky, head of the Provisional Government of Russia at the time of the Bolshevik revolution, was in exile in London at that time. From there he was calling for the recognition of the Directorate by Britain and France.

On November 18, 1918, Admiral Kolchak was declared the "Supreme Ruler of Russia." Kolchak had carried out a coup d'état and replaced the Directorate with a one-man military dictatorship. Representatives of General Denikin travelled to Omsk to meet and consult with Kolchak. Kolchak, along with Denikin, Boldyrev, and others, formed their own government. They were hoping to be recognized by the "Big Five" (Britain, France, the United States, Italy, and Japan) at the Versailles peace conference in late 1918 and early 1919. No one, however, would receive them, let alone recognize Kolchak's newly formed government.

In the meantime, the Bolsheviks were expanding their area of influence and control over Russian territory. By the end of May 1919, all of the Ukraine was in the hands of the Bolsheviks. This event, coupled with Kolchak's advance toward Moscow, led the Big Five to recognize Kolchak's government in May of 1919.

The British Military Mission, sent to aid Denikin in the south, consisted of equipment, supplies, and personnel who would train and instruct the Russian forces in the operation of the equipment.

The magnitude of British aid to Denikin was enormous. From March 1919 to March 1920 the Russians received 1200 guns, nearly two million shells, 6100 machine guns, 200,000 rifles, 500 million rounds of SAA, hundreds of trucks and motorcycles, seventy-four tanks, and 100 aircraft, plus uniforms and many other stores. Only a part of this vast amount of material reached front-line units; the commander of the British Mission, Major-General H. C. Holman, complained in his final report that "the incompetence and corruption of the administrative services and departments could not be overcome by any scheme." It was Denikin's successes in an offensive during the summer that persuaded the British government to maintain its support for him, despite his own excesses and rising criticism at home. Even so, domestic political pressure caused the British to withdraw 47 Squadron from Russia; its members instead were

Library and Archives Canada, PA-203553.

Major Raymond Collishaw, Commanding Officer, No. 47 Squadron, RAF.

asked to volunteer for the Mission. The squadron was disbanded on 1 October 1919 and in its place appeared 'A' Detachment, RAF Mission, with the same organization, personnel, equipment, and task.[1]

There was to be no armed intervention on the part of the British and Commonwealth forces. All recruits were to be volunteers. This provision applied to No. 47 Squadron, which had finished the war flying against the Bulgarians in Macedonia. This squadron had been selected by the British to support Denikin's operations in South Russia.

> The Chief of the Air Staff at the Air Ministry appointed Major R. Collishaw to recruit officers and men for special service in South Russia. A special appeal was sent out in Major Collishaw's name, to thousands who had recently been de-mobilized from R.A.F. Squadrons, and a careful selection was made to fill the establishment. The airmen were exclusively English, while the pilots were principally Canadian.[2]

Collishaw visited many RAF units in Britain to recruit members for this force. He put together a fine group of men which then travelled through France on a special train, then took a ship in Italy for the Black Sea port of Novorissisk in South Russia. They arrived in Novorissisk on June 8, 1919.

Also joining Collishaw was Harold "Gus" Edwards, a Nova Scotian who had been shot down and made a prisoner of war in 1917. He was repatriated at the end of the war and had volunteered to be with Collishaw and No. 47 Squadron. Edwards's duties in South Russia included being a motor transport officer to the Aviation Section, and in December 1919 he became the Adjutant of 'A' Detachment (No. 47 Squadron). Gus would be awarded two Imperial Russian decorations for his contribution to the war against the Bolsheviks. Gus Edwards would eventually become an Air Marshal of the Royal Canadian Air Force.

Edwards's friend and fellow pilot Herbert Seton Broughall of Toronto was, like Edwards, shot down and made a prisoner of war. Together on April 12, 1919 they joined 'C' Flight of No. 47 Squadron and then travelled to Krasnodar in South Russia. It should be noted that Broughall would become Collishaw's senior staff officer in the Western Desert Campaign of the Second World War and then would go on to Burma to serve as the Officer Commanding the RAF forces there. Another notable addition to Collishaw's team was fellow RNAS pilot Lionel Lodge Lindsay of Calgary. Lindsay would eventually be awarded the Imperial Russian Order of Saint Stanislas.

Author's Collection.

Imperial Russian Order of Saint Stanislas, similar to the one Collishaw received from the White Russian forces.

Library and Archives Canada, PA-203554.

D.H.9 aircraft of 'C' Flight, No. 47 Squadron, RAF, Ekaterinodar, Russia, 1919.

In the meantime, during April 1919, a party of twenty-one of No. 47 Squadron's officers and ground crew sailed from Salonika in Greece and also landed at Novorissisk, located east of the Crimea. The squadron headquarters was established at Ekaterinodar, on a rail line some 60 miles to the northeast of Novorissisk. The squadron was under the temporary command of Captain Sidney G. Frogley who faced many difficulties overseeing the assembly of the unit's aircraft and getting ready for operations against the Bolsheviks. Overall command of the RAF in South Russia fell to Brigadier-General Maund, DSO. Earlier in the year Maund took charge of an RAF instructional group consisting of about 130 RE8 two-seaters also based at Ekaterinodar. The goal was to teach members of Denikin's forces to fly and to operate their own squadrons.

> ... according to Air Vice-Marshal Collishaw's recollections there was a "severe dragging of heels" at the squadron's base at Ekaterinodar (now Krasnodar) in the assembling of the squadron's D.H.9s. The squadron went to the Volga front in early June 1919. In order to release officers desiring demobilization Collishaw, then a Major, was sent out to command 47 Squadron, and he brought with him a party of volunteers ... and was joined by two other Canadians, Captains W.F. Anderson of Toronto and J.L. MacLennan of Montreal.[3]

Denikin's forces were organized into three armies. The Kuban and Terek Cossack Army, under General Wrangel, formed the right wing at and along the Volga River. Their objective was the capture of Tsaritsyn (later Stalingrad). The second army, under the leadership of General Sidorin, consisted of the Don Cossacks and held the centre. Its objective was the capture of Kharkov. The third army was composed of an irregular volunteer army under General Mai-Maievsky whose objective was the capture of Kiev. Masses of ex-Czarist officers served along with Mai-Maievsky. Baron Peter Wrangel was an officer of an aristocratic guards regiment during the First World War and had acquired a great deal of fame early in the war in a cavalry attack against a German gun battery. Since the spring of 1917 he had been involved in a number of plots to replace Kerensky's Provisional Government with a military dictatorship.

Collishaw's No. 47 Squadron was made up of three flights, one equipped with D.H.9 two-seater bomber/reconnaissance biplanes, another with D.H.9a bombers (a variant of the D.H.9), and the third flight composed of Sopwith Camel fighters. Each flight was assigned their own special train equipped with workshops and other facilities, which enabled them to operate as self-contained operating units. A fourth train was to be used for headquarters staff.

The de Havilland D.H.9 had a wingspan of 41 feet, 4 5/8 inches, and a length of 30 feet, 5 inches. It stood over 11 feet tall and was powered by a 230-horsepower Siddeley Puma engine. This gave the D.H.9 a top speed of 109.5 miles per hour and a ceiling of 15,500 feet. It could carry almost 1,000 pounds of bombs and had a forward-firing .303-inch Vickers machine gun for use by the pilot, and either one or two rear-firing .303-inch Vickers machine guns for the observer.[4]

Unlike the static trench warfare of the First World War, the war in Russia was very fluid, with the front sometimes changing by tens of miles a day. The vastness of the land was a major challenge for both sides of the conflict, making it difficult to maintain the control over any given territory. What mitigated the expanse of the open steppes of the southern Russian territory was the advanced system of railways that had been developed over the years. Troops were moved by train and so too were their supplies and equipment. Military operations on the ground were often confined to an area of between 10–15 miles on either side of the railway lines. The trains also transported the aircraft from place to place. They would be partly disassembled, loaded on to the rail cars, and then off-loaded and reassembled where required. Makeshift aerodromes for the aircraft to fly from were quickly constructed nearby.

On June 10, two days after Collishaw's arrival at Novorossisk, 'C' Flight, with five D.H.9s, left Ekaterinodar by train for the Tsaritsyn front. Wet weather and considerable congestion on the rail lines hampered their movements. In spite of this, on June 20, the D.H.9s of 'C' Flight arrived at the village of Gniloakaiskaya, some 315 miles northeast of Ekaterinodar, where they operated out of an improvised aerodrome near the railway siding. They successfully carried out several bombing raids and reconnaissance flights, their first one taking place on June 23, 1919. By the end of the month the flight had carried out daily raids, during which they strafed enemy barges, rail transportation, groups of cavalry, and troops assembled in and around Tsaritsyn. They even dropped a bomb on a building that housed the local Soviet officials, killing most of them. Other bombing attacks were made on the naval vessels and supply barges along the Volga.

By the time Wrangel's forces had captured Tsaritsyn, the Don Cossack Army had captured Kharkov and the volunteer army had captured Kiev.

After the fall of Tsaritsyn, 'C' Flight moved north on July 6 to a town called Beketovka, some 12 miles south of Tsaritsyn. From there they were able to carry out bombing raids and reconnaissance missions around Kamyshin, on the Volga River northeast of Tsaritsyn.

On July 11, Major Collishaw arrived in Ekaterinodar with seven officers and 179 other ranks. A large amount of work was carried out re-assembling the aircraft, which had been delivered in pieces by train. Then trains had to be obtained to transport the flights to their various destinations. 'B' Flight, for example, left on July 15 for Kharkov to the northwest of Ekaterinodar.[5] Five days later Collishaw received orders to recall 'C' Flight from the Volga front and replace it with 'B' Flight. 'B' Flight returned to Ekaterinodar and on July 21 left for Beketovka. 'C' Flight, upon its return to Ekaterinodar, was disbanded, making 'B' Flight the new 'C' Flight, under the command of Captain Frogley. The new 'C' Flight carried out its first bombing raid on July 23, 1919, against Kamyshin and Tcherni-Yar on the Volga River to the southeast of Tsaritsyn. 'C' Flight's bombing raids on these two targets continued for the rest of the month.

The squadron's first aerial victory in South Russia occurred on July 25. Two of 'C' Flight's D.H.9s took off early that morning for a bombing raid. They unloaded ten 20-pound and two 112-pound bombs on barges and at the railway station. They then strafed ground positions. When they were turning for home they were attacked by a Bolshevik Nieuport scout. Because his front-firing Vickers machine gun was jammed, Pilot Lieutenant J. R. Hatchett manoeuvred the D.H.9 so that his observer, Lieutenant H. E. Simmons, could get away a clean shot on the Red machine. Simmons fired a burst of fifty rounds into the Nieuport. It veered away sharply, went down out of control, and crashed. The Red Air Fleet at that time numbered about a hundred aircraft, made up of French, Russian, and some German machines.

On July 30, what started out as a regular bombing and strafing run turned out quite differently. Three D.H.9s took off in the afternoon for Tcherni-Yar to bomb river barges and to strafe cavalry. After completing the mission, one D.H.9, flown by Captain Walter F. Anderson, with Lieutenant John Mitchell as his observer, had been instructed to take aerial photos behind enemy lines at about 1,000 feet. A second D.H.9 piloted by Captain William Elliott, with observer Lieutenant H. S. Laidlaw, flew as an escort to Anderson's machine. While Mitchell was taking the photos both machines came under heavy machine-gun fire from enemy troops on the ground. Anderson's plane was hit by a number of bullets in the fuel tank, so Mitchell climbed out onto the wing and stopped the leaks by placing his hand over the holes in the tank. Meanwhile, Elliot's aircraft had been hit in the engine and was forced to land. Elements of the Red cavalry saw the machine go down so they charged towards the D.H.9. Laidlaw fired his Lewis gun at them causing them to retreat out of range. Anderson landed to rescue Elliot and Laidlaw. The two observers, each firing their own machine gun, kept the Bolshevik cavalry back while Elliot set fire to his D.H.9. He and Laidlaw then dashed across to Anderson's aircraft and scrambled into the rear cockpit of Anderson's plane. Mitchell held onto the struts and stood on the lower wing. Anderson gunned his engine and the D.H.9 took off with the Red cavalry in hot pursuit. For their heroic deeds that day both Anderson and Mitchell were awarded the DSO.

Luckily the four flyers were not captured, as the Bolsheviks had made a point to advertise by way of posters and their local press, what would happen to anyone made prisoner: they would be nailed to a tree by their genitals, disembowelled, and finally, if that was not enough, hacked to death by cavalry sabres.

August saw further bombing, strafing, and reconnaissance missions from Beketovka, but it also saw the buildup of D.H.9s available for service. Collishaw supervised this work at the Ekaterinodar headquarters. Twenty-one machines were assembled or overhauled during the month for service at the front. Thirteen D.H.9s (including some D.H.9as) arrived at the port of Novorossisk (having been transported aboard the carrier *Ark Royal*), and were later unloaded at squadron headquarters. Further work on these machines was held up due to a shortage of parts, having been either lost or stolen in transit.[6]

The RAF's Training Mission, whose job it was to teach the Russians to fly and to help them in forming squadrons from the RE8s, shared the Chernomorskt field with Collishaw's No. 47 Squadron. Many of the Russian pilots were hopelessly inept, resulting in many crashes and injuries. Others resented taking instructions from officers of a lesser rank, and some even refused to show up for duty.

Along the front lines Wrangel's forces pushed north and southeast along the Volga following the capture of Tsaritsyn and managed to take Kamyshin early in August. 'C' Flight's role at this time was to bomb and strafe Bolshevik naval vessels and barges on the Volga. It also carried out bombing raids on Tcherni-Yar to the southeast of Tsaritsyn.

In two days during the first week of August they had dropped 181 bombs of various weights and fired 7,800 rounds of SAA. In the second and third week of August, eight bombing raids were carried out on Tcherni-Yar and also on Staritskoe. During the last week of August, eleven combined bombing raids and reconnaissance missions were carried out on Tcherni-Yar, Startitskoe, Bilklei, and Duvovka.[7]

General Denikin and his Generals were very pleased with the work of No. 47 Squadron, as can be seen in the following extract from General Holman's command orders, dated August 18, 1919, and received from the general commanding Russian aviation:

These last few days I have had the pleasure of reading the daily report of flying of No. 47 Squadron RAF about the extraordinary work of the British pilots and especially Major Collishaw. I beg you to accept and transmit to Major Collishaw from the whole Russian aviation, our sincere admiration of his brilliant activity.
— Kravtsevich, Major General[8]

Some notable air combats took place in August. On August 20, a D.H.9 flown by Canadian Lieutenant E.J. Cronin with Lieutenant H. Mercer as observer, was carrying out an early morning bombing raid on Tcherni-Yar when the pilots spotted an enemy Nieuport. Lieutenant Cronin's report of the engagement is as follows:

… an enemy Nieuport was seen to dive on me on rear right. My front gun not working. [sic] I circled round to give my obs a field of fire. After 10 minutes fighting during which four bursts of fire were exchanged from about 50 to 100 yards the enemy was seen to go down in control after a burst of fire into his left wing out of which splinters flew. He was observed to go down over the marshes NE of Tcherni-Yar and was then lost sight of. He was undoubtedly badly shot up.[9]

On August 25, on a bombing raid and reconnaissance mission, pilot Lieutenant A. Hatchett and observer Lieutenant G. Simmons encountered an enemy Nieuport scout. This one had a red nose, a red disc on its rudder, and a black cross on its fuselage. Lieutenant Hatchett described what happened next.

The Nieuport was seen taking off. We waited our time for him to gain height. The hostile machine climbed to 500 feet above us and then dived. 50 rounds fired from the back gun striking hostile in fuselage but doing no damage. The back gun jammed and we broke off the fight.[10]

Squadron 47's first battle casualty was Captain J.L. MacLennan. Flying as an observer in Captain Anderson's D.H.9 on August 28, 1919, they attacked an enemy observation balloon north of Tsaritsyn. The balloon was set on fire and totally destroyed by the D.H.9, despite intense ground fire. Upon their return to Beketovka, Anderson discovered Captain McLennan dead in the rear cockpit, killed from bullet wounds.

Of the additional D.H.9 machines received in August some were sent up to 'C' Flight on the Volga front, whereas the D.H.9as were slated for 'A' Flight. The Sopwith Camels, sent from the one-time RNAS base at Mudros in the Aegean, were used to equip 'B' Flight. Its commander was Captain Samuel M. Kinkead, an experienced RNAS fighter pilot that Collishaw had met in France.

Personnel of No. 47 Squadron, RAF. Major Collishaw is seventh from left in the centre row.

Library and Archives Canada, PA-203555.

The Camels arrived at squadron headquarters on September 19, 1919, and by September 27 three of them left for the front. A fourth left the next day. Having organized and prepared all three flights of No. 47 Squadron, Major Raymond Collishaw was able to proceed to the front, which he did on September 14.

Towards the end of August the Bolsheviks had recaptured Kamyshin from the White Russian counter-revolutionaries. This meant 'C' Flight had to pull back from Beketovka to a village called Gnileaksayskaya, on the rail line further south. This is where Collishaw joined the flight. 'C' Flight lived on its special train that had pulled up on a siding adjacent to a flat area of land, which was used as the aerodrome. It was equipped with sleeping coaches, a kitchen, a bakery, and even a sick bay.

The aircraft normally flew from point to point with the train rendezvousing with them at each designated point. If this was not possible, the machines would be partially disassembled and loaded onto the train's flatbeds. The Russian railway system provided a truly mobile strike force.

Collishaw was happy to be away from the administrative problems and frustrations of squadron headquarters and took full advantage of being at the front. He flew a D.H.9 twice on the day he arrived. Lieutenant Greenwood was Major Collishaw's observer for most of September and into October, 1919. They went on numerous bombing runs in D.H.9s against Bolshevik cavalry near the town of Eslaterslov and bombed and strafed enemy positions along the Volga north of Tsaritsyn. Their task was also to carry out reconnaissance missions behind the Red positions.

The Bolsheviks had amassed numerous naval gunships and other vessels on the Volga, both north of Tsaritsyn and south near Tcherni-Yar. Wrangel had no river craft to counter these forces, just heavy artillery mounted on railway trucks which were of no use unless they were in the vicinity of Tsaritsyn. Therefore, No. 47 Squadron and several Russian units were engaged to bomb these Red flotillas. All three flights of the squadron flew out of Beketovka, only minutes from their targets. They bombed the ships daily with 112- and 230-pound bombs and strafed them with their machine guns. The D.H.9s and D.H.9as of 'C' and 'A' Flights took off to attack the fleet again and again, in spite of the heavy anti-aircraft fire. The Camels of 'B' Flight bombed the vessels with their 20-pound bombs and strafed them with machine-gun fire as well. Few enemy aircraft appeared and what did show up was driven away by the Camels. After two days of bombing, eleven of the ships had been sunk. The rest retreated up river and stayed out of the rest of the conflict.

Collishaw was a part of these numerous raids made against the naval forces along the Volga. Shortly after his arrival in the area, Collishaw, with Greenwood as the observer, dropped two 230-pound bombs on a Red destroyer north of Tsaritsyn and sank it.

Throughout the month of September, 'C' Flight carried out recce (reconnaisance missions) and bombing raids. On some raids they came upon enemy aircraft. For example, on September 16 two D.H.9s were attacked by an enemy Nieuport, which was driven off by machine-gun fire and forced to land. Later in the month two D.H.9s piloted by Lieutenants E.J. Cronin and A.W. Day (with observers Lieutenant A. Mercer and Lieutenant H. Buckley, respectively) also encountered an enemy scout. Their report on the engagement reads as follows:

> While over Chirokoe we were flying north when an enemy machine was observed four miles in the rear

and flying towards us. The two DH9's immediately turned to meet him. The enemy scout dived in between the tails of our machines, and was met by heavy and effective cross fire from the Lewis guns. His propeller was seen to stop and he went down in a long, steep dive followed by our machines, which were unable to overtake him. The enemy scout was last seen ten feet above the ground over Dubovka, and was flying south. Our machines then continued their recce.[11]

Dubovka was the site of a Red aerodrome and seaplane base on the Volga, about 50 miles north of Tsaritsyn. A number of raids on these targets were flown in September, including a significant one on September 17 by two D.H.9s flown by Walter Anderson, and Lieutenant A.W. Day. They had as observers Lieutenants H.W.L. Buckley and R. Addison, MC, respectively. The two bombers dropped four 112-pound bombs and a number of 20-pounders on a barge carrying eight flying boats and Nieuports that were parked at a nearby aerodrome. Once their bombs were let loose they strafed the area with machine-gun fire.

Toward the end of the month, 'B' Flight, made up of Sopwith Camels, moved up to Beketovka. On September 30, Captain S. Kinkead of 'B' Flight shot down an enemy Nieuport into the Volga River. This was 'B' Flight's first aerial victory.

All was not well back in Britain, though. Support for the mission in South Russia was dwindling. Many questioned the need to prop up a feudal aristocracy that was fighting a popular revolution of the people. One proposal suggested Collishaw withdraw his squadron from the Volga front and attach it to the RAF Training Mission as a strictly instructional unit. Both Collishaw and his superior Brigadier-General Maund opposed the plan vigorously.

Collishaw continued to fly D.H.9s with Lieutenant Greenwood into the month of October. However, on October 7 he switched aircraft and started to fly Camel No. 6396. That day and the following one Collishaw tangled with an Albatros D. V. It was the third D. V he had seen over Tsaritsyn and Tcherni-Yar. On October 9, flying the same Camel, Collishaw tangled again with an Albatros D. V about 20 miles

Library and Archives Canada, PA-203556.

Personnel of 'C' Flight, No. 47 Squadron, RAF, Tsaritsyn, Russia. Collishaw is in the middle of the centre row.

north of Tsaritsyn. He managed to shoot it down out of control and it crashed on the bank of the Volga River. This was Raymond Collishaw's sixty-first victory.

In early October, the Red Army launched another attack on Tsaritsyn. Large numbers of cavalry attacked from the north, supported by reinforced naval units and armoured trains. Other Bolshevik forces southeast of the city tried to encircle Tsaritsyn. General Wrangel's Caucasian Army and North Caucasian Army, made up of Kuban and Terek Cossacks, tried desperately to hold on. The D.H.9s from 'A' flight quickly moved up to Beketovka, along with its special support train. 'B' Flight, already at Beketovka, flew escort missions with the D.H.9s. On October 6, two D.H.9as, escorted by Camels bombed armoured trains, obtaining direct hits. On October 7 Captains Kinkead and Thomson, escorting D.H.9as in their Camels, engaged two enemy Nieuports and drove them down.[12]

The Camels were also put to good use during the bombing and strafing of Red cavalry. Dumenko, the Red cavalry commander, and his forces were approaching Tsaritsyn, having forced a wedge between Wrangel's army and the Don Cossack Army. No White forces were between the Red cavalry, so General Wrangel called on Collishaw's No. 47 Squadron to assist. In October, all available Camels were sent aloft to bomb and strafe the cavalry. Collishaw and the other three Camel pilots flew five missions on October 10, 1919, against the cavalry. Dumenko's forces had no place to hide as the countryside around the town was flat. They stood little chance against the Camels. It was estimated there were approximately 1,600 Red casualties that day. Tsaritsyn was saved.

In the meantime, General Mai-Maievsky and his volunteer army were marching north from Kharkov to the town of Orel.

On 13 October Denikin reached his high-water mark upon entering Orel, only 250 miles from Moscow. General Wrangel suggested that the RAF bomb the capital, but the War Office forbade such an attempt, "as there is no military value in this operation." Within a few days the bombing of Moscow became physically impossible for on 20 October Denikin was compelled to withdraw from Orel, and a long retreat commenced, ultimately to end in the extinction of his army along the shores of the Black Sea. During the first stages of Denikin's retreat 'A' Detachment flew on the Volga front, around Tsaritsyn. Collishaw joined frequently in fighter patrols.[13]

Things were not well for Collishaw personally. By mid-October he was running a high fever, and although he had not yet been diagnosed with it, he was suffering from typhus. Unfit for duty, he was put on a train back to Ekaterinodar where his condition got much worse. The train stopped at a village on the line and, luckily for Collishaw, word of his condition had reached an elderly Russian countess who had a small cottage nearby. She took Collishaw in and nursed him back to health. He lay unconscious as the countess tried to get his fever under control. When he recovered consciousness he was so weak that he could barely move. Eventually, Collishaw was discovered by his colleagues and moved to a nearby hospital. He never did find out the identity of his benefactor.

Although the notice appeared on September 20, 1919, in the *London Gazette*, Collishaw was informed while he was recuperating in hospital that he had been awarded the Order of the British Empire. What follows is the formal announcement.

> The Register of the Order of the British Empire presents his compliments and has the honour to enclose the warrant of appointment to the most excellent order to Major Collishaw. Major Collishaw was awarded the OBE (Military) for conspicuous gallantry and devotion to duty during active service flying operations in South Russia, in command of No. 47 squadron RAF operating under the operational control of the C in C Armed Forces.[14]

Collishaw also later found out that he had been recognized by his Russian compatriots with the award of the Order of St. Anne. The certification read as follows:

> This is to certify that the Commander in Chief Russian Volunteer Army awarded the Order of St. Anne II Class (with swords) to Major R. Collishaw, Commanding No. 47 squadron Royal Air Force on October 19, 1919 for flying services with the Caucasian Army at Tzaritsan.
> — W.A. Sivoloboff, Russian Liaison Officer, General Staff[15]

The Order of St. Anne is a beautifully designed, colourful example of Imperial Russian orders. The obverse is formed by a gold-edged red, dark red, or black-enamelled cross, and in the middle is a medallion that displays St. Anne standing in an open field with trees in the background. Between the arms of the cross is gold filigree work.

Collishaw recuperated at the base hospital at Taganrog along with other RAF officers. Many of the women volunteers who nursed these officers were from the upper class of the former Czarist Empire. Collishaw recollects one particular woman, a most beautiful Russian Countess, with whom a British RAF officer had fallen deeply in love. However, another suitor, Canadian RAF officer Gus Edwards, was very jealous of the two and desired the affections of the Countess. She proposed a duel between her two suitors the following morning to settle who she would choose. When Collishaw heard about the dual he put a stop to it, much to the anger of the two officers. It was all for nought anyway as the Countess ran off with a Russian officer the next day without telling anyone. It is interesting but not surprising this incident is not mentioned in the biography of Gus Edwards, *Gus, From Trapper Boy To Air Marshal* written by his daughter.

Much had changed by the time Collishaw had returned to Beketovka on November 27, 1919. Denikin's offensive drive to Moscow had been stalled at Orel. His lines were thin and spread out, making it easy for a Red counterattack. Orel fell to the Bolsheviks and Denikin's offensive was in tatters. His centre was in retreat causing his forces on either flank to retreat as well.

At 'A' Detachment (old No. 47 Squadron) headquarters at Ekaterinodar, work was underway for its evacuation. During late October and into November, many spare parts and stores had been dispatched to Taganrog and Tsaritsyn in spite of the absence of sufficient quantities of rolling stock. By mid-November, a train comprising twenty-two railway cars was being readied to proceed to Beketovka. On November 10 some personnel from 'C' Flight were on their way back to Novorossick in order to leave for Britain. The HQ train, comprised of an orderly room, general stores, transport, and armoury left Ekaterinodar on November 16 and arrived at Beketovka on November 21.[16]

For the first time in the South Russia campaign, all three flights were at one location: Beketovka. 'C' Flight, because of its change in personnel, had been re-equipped with RE8s. The D.H.9s had been turned over to the Russians. The common location for the three flights did not last long as the planes were to move to the Kharkov front. They were taken apart and loaded on to a train which would transport them to the front where they would be re-assembled. 'B' Flight and its Camels left Beketovka on November 27. 'A' Flight left three days later with 'C' Flight remaining on the Volga front, flying in support of Wrangel's troops.

The end of November brought confirmation that Collishaw was to receive yet another decoration, this time the Order of St. Vladimir. The announcement appears below.

This is to certify that the Commander-in-Chief Russian Volunteer Army awarded to Major R. Collishaw, commanding No. 47 Squadron Royal Air Force: Order of St. Vladimir 4th class (with swords and bow) on November 28th, 1919: for flying services with the Caucasian Army on the Tzaritsan front.

— W.A. Sivoloff, Russian Liason Officer,

General Staff[17]

Similar to the Order of St. Anne, the Order of St. Vladimir has a red-enamelled cross. The obverse is a red, dark red, or black-enamelled cross with a gold and black border. In the centre of the cross is a black-enamelled, gold-rimmed medallion which bears the crowned Imperial mantle of ermine with the saint's initials "SV." The reverse of the badge is similar to its obverse except that the medallion bears the date of the foundation of the Order: "22 September 1782." Crossed swords were added between the arms of the cross if the order was awarded in times of war.

A new 'Z' Flight had been formed on November 30, 1919, out of volunteers of the training mission. They were equipped with RE8s and under the command of Sub-Lieutenant J.O. Archer. 'Z' Flight was proceeding to Kharkov as well. 'B' Flight arrived at Veluiki on December 1, but because of the Red army advance had to pull back to Peschanoe, northeast of Kharkov. 'Z' Flight arrived at another location called Kislovka on the evening of December 5. 'A' Flight arrived at Peschanoe on December 8, but owing to the retreat of Denikin's Volunteer Army, had to pull back further south to Svatovo, arriving there on December 10. 'B' Flight left Peschanoe on December 10 on their way south. With both flights in retreat they managed to find an aerodrome six *versts* south of Kremmenaya on December 11. 'B' Flight then continued south to Taganrog to refit their machines.

General Holman, General Officer Commanding of all the British forces in South Russia, was aboard 'Z' Flight's train. On a number of occasions he went up in aircraft to have a first-hand look at the state of affairs.

> Holman flew personally as the convalescent Collishaw's observer on a number of bombing flights, but it soon became evident that irretrievable disaster was overtaking Denikin's forces. Amid scenes of extraordinary confusion, the various elements of the RAF Mission made their separate ways to the Crimea, Rostov, and the Kuban.[18]

Holman gave the order to retire. All flights ('A', 'B', and 'Z') along with the HQ staff, retreated in their separate trains along the rail lines towards Rostov near the Black Sea. 'B' Flight continued to head for Taganrog on the Sea of Azov, just west of Rostov, to refit. At each stop 'A' Flight made along the railway, the D.H.9s had to be taken off the flatbeds and re-assembled in order to carry out reconnaissance or bombing missions. It was a fighting retreat. When the trains stopped, the planes would take to the air to bomb the advancing Red cavalry, which were within 20 miles of Collishaw's train.

Bombing and reconnaissance missions continued as the flights moved south, and the Volunteer Army was seen to be in retreat.

> On December 17 Lts. Grigson and Breakey with their respective observers Gordon and Spalton made a bombing/reconnaissance run in the area Novo-Yekaterinoslav and Muzemovka. Light bombs only were dropped on massed troops causing panic and disorder. On this occasion great difficulty was experienced in distinguishing between friendly and enemy troops.[19]

Collishaw and other pilots carried out reconnaissance flights to determine troop movements, both of the Red Army and of the Volunteer Army. The information gathered was passed on to Geneeral Ulaga, commander of the local Volunteer Army forces.

Reconnaissance flights were also carried out in search of new aerodromes as the trains retreated south. Slow progress was made due to winter blizzard conditions and due to congested railways. The next day orders were received from General Ulaga to proceed further south to Krinichnaya, where a suitable aerodrome was found. The HQ and Flight trains reached it on December 24, 1919.

The day before, Lieutenant Slatter and observer Spalton carried out a very successful reconnaissance mission in the area of Listchansk.

> The large railway bridge of Listchansk was reported to have fallen into enemy hands intact and two armoured trains were already proceeding south to Popasnaya. This timely report to the Russian authorities undoubtedly saved many troops and much rolling stock from falling into enemy hands. Lts. Breakey and Gordon (observer) accompanied Lt. Slatter on this successful recce. Over Rubejnaya enemy machine gun bullets pierced the petrol tank causing the machine to descend in the area of enemy occupation, necessitating the burning of the machine. These officers joined the squadron on the 24th.[20]

Boxing Day found the retreating trains on a multi-track siding, alongside one another. Somehow fire broke out in the sleeping coach in which Collishaw, a number of the other headquarters staff, and 'A' Flight had their quarters. It was only through quick action that the whole of the headquarters train avoided being totally engulfed in flames and 'Z' Flight's train prevented from catching fire. The officers lost all of their kit in the fire, including a magnificent diamond from a once-wealthy aristocratic family fleeing the Bolsheviks, which Raymond Collishaw had purchased for a fragment of its worth.

Blizzard conditions prevented any further flying so, on December 28, Collishaw ordered the aircraft be dismantled and loaded onto the trains. They attempted their escape to Taganrog, but progress was very slow. On December 30, 1919, 'Z' Flight's train, with General Holman aboard, pulled up just outside of Ilovaiska.

Gen. Holman, with OC Flight (Archer), walked into Ilovaiska, in an attempt to get the train received there, as the refusal of this was the cause of the delay. Information received that 'A' Flight, also, were refused here, and sent down towards Crimea. On arrival at Ilovaiska the night was spent in telegraphing for train to come on as station had agreed to accept it, under pressure, from Corps Commander, whose train, fortunately, was in the station when we arrived, although it left about midnight.[21]

The next day further trouble was encountered, as a Russian officer from No. 6 Squadron refused to give up an engine that had been allocated to the 'Z' Flight's train, in spite of the fact that General Holman was aboard. The 'Z' Flight train finally left the crowded station at 1530 hours — just in time, as reports were received that the Bolsheviks had burnt a village 5 miles away and were headed in the direction of the station. By January 1, 1920, the train was within 20 miles of Taganrog. The 'Z' Flight train managed to continue on, crossing the big railway bridge over the Don River, and arrived at Rostov on January 5, 1920. Collishaw's train was not as fortunate. The Red cavalry had cut the rail line between the Rostov Bridge and the town of Rostov, forcing Collishaw's train to take another route south and then west to the Crimea.

The retreat to Sevastopol on the Crimea was becoming increasingly dangerous for Collishaw and his RAF personnel. With the collapse of the Volunteer Army and the Red forces on the attack, numerous troops and ex-Czarist officers and their families had been cut off and faced capture by the Bolsheviks. Collishaw had extra wagons attached to his train for these refugees. The train crews had deserted so the RAF's other ranks became engineers and firemen aboard the train. Machine guns from the aircraft were mounted on the roofs of some of the coaches. The local populace were Red sympathizers, so armed foraging parties had to be organized to obtain wood for fuel and snow to be dumped into the locomotive's water tanks. The women on board used their skirts to carry the snow to the train.

Library and Archives Canada, PA-207523.

Raymond Collishaw, circa. 1920s.

To make matters worse, typhus had broken out amongst the refugees on the train. To avoid the spread of the disease, and because the train could not stop to bury the dead, Collishaw ordered the bodies of the dead be thrown from the train as it proceeded to the Crimea.

On January 1, 1920, Collishaw's train stopped at a town called Balshoi-Tomak. There, their journey almost ended in disaster. Unbeknownst to Collishaw and his personnel, the Bolsheviks had sent an unmanned runaway train careening down the tracks toward them.

> ... serious damage was caused by a collision in the rear of our train, resulting in some eight or ten trucks

being telescoped on our train. All possible stores and material was salved [sic] from the damaged trucks before they were abandoned, remaining material all being rendered unserviceable.[22]

The train did manage to reach the Crimea on January 4 and continued further southward, reaching Sevastopol on January 6. There they managed to get coal from a British warship docked in port. They also ridded themselves of the refugees and stocked up on supplies and food. The remainder of the month was taken up with trying to find aircraft to put back into flying order to be able to continue the battle against the Reds. Only one D.H.9 was ready for flight by January 31, 1920.

In the meantime 'B' Flight's train had to quickly evacuate Tagonrog on December 28. The 'A' Flight stores train had managed to pass through Tagonrog before it was evacuated and arrived at Rostov on December 29, 1919. It was impossible to proceed further as the Red army was closing in fast. The train had to be abandoned. Lieutenant Slatter, Officer Allsebrook, and observer Officer Kesketh, under continuous and heavy shrapnel fire, rendered unserviceable all the aircraft and transport before evacuating the train.[23] 'C' Flight remained on the Tsaritsyn front, but was out of communication from the rest of 'A' Detachment.

After the retreat from Kharkov Collishaw had to reorganize his forces. 'A' Flight was re-designated the Crimean Group, under Collishaw's command. The remainder of the squadron and 'Z' Flight were at Ekaterinodar, the new headquarters of the RAF Mission, and were named the Kuban Group.

The retreating Russian forces managed to form a line of defence at the Perekop peninsula, which joins the Crimea to the mainland. On February 17 Collishaw was able to take his remaining aircraft by train from Sevastopol to the aerodrome at Djankoi, near Perekop. The next day, Collishaw was in the air in a D.H.9a making a long reconnaissance over the Red positions. On February 19, 1920, he led a bombing attack on a Bolshevik armoured train heading in the direction of Perekop. Again on February 22 he attacked a Red armoured train. This time it nearly resulted in Collishaw's capture by the Bolsheviks. His D.H.9 was hit by gunfire from the train and he had to land. He had to taxi along the ground for 20 miles, all the way back to his base at Djankoi. Thank goodness for the flat Russian steppes.

In March, a number of bombing and reconnaissance flights took place over the Perekop Penninsula. It appeared that the Red army was planning a large-scale attack on the Crimea. Collishaw managed to obtain a new Nieuport from the Russians, which he flew beginning on March 8, 1920. Two days later, a mercy mission was flown over the White Russian ship Kornilov, which was stuck in the ice in the Sea of Azov, dropping both food and ammunition. Throughout the month Collishaw and his pilots bombed and strafed Red army cavalry and troops in the Perekop area. It was becoming clear that fighting the Red army was a lost cause. Denikin's forces were in retreat once again. Ekaterinodar was abandoned and his forces were pulled back to the port of Novorossisk, where Denikin made one last stand. The retreat was a hasty one and disorganized. Many of the British officers, including Gus Edwards, had to leave their kits behind. Edwards lost his log book, beating a hasty retreat from the quickly advancing Bolsheviks. Members of the RAF Mission and the Kuban Group were evacuated from Novorossik during the last days of March. Denikin's armies and large numbers of refugees moved on to the Crimea. Collishaw, with another remnant of his squadron, carried out bombing and reconnaissance missions for Wrangel's Crimean army in February and March 1920. RAF participation in the Russian Civil War finally ended with the withdrawal of the British Military Mission in the late spring of 1920.[24]

The last bombing mission of Collishaw's forces occurred on March 28. Collishaw himself flew for the last time in Russia the next day, when he went out on a long recce over the whole front line. He confirmed the Reds were about to mount an offensive.

Collishaw received one last decoration from the appreciative Russians, the Order of St. Stanislaus. The notification is shown below:

… from the General Officer Commanding-in-Chief Armed Forces South Russia Order dated 27th, March 1920.

The Cross of St. Stanislaus 2nd Class with swords to
Major Collishaw No 47 British Aviation Squadron.

— Baron Wrangel

C. in. C.

Armed Forces South Russia[25]

The Order of St. Stanislaus is another example of a beautiful
Imperial Russian decoration. The obverse is formed by a gold-edged
red, dark red, or black-enamelled cross, tipped with golden ball finials.
Between the arms of the cross are golden Russian Imperial eagles. The
points of the cross are connected to each other by a golden arc. The
centre medallion is white and bears the entwined red or gold-edged
red cipher of the saint, "SS." It is encircled by a gold and green laurel
wreath. The reverse of the Order is entirely gold, with a medallion
similar to the obverse one.

Upon Collishaw's return from his last flight he received orders to
leave Russia. He and his squadron personnel handed everything over
to a White Russian squadron, then travelled by ship from the Crimea
to the port of Theodosia. Several days later a British transport took
them to Constantinople and then to England. Their Russian adventure
was over.

Was this Russian adventure worth it? Did No. 47 Squadron affect the
outcome of the Russian Civil War? Although one could argue it did not
effect the outcome of the civil war, it certainly provided Denikin's forces
with air superiority and made a significant contribution in that regard.

What motivated men like Collishaw to volunteer to fight in South
Russia? S.F. Wise says it best:

The RAF presence in Russia was, in the first instance,
an outgrowth of the exigencies of the First World War.
With the end of the war the British intervention was
transformed into a species of anti-Bolshevik crusade.
It is unlikely, however, that many of the Canadians
who found themselves flying over the White Sea, the
steppeland, or the Caucasus were motivated primarily
by ideological considerations. Most of them were

Collishaw with Muslim tribesmen from the Caucasus, part of Denikin's White Russian forces.

relatively inexperienced airmen who were in Russia because of the lottery of service postings. Among the volunteers some were military adventurers, others already professional airmen, and a few a combination of the two. For young men who had joined the armed forces directly from school or university, and had no trade or profession waiting for them in civilian life, Russian service was a chance to earn a permanent commission in the RAF or in the Canadian air force to come. For others, it was simply another opportunity to continue their love affair with the aeroplane.[26]

EPILOGUE

After arriving in England Raymond Collishaw was given three months leave, so he returned to Canada at the end of May 1920. Upon his return to England in August he was posted to Baghdad in Mesopotamia (now Iraq) and took command of No. 30 Squadron. Since the collapse of the White Russian forces of Denikin, the Bolsheviks controlled the entire Black and Caspian Seas, including the oil-rich Baku area. With the Bolsheviks threatening the British-held territory of Northern Persia (now Iran), the British government decided to send a strong land force there under the command of General Edmund Ironside who had his headquarters in Kasvin.

In the autumn of 1920 he sent for No. 30 Squadron to provide air cover for his troops. Raymond Collishaw arrived at Kasvin on January 18, 1921. Once again, Collishaw faced the Russians. The Bolsheviks wanted North Persia in their sphere of influence and wanted the British out.

By a pre-existing Anglo-Russian Treaty, Persia had been divided into two spheres of influence: the northern area controlled by the Russians, and the southern area under the influence of the British. However, General Ironside and his army had encroached upon the Russian sphere of influence by entering northern Persia. The Bolshevik forces advanced south through northern Persia.

Although the British and Bolshevik armies faced one another, it was No. 30 Squadron that provided the only examples of aggression. Without any Red aircraft in the region, Collishaw and his squadron of D.H.9as had air supremacy. They carried out reconnaissance missions over the Red lines. At times they bombed and machine-gunned the Russian troops. Their biggest challenge, however, was how to keep the landing areas free of snow and stay warm. The mountainous regions of Persia were subject to frequent storms and blizzards. Collishaw employed local owners of camels to have the animals go back and forth over the aerodrome to pack the snow down, so aircraft could take off. No. 30 Squadron was also the major means of communication between Ironside's forces and those in Baghdad. Collishaw's pilots would often have to make the trip from the frigid, sub-zero weather of north Persia to Baghdad's sweltering heat.

Air reconnaissance conducted by Collishaw's planes in northern Persia showed the Russians were massing forces for an attack against Kasvin. The British forces, not wanting a major confrontation, withdrew from Kasvin in the spring of 1921, once the snow was mostly melted.

No. 30 Squadron's new home was Baghdad. They joined No. 47 Squadron, equipped with D.H.9s and No. 70 Squadron, which flew massive Handley-Page bombers. Included in their duties was the establishment of an air corridor from Cairo in Egypt to Amman in the Trans-Jordan, and then on to Baghdad. The squadrons marked their route with a series of landing areas that were staked out for further use to carry supplies and mail between these three major centres.

When the country of Iraq was formed in late 1921, it was still under British mandate. The British put King Faisal on the throne to rule the protectorate. The Kurds in the north of the area, however, were not prepared to come under anyone's rule. A fiercely independent people, they rebelled against the British. The British would countenance no rebellion against them, and so sent Collishaw's and other RAF squadrons against the rebels. The squadrons bombed many villages, but the drone of oncoming aircraft gave the Kurds ample time to hide in the surrounding hills and caves nearby. Sheik Mamoud, the leader of the rebellion, defiantly anointed himself King of Kurdistan and announced a Holy War against the British. The British countered by sending some 5,000 mounted troops against Mamoud. Collishaw was the RAF Liaison Officer at the time. His job was to be in the forward echelon of the advancing column to scout out suitable landing sites for the squadrons, which kept the troops supplied. The parachuting of supplies was also employed due to the rugged nature of the countryside. This was one of the first examples of coordination between the Army and RAF, with the Army being completely dependent on supply from the air. After a six-week campaign the rebellion had fizzled out.

Collishaw left Iraq in the summer of 1923, having spent three years in the Persian-Mesopotamian area. Upon his return to England he was given three months' leave, marrying Neita Trapp that summer.

Recalled from leave in early October, Collishaw took over No. 41 Squadron at Northolt in Middlesex. He was then selected to attend the RAF Staff College at Andover in May of 1924. From there he was assigned to Henlow, north of London, to form and command No. 23 Squadron. The squadron later moved to RAF Station Kenley where it was mainly involved in night flying operations and air defence over London. Posted to the Department for Operations and Intelligence under Air Marshal Sir John Salmond in the fall of 1927, Raymond Collishaw was involved in the development of an air fighter force for the RAF.

In July 1929 Collishaw was sent to Malta to be the Senior RAF Officer aboard the aircraft carrier *Courageous*, where he was promoted to Wing Commander. He would spend three years aboard that ship. His major challenge at the time was to reconcile the differing views over the role of the RAF pilots on an aircraft carrier — were they to be an attack force to hunt down enemy ships and destroy them, or were they just a reconnaissance force to find the enemy ships so that the Royal Navy could destroy them? Collishaw worked hard to try to develop answers to this question.

Library and Archives Canada, PA-207524.

Raymond Collishaw with His Majesty King George V and Her Majesty Queen Mary at the RAF Station, Bircham Newton, 1934. Far left is Air Marshal H.R.M. Brooke-Popham, far right is Air Vice-Marshal Nicol.

Collishaw left the *Courageous* in September of 1932 to command Station Bircham Newton near Sandringham, one of the homes of the Royal Family. The King made several visits to the station, including attending an air show and inspection of the different aircraft and their capabilities in 1934.

Collishaw was promoted to group captain in 1935 and sent to command the RAF station in Oxfordshire. With the threat of Mussolini's forced invading Abyssinia, Collishaw was transferred to the Sudan and took command of No. 5 Wing under the RAF's Middle East Command. No. 5 Wing consisted of three squadrons, two of bombers, and one squadron of fighters. The danger of war with Italy became remote, so the Wing was disbanded. Collishaw then moved on to the station at Heliopolis, just outside of Cairo.

This proved to be one of the most pleasant of Collishaw's postings. His wife Neita and their two daughters joined him. Raymond Collishaw and family were able to take many tours of the area on his days of leave. For example, they visited Libya, then in the hands of the Italians. They were also able to see the pyramids and many other historical sites around Cairo.

Britain's RAF contingent in Egypt was strengthened, as war with Hitler's Germany was becoming more certain. As a result, Collishaw was promoted to Air Commodore in April of 1939 to command what was called Egypt Group, which consisted of all the RAF personnel, planes, and equipment in the region. Collishaw and his force of nine bomber and fighter squadrons were responsible for the defence of Egypt and the Suez Canal in the event of war. Egypt Group was also charged with defending the desert area west of Cairo, all the way to the border of Libya. In this regard, Collishaw and his staff developed a system of landing areas and support facilities across the desert and up to the frontier of Libya.

The coming of the Second World War meant the end of Raymond and Neita Collishaw's idyllic life in Egypt. He sent his wife and family back to England, and then on to Canada where they would spend the rest of the war. In the meantime, preparations for war continued. Raymond Collishaw oversaw a number of exercises meant to test his forces in the event of war. Much was learned from these exercises, including how limited his squadron's strengths and capabilities were. He could by no means provide protection for all of Egypt and provide support of the British naval base in Alexandria as well. His resources were too limited.

When war was declared in September of 1939, Egypt Group was divided into 202 Group and the advance wing became No. 253 Wing. Collishaw and his staff moved to Maaten Bagush and set up headquarters there, about 160 miles from the Libyan frontier. His nine squadrons consisted of old aircraft such as the Gloster Gladiator fighter, Blenheim bombers, Lysanders, and a single Hawker Hurricane — some 150 aircraft in all. These forces were facing 300 to 400 Italian airplanes. Two squadrons of Gloster Gladiators were in the rear area to defend Cairo and the Canal. Collishaw's forces were limited, and no reinforcements or replacement planes were available. Notwithstanding their small numbers, Collishaw planned to make a series of offensive strikes against the Italian Air Force at different locations.

War with Italy commenced on June 10, 1940. Available to Collishaw at this time were Squadrons 33, 80, and 112, all equipped with Gloster Gladiator biplanes. As well, Squadron 80 had the sole Hawker Hurricane. Squadrons 3, 45, 55, 211, and 113 consisted of Bristol Blenheim bombers of the Mark 1 and newer Mark 4 models. The Gladiators had a top speed of 253 miles per hour and were armed with three .303-inch Browning machine guns. The Blenheims could reach a top speed of 285 miles per hour and carried a forward-firing .303 Browning and a Vickers machine gun in the turret.

Collishaw immediately ordered three squadrons of Blenheims, 45, 55, and 113, to bomb the Italian airfield at El Adem near Tobruk. Three of his bombers were lost in this raid due to anti-aircraft fire. A second raid was made during the day on the same airfield, resulting in eighteen Italian aircraft destroyed. Throughout the month of June, Collishaw's forces struck at the harbour facilities of Tobruk and Bardia, as well as numerous enemy airfields and troop detachments. Collishaw's squadrons also provided air support for the British Navy's bombardment of Bardia by sea. The Italian airforce conducted a bombing raid against the port of Alexandria and a maintenance depot on June 21, 1940, but the slow Gladiators were no match for the modern Italian bombers. To try to convince the enemy that Collishaw's forces were more numerous than they were, the sole Hurricane was moved around from airfield to airfield, to give the impression he had a squadron of Hurricanes and not just one sole fighter of this kind. As well, dummy aircraft made of wood were built and placed at forward locations. They too were moved around, again to give the impression of strength.

Operations during July were similar, however, as the Italians were building up their strength to four divisions of infantry in Eastern Libya, known as the Cyrenaica.

Up to September 1940 the Commonwealth forces had the upper hand, having carried out many raids and inflicted very heavy losses while suffering few casualties, in the ratio of about twenty to one. On September 13, 1940, Italian Marshal Graziani, with hundreds of tanks and four divisions, crossed the border and entered Egypt. His army halted when it reached Sidi Barrani. Collishaw's air forces were able to harass the enemy such that they reverted into a defensive role, providing air support for the Italian army rather than flying offensive sorties against Collishaw's airfields and supply depots.

With the Italian declaration of war against Greece on October 28 came the request from the Greek government for military assistance. Collishaw's No. 30 Squadron of Blenheim bombers and fighters left for Greece on November 1, further depleting his forces. By December, five other squadrons from Collishaw's wing would be bound for Greece. To replace these departing squadrons, two Hawker Hurricane squadrons arrived, as well as three Wellington bomber squadrons. Collishaw had ten squadrons in all. Even with these reinforcements he was outnumbered by the Italian Air Force two to one.

On December 9, 1940, General Archibald Wavell, Commander-in-Chief of the British forces, and his General, Richard O'Connor, organized and began an offensive against the Italian forces at Sidi Barrani. The push was an unqualified success, throwing the Italians into complete confusion, and quickly the reconnaissance in force became a full-scale advance. Collishaw's Wellington bombers flew raids against positions behind the Italian lines, while Collishaw's two Hurricane squadrons provided air support for Wavell's troops. Collishaw and his squadrons managed to keep the skies clear of Italian aircraft and Sidi Barrani was taken by the British on December 11. The retreating Italian infantry and their transport vehicles were a perfect target for Collishaw's fighters to strafe. During the British offensive, Collishaw's planes shot down seventy-five enemy planes with the loss of only ten of his own. By January 5, 1941, the town of Bardia surrendered to the British. In the meantime, Air Marshal Arthur Tedder had taken over 202 Group from Collishaw. They did not see eye to eye, with each preferring different air tactics.

The army of General O'Connor continued to Tobruk, which fell to the British on January 22, 1941. They entered Benghazi on February 6. Both General Wavell and General O'Connor sent Air Commodore Raymond Collishaw messages of thanks for the support the RAF had provided in the offensive. Another message Collishaw received at that time was that he had been made a Companion of the Order of the Bath.

The Most Honourable Order of the Bath is an ancient British Order that was established in 1399. It got its name from an old ceremony for Esquire's who wanted to become Knights. The ceremony required the hopeful Esquire to bathe in the presence of several of the Knights of the Order. The Order was revived in 1725 and remodelled in 1815, and again in 1847. The First Class of the Order is the Knights Grand Cross (G.C.B.), the Second Class of the Order is the Knights Commanders (K.C.B.), and the Third Class, the one that Collishaw received, is the Companions of the Order (C.B.). The badge of the Order is a gold Maltese cross of white enamel, with eight points. The points each end with a gold ball. In the centre are a rose, thistle, and shamrock coming out of a gold sceptre, between three Imperial crowns, all within a red circle.

The retreating Italians called on Hitler's Germany for assistance. That came in the form of Rommel's Afrika Corps and numerous squadrons of German fighters and bombers. At the same time, early in 1941, three more of Collishaw's squadrons were taken from him and sent to Greece. Collishaw was in favour of continuing the attack and pursuing the fleeing Italian army further into Libya. His opinion was not shared by the British Army Generals, who decided to stop the advance at Benghazi. In mid-February, 1941 three squadrons of 202 Group moved back to Egypt for refitting and to be ready in case they too were needed in Greece. That left four squadrons to face the enemy on the Cyrenaica (northern Libya) front.

On March 31, 1941, Rommel launched a reconnaissance in strength, similar to the one launched on Marsh Brega by Wavell the previous December. Benghazi had to be evacuated on April 3, with Collishaw's two Hurricane squadrons providing air cover for the withdrawal. These same Hurricanes had destroyed over seventy enemy machines, either in air combat or through strafing missions in the recent combat, with the loss of only a little over twenty of their own aircraft. On April 12, Collishaw's squadrons became 204 Group which was headquartered in Maaten Bagush. Collishaw was back where he started.

The final air battle over Tobruk occurred on the April 23, with Collishaw's squadrons facing Messerschmitt 109s and 110s, as well as Stuka Ju 87s. The RAF suffered heavy losses by such German aces as Marseille. On May 3 Air Marshal Tedder took over from Longmore as Air Officer Commanding, RAF Middle East. Collishaw now reported to Air Marshal Tedder. By mid-May, the British launched the first offensive against the German army, using Collishaw's squadrons to fly ground-strafing missions. Around the same time, a convoy, complete with fifty new Hurricane aircraft, had docked at the port of Alexandria, providing reinforcements for 202 Group. On July 1, 1941, Beaufighters from 272 Squadron arrived at Abu Sueir from Malta.

Other squadrons arrived in early June, including 229 Squadron, which arrived at Mersa Matruh after a flight from Gibraltar. Another squadron, 250, arrived in the Alexandria area and was equipped with American Curtiss Tomahawk fighters, a fairly manoeuvrable machine that carried two .50-inch machine guns in the nose above the engine and four .303-inch guns in the wings. It had a top speed of 352 miles per hour. The Tomahawk was an improvement over the older Hurricanes and was a match for the Me 109E. With ten re-equipped squadrons, the RAF was ready to support the Army in a new offensive known as Operation "Battleaxe," which began on June 14, 1941. In the lead up to the battle, Collishaw's Wellington bombers hit the Benghazi harbour nightly while the smaller Blenheims bombed nearby airfields. By day, the Blenheims attacked troop convoys. Collishaw's forces had air superiority at the start of the battle, but by June 17 the British forces had been beaten back across the Egyptian frontier to the Sidi Barrani-Sofafi line. Three dozen of Collishaw's fighters and bombers were lost in the process.

At the end of July 1941, Raymond Collishaw turned over his command to another ace of the First World War, Air Vice Marshal Sir Arthur Coningham, and returned to England to work in the headquarters of Fighter Command.

However, in spite of this outstanding victory over an entire enemy air force, Collishaw runs afoul of the new Commander of the RAF Middle East, Air marshal Arthur Tedder. Collie had followed his First World War instincts, when the pilots were not tethered by radio and radar and aggressively ran their own show once airborne. Tedder believes in detailed planning and preparation and finds Collishaw impulsive in overlooking "proper" administration.[1]

Department of National Defence.

Collishaw in later life.

In March 1942 he was promoted to Air Vice Marshal and sent to Scotland to command No. 14 Fighter Group. Collishaw retired from the RAF mid-1943 after almost twenty-seven years of service. Thus ended an illustrious career in the air force.

At the end of the war, Collishaw returned to Canada and settled down to a life with his family in Vancouver, British Columbia. He was involved in a number of mining enterprises and was President of Craigmont Mines Ltd. for five years. Raymond Collishaw passed away in September 1976.

Looking back on the career of this often-forgotten air ace, one sees a man of great bravery and integrity. He was highly thought of, as can be seen by the quotation below.

> Major Raymond Collishaw, D.S.O., D.S.C., D.F.C., served under my command in the 1st Brigade R.F.C. and R.A.F. in France from March to Nov. 11th, 1918. During this period he was in command of No. 3 Naval Squadron and No. 203 Squadron R.A.F.
>
> I cannot speak too highly of his qualities as a Squadron Commander. He showed the greatest tact and power of command in dealing with all ranks under him and however unpleasant was the job given to him and his Squadron, it was always performed promptly and cheerfully. In addition, he set a very fine personal example of flying courage in aerial fighting: bringing his total of Huns crashed, up to Armistice Day, to 59.
>
> I consider Major Collishaw one of the best Squadron Commanders in the R.A.F.
>
> — D. Pitcher, Commander, 1st Brigade R.A.F.
> Dated May 5th, 1919[2]

During the 1960s and into the early 1970s, Collishaw corresponded with R.V. Dodds, who was then with the RCAF's historical section in Ottawa. Dodds collaborated with Collishaw on Collishaw's autobiography, and also wrote *The Brave Young Wings*. Dodds' view of Collishaw's career is important to note.

> Collishaw's place amongst the fighter pilots cannot be assessed simply on the basis of comparative "scores." Equally important were his ability to lead and inspire

others, both as a flight and squadron commander, and the achievements of those units which he commanded. If these factors are taken into account, as indeed they must be, Collishaw was unsurpassed by any of the many Canadians who flew as fighter pilots during the First World War.[3]

Undoubtedly, Raymond Collishaw's contributions to the air battles of the First World War are extremely significant. His dedication to the RNAS and RAF and to the men he commanded is unquestionable, as is the fact that he should be remembered and celebrated often as a truly great Canadian hero.

NOTES

Chapter One

1. J. Allen Snowie, *Collishaw and Company: Canadians in the Royal Naval Air Service 1914–1918* (Bellingham, WA: Nieuport Publishing Inc., 2010), xviii. Used by permission.
2. David Perkins, *Canada's Submariners 1914–1923* (Erin, ON: The Boston Mills Press, 1989), 16.

Chapter Two

1. Ralph Barker, *The Royal Flying Corps in World War I* (London: Constable and Robinson Ltd., 2002), 13. Used by permission.
2. *Ibid.*, 13.
3. *Ibid.*, 13.
4. Ronald Dodds, *The Brave Young Wings* (Stitsville, ON: Canada's Wings, Inc., 1980), 7. Used by permission.
5. S.F. Wise, *Canadian Airmen and the First World War: The Offi-*

cial History of the Royal Canadian Air Force, Volume 1 (Toronto: University of Toronto Press in cooperation with the Department of National Defence and the Canadian Government Publishing Centre, Supply and Services Canada, 1980), 31. Used by permission.

6. *Ibid.*, 31.
7. *Ibid.*, 31.
8. *Ibid.*, 31.
9. *Ibid.*, 39
10. *Ibid.*, 32.
11. *Ibid.*, 33.
12. Library and Archives Canada, MG30E280, Volume 9, Pre-1916 Biographical Research Notes.
13. *Ibid.*
14. *Ibid.*
15. *The Brave Young Wings*, 14–15. Used by permission.

Chapter Three

1. *Canadian Airmen*, 144. Used by permission.
2. *The Brave Young Wings*, 20. Used by permission.
3. Bernard Fitzsimons, editor, *Warplanes and Air Battles of World War 1* (New York: Beekman House, 1973), 15.
4. K.M. Molson, *Canada's National Aviation Museum, Its History and Collections* (Ottawa: National Aviation Museum, National Museum of Science and Technology, 1988), 150.
5. Peter Cooksley, *Sopwith Fighters in Action* (Carrollton, TX: Squadron/Signal Publications, Inc., 1991), 14. Used by permission. Courtesy of Squadron/Signal Publications, Carrollton, Texas, USA.
6. *The Brave Young Wings*, 141. Used by permission.

Chapter Four

1. *Canadian Airmen*, 142. Used by permission.
2. *Ibid.*, 142.
3. *Ibid.*, 143.
4. *The Brave Young Wings*, 140. Used by permission.
5. Library and Archives Canada, MG30E280, Volume 5, File: Air Historical Subjects Texts by Collishaw (File 1), Report from Elder

to Admiralty dated 24 May 1917.

6. *Ibid.*

7. *Ibid.*

8. Library and Archives Canada, MG30E280, Volume 9, File: No. 3 Wing RNAS Research Material and Correspondence, Pt. 1.

9. *The Brave Young Wings*, 142. Used by permission.

10. *Ibid.*, 140–41.

11. *Canadian Airmen*, 167. Used by permission.

12. Library and Archives Canada, MG30E280, Volume 9, File: No. 3 Wing RNAS Research Material and Correspondence N/D 1916–1972, Pt. 2, Wing Commander R. Bell Davies' report of the Oberndorf raid to the Admiralty.

13. *Canadian Airmen*, 266. Used by permission.

14. Library and Archives Canada, MG30E280, Volume 9, File: No. 3 Wing RNAS Research Material and Correspondence N/D 1916–1972, Pt. 2, Condensed Report Regarding the Expedition on October 12 on Mauser Factory at Oberndorf, translated from the French version.

15. *Canadian Airmen*, 266. Used by permission.

16. Library and Archives Canada, MG30E280, Volume 9, File: No. 3 Wing RNAS Research Material and Correspondence N/D 1916–1972, Pt. 2, Wing Commander R. Bell Davies' report of the Oberndorf raid to the Admiralty.

17. Library and Archives Canada, MG30E280, Volume 9, File: No. 3 Wing RNAS Research Material and Correspondence N/D 1916–1972, Pt. 2.

18. *The Brave Young Wings*, 143. Used by permission.

19. Library and Archives Canada, MG30E280, Volume 9, File: No. 3 Wing RNAS Research Material and Correspondence N/D 1916–1972, Pt. 2, Condensed Report Regarding the Expedition on October 12 on Mauser Factory at Oberndorf, translated from the French version.

20. *The Brave Young Wings*, 143. Used by permission.

21. Library and Archives Canada, MG30E280, Volume 9, File: No. 3 Wing RNAS Research Material and Correspondence N/D 1916–1972, Pt. 2, Wing Commander R. Bell Davies' report of the Oberndorf raid to the Admiralty.

22. *The Brave Young Wings*, 144. Used by permission.

23. *Ibid.*, 144.
24. *Ibid.*, 144.
25. Library and Archives Canada, MG30E280, Volume 9, File: No. 3 Wing RNAS Research Material and Correspondence N/D 1916–1972, Pt. 2, Wing Commander R. Bell Davies' report of the Oberndorf raid to the Admiralty.
26. *Ibid.*
27. Library and Archives Canada, MG30E280, Volume 9, File: No. 3 Wing RNAS Research Material and Correspondence N/D 1916–1972, Pt. 2, Summary of raids carried out by No. 3 Wing, RNAS between 30 July and 14 April, 1917.
28. *The Brave Young Wings*, 146. Used by permission.
29. Library and Archives Canada, MG30E280, Volume 9, File: No. 3 Wing RNAS Research Material and Correspondence N/D 1916–1972, Pt. 2, Summary of raids carried out by No. 3 Wing, RNAS between 30 July and 14 April, 1917.
30. *Ibid.*
31. *Ibid.*
32. *Ibid.*
33. *The Brave Young Wings*, 148. Used by permission.
34. Library and Archives Canada, MG30E280, Volume 9, File: No. 3 Wing RNAS Research Material and Correspondence N/D 1916–1972, Pt. 2, Summary of raids carried out by No. 3 Wing, RNAS between 30 July and 14 April, 1917.
35. *Ibid.*
36. Library and Archives Canada, MG30E280, Volume 9, File: No. 3 Wing RNAS Research Material and Correspondence, Pt.1.
37. Library and Archives Canada, MG30E280, Volume 9, File: No. 3 Wing RNAS Research Material and Correspondence N/D 1916–1972, Pt. 2, Summary of raids carried out by No. 3 Wing, RNAS between 30 July and 14 April, 1917.
38. Library and Archives Canada, MG30E280, Volume 5, File: Air Historical Subjects Texts by Collishaw (File 1), Report from Elder to Admiralty dated 24 May 1917.
39. Library and Archives Canada, MG30E280, Volume 9, File: No. 3 Wing RNAS Research Material and Correspondence N/D 1916–

1972, Pt. 2, Summary of raids carried out by No. 3 Wing, RNAS between 30 July and 14 April, 1917.

40. Library and Archives Canada, MG30E280, Volume 5, File: Air Historical Subjects Texts by Collishaw (File 1), Report from Elder to Admiralty dated 24 May 1917.

41. *The Brave Young Wings*, 151. Used by permission.

42. *Canadian Airmen*, 260. Used by permission.

43. *Ibid.*, 276.

Chapter Five

1. *The Brave Young Wings*, 119. Used by permission.

2. Leonard H. Rochford, *I Chose the Sky* (London: William Kimber, 1977), 55.

3. *The Brave Young Wings*, 113–14. Used by permission.

4. *Ibid.*, 118–19.

5. *Canadian Airmen*, 396. Used by permission.

6. Peter Cooksley, *Sopwith Fighters in Action* (Carrollton, TX: Squadron/Signal Publications, Inc., 1991), 20. Used by permission. Courtesy of Squadron/Signal Publications, Carrollton, Texas, USA.

7. Norman Franks, *Osprey Aircraft of the Aces: Albatros Aces of World War 1* (Oxford, England: Osprey Publishing, 2000), 8. Used by permission.

8. *Ibid.*, 8.

9. Peter Kilduff, *Richthofen: Beyond the Legend of the Red Baron* (Toronto: John Wiley & Sons, Inc., 1993), 77. Used by permission.

10. Ralph Barker, *A Brief History of The Royal Flying Corps in World War 1* (London: Constable & Robinson Ltd., 2002), 170. Used by permission.

11. *Ibid.*, 170.

12. *I Chose the Sky*, 66.

13. Library and Archives Canada, MG30E280, Volume 5, File: Collishaw's Air Combats — Chronological Listing (File 5–9), extracted from the Air Historical Branch, Air Ministry.

14. *I Chose the Sky*, 69.

15. *Ibid.*, 74.

16. *Canadian Airmen*, 395. Used by permission.

Chapter Six

1. *Canadian Airmen*, 395. Used by permission.
2. Library and Archives Canada, MG30E280, Volume 9, File: No. 10 Naval Squadron (Black Flight), Pt. 1, N/O 1917–1973.
3. Norman Franks *Osprey Aircraft of the Aces: Sopwith Triplane Aces of World War 1* (Oxford, England: Osprey Publishing, 2004), 7. Used by permission.
4. Peter Cooksley, *Sopwith Fighters in Action, Aircraft Number 110* (Carrollton, TX: Squadron/Signal Publications, 1991), 28. Used by permission. Courtesy of Squadron/Signal Publications, Carrollton, TX, USA.
5. Peter Hart, *Bloody April Slaughter in the Skies over Arras, 1917* (London: Cassell Military Paperbacks, a division of The Orion Publishing Group, 2005), 249, 250. Used by permission.
6. Library and Archives Canada, MG30E280, Volume 9, File: No. 10 Naval Squadron (Black Flight), Pt. 1, N/O 1917–1973, Letter to R. Dodds from W. M. Alexander, dated 10 August, 1972.
7. Deborah Lake, *The Zeebrugge and Ostend Raids 1918* (Barnsley, South Yorkshire: Leo Cooper Pen and Sword Books Ltd., 2002), 6.
8. *Ibid.*, 10.
9. Library and Archives Canada, MG30E280, Volume 9, File: No. 10 Naval Squadron (Black Flight), Pt. 1, N/O 1917–1973.
10. *Canadian Airmen*, 175. Used by permission.
11. *The Brave Young Wings*, 59. Used by permission.
12. *Ibid.*, 60.
13. Library and Archives Canada, MG30E280, Volume 9, File: No. 10 Naval Squadron (Black Flight), Pt. 1, N/O 1917–1973, letter to Ken Molson from Robert (Bob) Dodds, dated 24 November, 1964.
14. Library and Archives Canada, MG30E280, Volume 9, File: No. 10 Naval Squadron (Black Flight), Pt. 1, N/O 1917–1973.
15. Library and Archives Canada, MG30E280, Volume 9, File: No. 10 Naval Squadron (Black Flight), Pt. 1, N/O 1917–1973, Squadron Record Book — No. 10 Naval Squadron — May 1917 to March 1918.
16. Library and Archives Canada, MG30E280, Volume 9, File: No. 10 Naval Squadron (Black Flight), Pt. 1, N/O 1917–1973, XI Wing, RFC, Combat Record Book —3 May, 1917 to 8 June, 1917.

17. *Ibid.*
18. Library and Archives Canada, MG30E280, Volume 9, File: No. 10 Naval Squadron (Black Flight), Pt. 1, N/O 1917–1973, RNAS Operations Reports, No. 10 Naval Squadron, Report No. 34.

Chapter Seven

1. *Richthofen*, 107.
2. *Ibid.*, 125–27.
3. Norman Franks, *Osprey Aircraft of the Aces: Albatros Aces of World War 1* (Oxford, England: Osprey Publishing, 2000), 30. Used by permission.
4. Library and Archives Canada, MG30E280, Volume 9, File: No. 10 Naval Squadron (Black Flight), Pt. 1, N/O 1917–1973, Squadron Record Book — No. 10 Naval Squadron — May 1917 to March 1918.
5. Library and Archives Canada, MG30E280, Volume 9, File: No. 10 Naval Squadron (Black Flight), Pt. 1, N/O 1917–1973, XI Wing, RFC, Combat Record Book — 3 May, 1917 to 8 June, 1917.
6. Library and Archives Canada, MG30E280, Volume 9, File: No. 10 Naval Squadron (Black Flight), Pt. 1, N/O 1917–1973.
7. *Ibid.*
8. Library and Archives Canada, MG30E280, Volume 9, File: No. 10 Naval Squadron (Black Flight), Pt. 1, N/O 1917–1973, Squadron Record Book — No. 10 Naval Squadron — May 1917 to March 1918.
9. Library and Archives Canada, MG30E280, Volume 5, File: Possible German Casualties, 5–10.
10. Library and Archives Canada, MG30E280, Volume 9, File: No. 10 Naval Squadron (Black Flight), Pt. 1, N/O 1917–1973, Squadron Record Book — No. 10 Naval Squadron — May 1917 to March 1918.
11. John Keegan, *The First World War* (Toronto: Vintage Canada, 2000), 356–57. From *The First World War* by John Keegan, copyright © 1998 by John Keegan. Used by permission of Alfred A. Knopf, a division of Random House, Inc.
12. *Canadian Airmen*, 408–09. Used by permission.
13. Library and Archives Canada, MG30E280, Volume 9, File: No. 10 Naval Squadron (Black Flight), Pt. 1, N/O 1917–1973, Squadron Record Book — No. 10 Naval Squadron — May 1917 to March 1918.

14. *The Brave Young Wings*, 62–63. Used by permission.
15. Library and Archives Canada, MG30E280, Volume 5, File: Possible German Casualties, 5–10.
16. Library and Archives Canada, MG30E280, Volume 9, File: No. 10 Naval Squadron (Black Flight), Pt. 1, N/O 1917–1973, Gazette, 20 July 1917.
17. Library and Archives Canada, MG30E280, Volume 9, File: No. 10 Naval Squadron (Black Flight), Pt. 1, N/O 1917–1973, RNAS Operations Reports, No. 10 Naval Squadron, Report No. 35.
18. Library and Archives Canada, MG30E280, Volume 9, File: No. 10 Naval Squadron (Black Flight), Pt. 1, N/O 1917–1973, No. 10 Naval Squadron, Decisive Combats by Flight Lieutenant Collishaw.
19. Library and Archives Canada, MG30E280, Volume 9, File: No. 10 Naval Squadron (Black Flight), Pt. 1, N/O 1917–1973, Report of Operations carried out by Naval Squadron No. 10, between 17 June and 30 June.
20. *Richthofen*, 128.
21. *Ibid.*, 129.
22. *The Brave Young Wings*, 63–64. Used by permission.
23. Library and Archives Canada, MG30E280, Volume 5, File: Possible German Casualties, 5–10.
24. Library and Archives Canada, MG30E280, Volume 9, File: No. 10 Naval Squadron (Black Flight), Pt. 1, N/O 1917–1973, No. 10 Naval Squadron, Decisive Combats by Flight Lieutenant Sharman and Commanding Officer Naval Squadron No. 10 report dated 1 July 1917.
25. *Richthofen*, 128.
26. Thomas R. Funderburk, *The Fighters: The Men and Machines of the First Air War* (New York: Gosset & Dunlap Publishers, 1965), 109. Used by permission.
27. *Richthofen*, 127, 128.
28. Library and Archives Canada, MG30E280, Volume 5, File: Collishaw's Air Combats, 5–9.
29. Library and Archives Canada, MG30E280, Volume 9, File: No. 10 Naval Squadron (Black Flight), Pt. 1, N/O 1917–1973, Commanding Officer, Naval Squadron No. 10, Report of 1 July 1917.

30. Library and Archives Canada, MG30E280, Volume 9, File: No. 10 Naval Squadron (Black Flight), Pt. 1 N/O 1917–1973, Squadron Record Book — No. 10 Naval Squadron — May 1917 to March 1918.

31. Library and Archives Canada, MG30E280, Volume 5, File: Collishaw's Air Combats, 5–9, extracted from the Air Historical Branch, Air Ministry.

32. *The Fighters*, 110.

33. Library and Archives Canada, MG30E280, Volume 9, File: No. 10 Naval Squadron (Black Flight) Research Material and Correspondence, Pt. 2, N/D 1917–1973, Squadron Record Book — No. 10 Naval Squadron, 28 June 1917.

34. Library and Archives Canada, MG30E280, Volume 9, File: No. 10 Naval Squadron (Black Flight), Pt. 1, N/O 1917–1973, RNAS Operations Reports, No. 10 Naval Squadron, Report No. 36.

35. *Canadian Airmen*, 412. Used by permission.

Chapter Eight

1. Bernard Fitzsimons, editor, *Warplanes and Air Battles of World War 1* (New York: Beekman House, 1973), 46.

2. Leon Bennett, *Gunning for the Red Baron* (College Station, TX: Texas A&M University Press, 2006), 185. Reprinted from *Gunning for the Red Baron* by Leon Bennett by permission of the Texas A&M University Press. Copyright © 2006 Leon Bennett.

3. William D. Mathieson, *My Grandfather's War: Canadians Remember the First World War, 1914–1918* (Toronto: Macmillan of Canada, 1981), 215–16.

4. Library and Archives Canada, MG30E280, Volume 9, File: List of Collishaw's air combats (also victories and distinctions) N/D, 1964.

5. *Richthofen*, 129.

6. Dale M. Titler, *The Day the Red Baron Died* (New York: Bonanza Books, 1970), 67.

7. *Richthofen*, 132–33.

8. *The Day the Red Baron Died*, 68.

9. *Richthofen*, 133.

10. *The Brave Young Wings*, 65. Used by permission.

11. Library and Archives Canada, MG30E280, Volume 5, File: Collishaw's Air Combats, 5–9, extracted from the Air Historical Branch, Air Ministry.

12. Library and Archives Canada, MG30E280, Volume 9, File: No. 10 Naval Squadron (Black Flight), Pt. 1, N/O 1917–1973, Gazette, 11 August 1917.

13. *Ibid.*

14. Library and Archives Canada, MG30E280, Volume 9, File: No. 10 Naval Squadron (Black Flight), Pt. 1, N/O 1917–1973, RFC Headquarters reports to RNAS HQ. Report dated 16 July 1917.

15. Library and Archives Canada, MG30E280, Volume 7, File: 7–13 Roster of Victors and Casualties to the Naval Fighter Squadrons, No.'s. 1, 8, and 10, during the operational period with Sopwith Triplanes.

16. Ralph Barker, *A Brief History of the Royal Flying Corps in World War 1* (London: Constable & Robinson Ltd., 2002), 310. Used by permission.

17. Library and Archives Canada, MG30E280, Volume 9, File: No. 10 Naval Squadron (Black Flight), Pt. 1, N/O 1917–1973, Report from Commanding Officer Naval Squadron No. 10 to Commanding Officer 22 Wing Royal Flying Corps, dated 29 July 1917.

18. Library and Archives Canada, MG30E280, Volume 9, File: No. 10 Naval Squadron (Black Flight), Pt. 1, N/O 1917–1973, RNAS Operations Reports, No. 10 Naval Squadron.

19. *Ibid.*

20. Library and Archives Canada, MG30E280, Volume 5, File: Collishaw's Air Combats, 5–9, extracted from the Air Historical Branch, Air Ministry.

21. Library and Archives Canada, MG30E280, Volume 9, File: No. 10 Naval Squadron (Black Flight), Pt. 1, N/O 1917–1973, Report from Commanding Officer Naval Squadron No. 10 to Commanding Officer 22 Wing Royal Flying Corps, dated 29 July 1917.

22. Library and Archives Canada, MG30E280, Volume 9, File: No. 10 Naval Squadron Research Material, Casualties, N/D, 1964–1966, logbook of Mr. W. M. Alexander.

23. Library and Archives Canada, MG30E280, Volume 5, File: Collishaw's Air Combats, 5–9, extracted from the Air Historical

Branch, Air Ministry.

24. Library and Archives Canada, MG30E280, Volume 5, File: Possible German Casualties, pages 5–10.

25. *Richthofen*, 139.

26. Library and Archives Canada, MG30E280, Volume 5, File: Collishaw's Air Combats, 5–9, extracted from the Air Historical Branch, Air Ministry.

27. *The Brave Young Wings*, 67. Used by permission.

28. Library and Archives Canada, MG30E280, Volume 9, File: No. 10 Naval Squadron (Black Flight), Pt. 1, N/O 1917–1973, Report from Commanding Officer Naval Squadron No. 10 to Commanding Officer 22 Wing Royal Flying Corps, dated 29 July 1917.

29. Library and Archives Canada, MG30E280, Volume 9, File: No. 10 Naval Squadron (Black Flight), Pt. 1, N/O 1917–1973, Letter from Brigadier-General commanding 5 Brigade, Royal Flying Corps to Headquarters, 15 and 22 Wings RFC, dated 24 July 1917.

30. Library and Archives Canada, MG30E280, Volume 9, File: No. 10 Naval Squadron (Black Flight), Pt. 1, N/O 1917–1973, Squadron Record Book — No. 10 Naval Squadron — May 1917 to March 1918.

31. Library and Archives Canada, MG30E280, Volume 9, File: No. 10 Naval Squadron (Black Flight), Pt. 1, N/O 1917–1973, Report from Commanding Officer Naval Squadron No. 10 to Commanding Officer 22 Wing Royal Flying Corps, dated 29 July 1917.

32. Library and Archives Canada, MG30E280, Volume 7, File: 7–13 Roster of Victors and Casualties to the Naval Fighter Squadrons, No.s. 1, 8, and10, during the operational period with Sopwith Triplanes.

33. Library and Archives Canada, MG30E280 Volume 9, File: No. 10 Naval Squadron (Black Flight), Pt. 1, N/O 1917–1973, Squadron Record Book — No. 10 Naval Squadron — May 1917 to March 1918.

34. Library and Archives Canada, MG30E280, Volume 9, File: No. 10 Naval Squadron (Black Flight), Pt. 1, N/O 1917–1973, Report from Commanding Officer Naval Squadron No. 10 to Commanding Officer 22 Wing Royal Flying Corps, dated 28 July 1917.

35. *Ibid.*

36. Library and Archives Canada, MG30E280, Volume 9, File: No. 10 Naval Squadron (Black Flight), Pt. 1, N/O 1917–1973, RNAS Operations Reports, No. 10 Naval Squadron, Report No. 38.

37. *Gunning for the Red Baron*, 174. Reprinted from *Gunning for the Red Baron* by Leon Bennett by permission of the Texas A&M University Press. Copyright © 2006 Leon Bennett.

38. *Canadian Airmen*, 426. Used by permission.

Chapter Nine

1. Library and Archives Canada, MG30E280, Volume 9, File: No. 10 Naval Squadron (Black Flight), Pt. 1, N/O 1917–1973, Notes from R.V. Dodds, December 1970.

2. *Canadian Airmen*, 179. Used by permission.

3. *Ibid.*, 175.

4. Library and Archives Canada, MG30E280, Volume 9, File: No. 10 Naval Squadron (Black Flight), Pt. 1, N/O 1917–1973, Letter to S.F. Wise from W. M. Alexander, dated February 9, 1973.

5. Norman Franks, *Osprey Aircraft of the Aces: Sopwith Camel Aces of World War 1* (Oxford, England: Osprey Publishing, 2003), 7.

6. *The Fighters*, 121.

7. *Canadian Airmen*, 416. Used by permission.

8. Library and Archives Canada, MG30E280, Volume 9, File: List of Collishaw's Air Combats (Also Victories and Distinctions) N/D, 1964.

9. *Warplanes and Air Battles of World War 1*, 102.

10. Library and Archives Canada, MG30E280, Volume 9, File: List of Collishaw's Air Combats (Also Victories and Distinctions) N/D, 1964.

11. Library and Archives Canada, MG30E280, Volume 9, File: No. 13 (213) Squadron Research Material and Correspondence, N/D 1917–1972.

12. Library and Archives Canada, MG30E280, Volume 9, File: List of Collishaw's Air Combats (Also Victories and Distinctions) N/D, 1964.

13. *Canadian Airmen*, 179. Used by permission.

14. *The Brave Young Wings*, 68. Used by permission.

Chapter Ten

1. *The Brave Young Wings*, 69. Used by permission.

2. *Ibid.*, 69.

3. *I Chose the Sky*, 132.
4. *Ibid.*, 130, 131.
5. *Ibid.*, 134, 135.
6. John J. Pershing, *My Experiences in the World War, Volume 1* (New York: Frederick A. Stokes Company, 1931), 319.
7. *The First World War*, 393–94. From *The First World War* by John Keegan, copyright © 1998 by John Keegan. Used by permission of Alfred A. Knopf, a division of Random House, Inc.
8. *Brave Young Wings*, 69. Used by permission.
9. *Canadian Airmen*, 179. Used by permission.
10. *I Chose the Sky*, 139.
11. *Ibid.*, 138.
12. *The Brave Young Wings*, 69. Used by permission.
13. *The Fighters*, 126.
14. *Ibid.*, 128.
15. *The First World War*, 396, 400. From *The First World War* by John Keegan, copyright © 1998 by John Keegan. Used by permission of Alfred A. Knopf, a division of Random House, Inc.
16. *I Chose the Sky*, 142.
17. *Canadian Airmen*, 507. Used by permission.
18. *Richthofen*, 189.
19. *The First World War*, 403. From *The First World War* by John Keegan, copyright © 1998 by John Keegan. Used by permission of Alfred A. Knopf, a division of Random House, Inc.
20. Joshua Levine, *On a Wing and a Prayer* (London: Collins, 2008), 299–301. Reprinted by permission of HarperCollins Publishers Ltd. © 2008 Joshua Levine.
21. *The Royal Flying Corps in World War I*, 418. Used by permission.
22. *Ibid.*, 418.
23. *Canadian Airmen*, 192–93. Used by permission.

Chapter Eleven

1. *Canadian Airmen*, 511. Used by permission.
2. *Ibid.*, 511.
3. *Ibid.*, 511.
4. *Ibid.*, 512.

5. *I Chose the Sky*, 152.
6. *Canadian Airmen*, 513. Used by permission.
7. *Ibid.*, 514.
8. *Richthofen*, 197.
9. Dan McCaffery, *Air Aces: The Lives and Times of Twelve Canadian Fighter Pilots* (Toronto: James Lorimer & Company, 1990), 15.
10. *Richthofen*, 202–03.
11. *Canadian Airmen*, 516–17. Used by permission
12. *I Chose the Sky*, 157.
13. *Ibid.*, 157.
14. *Ibid.*, 164.
15. *Canadian Airmen*, 517. Used by permission.
16. *I Chose the Sky*, 170.
17. Library and Archives Canada, MG30E280, Volume 1, File: Collishaw Career 1–1, Gazette, 3 August 1918.
18. *I Chose the Sky*, 174.
19. *The Brave Young Wings*, 71. Used by permission.
20. Library and Archives Canada, MG30E280, Volume 1, File: Collishaw Career 1–1, Gazette, 21 September 1918.
21. Library and Archives Canada, MG30E280, Volume 9, File: List of Collishaw's Air Combats (Also Victories and Distinctions) N/D, 1964.
22. *I Chose the Sky*, 176, 177.
23. *Canadian Airmen*, 520. Used by permission.
24. *Ibid.*, 521.
25. *I Chose the Sky*, 178.
26. Library and Archives Canada, MG30E280, Volume 5, File:Collishaw's Air Combats, 5–9, extracted from the Air Historical Branch, Air Ministry.
27. *I Chose the Sky*, 181.
28. *Warplanes & Air Battles of World War 1*, 159.
29. *Canadian Airmen*, 550. Used by permission.
30. Library and Archives Canada, MG30E280, Volume 9, File: List of Collishaw's Air Combats (Also Victories and Distinctions) N/D, 1964.
31. *I Chose the Sky*, 189–90.
32. *Canadian Airmen*, 562. Used by permission.
33. Peter Hart, *Aces Falling: War Above the Trenches, 1918* (London:

Phoenix, a division of Orion Publishing Group, 2007), 204. Used by permission. Copyright © Peter Hart 2007

34. *The Brave Young Wings*, 71. Used by permission.
35. *Canadian Airmen*, 574. Used by permission.
36. *Ibid.*, 574.

Chapter Twelve

1. *Canadian Airmen*, 626–27. Used by permission.
2. Library and Archives Canada, MG30E280, Volume 5, File: Collishaw in South Russia 1919–1920, A review of the counter-revolution in South Russia in the period 1917–1918.
3. *Canadian Airmen*, 626. Used by permission.
4. Peter Cooksley, *De Havilland D.H-.9 in Action* (Carrollton, TX: Squadron/Signal Publications, 1996), 15. Used by permission. Courtesy of Squadron/Signal Publications, Carrollton, Texas, USA.
5. Library and Archives Canada, MG30E280, Volume 5, File: Collishaw in South Russia 1919–1920, 47 Squadron War Diary, South Russia, extracted from the Air Historical Branch, Air Ministry.
6. Library and Archives Canada, MG30E280, Volume 5, File: Collishaw in South Russia 1919–1920, 47 Squadron War Diary, South Russia, extracted from the Air Historical Branch, Air Ministry.
7. *Ibid.*
8. Library and Archives Canada, MG30E280, Volume 5, File: Collishaw in South Russia 1919–1920.
9. *Ibid.*
10. *Ibid.*
11. Library and Archives Canada, MG30E280, Volume 5, File: Collishaw in South Russia 1919–1920, 47 Squadron War Diary, South Russia, extracted from the Air Historical Branch, Air Ministry.
12. Library and Archives Canada, MG30E280, Volume 5, File: Collishaw in South Russia 1919–1920, Resume of Operations — RAF South Russia, June 1919 to May 1920, extracted from the Air Historical Branch, Air Ministry.
13. *Canadian Airmen*, 627. Used by permission.
14. Library and Archives Canada, MG30E280, Volume 5, File: Collishaw in South Russia 1919–1920, London Gazette September 20, 1919.

15. Library and Archives Canada, MG30E280, Volume 5, File: Collishaw in South Russia 1919–1920.
16. Library and Archives Canada, MG30E280, Volume 5, File: Collishaw in South Russia 1919–1920, Resume of Operations — RAF South Russia, June 1919 to May 1920, extracted from the Air Historical Branch, Air Ministry.
17. Library and Archives Canada, MG30E280, Volume 5, File: Collishaw in South Russia 1919–1972.
18. *Canadian Airmen*, 627. Used by permission.
19. Library and Archives Canada, MG30E280, Volume 5, File: Collishaw in South Russia 1919–1920, RAF Mission War Diary, South Russia, November 1919–January1920, extracted from the Air Historical Branch, Air Ministry.
20. *Ibid.*
21. *Ibid.*
22. Library and Archives Canada, MG30E280, Volume 5, File: Collishaw in South Russia 1919–1920, RAF Mission War Diary, South Russia, November 1919–January 1920, extracted from the Air Historical Branch, Air Ministry.
23. *Ibid.*
24. *Canadian Airmen*, 627. Used by permission.
25. Library and Archives Canada, MG30E280, Volume 5, File: Collishaw in South Russia 1919–1920.
26. *Canadian Airmen*, 628. Used by permission.

Epilogue

1. *Collishaw and Company*, 194. Used by permission.
2. Library and Archives Canada, MG30E280, Volume 5, File: Collishaw's Air Combats.
3. *Brave Young Wings*, 72. Used by permission.

BIBLIOGRAPHY

Books

Barker, Ralph. *The Royal Flying Corps in World War I*. London: Constable & Robinson Ltd., 2002.

Bashow, Lt. Col. David L. *Knights of the Air: Canadian Fighter Pilots in the First World War*. Toronto: McArthur & Company, 2000.

Bell Davies, Vice Admiral Richard. *Sailor in the Air*. London: Peter Davies, 1967.

Bennett, Alan. *Captain Roy Brown — A True Story of the Great War, 1914–1918 Volumes I and II*. New York: Brick Tower Press, 2011.

Bennett, Leon. *Gunning for the Red Baron*. College Station: Texas A&M University Press, 2006.

Bishop, Arthur. *True Canadian Heroes in the Air*. Toronto: Prospero Books, 2004.

Bowen, Ezra. *Knights of the Air*. Alexandria Virginia: Time-Life Books, 1980.

Clarke, John D., *Gallantry Medals and Awards of the World*. Somerset: Patrick Stephens Limited, 1993.

Collishaw, Raymond and R.V. Dodds. *Air Command: A Fighter Pilot's Story*. London: William Kimber, 1973.

Cooksley, Peter. *De Havilland D.H.9 in Action: Aircraft Number 164*. Carrollton, TX: Squadron/Signal Publications, Inc., 1996.

_____. *Sopwith Fighters in Action: Aircraft Number 110*. Carrollton, TX: Squadron/Signal Publications, Inc., 1991.

Dancocks, Daniel G. *Legacy of Valour: The Canadians at Passchendaele*. Edmonton: Hurtig Publishers, 1986.

Dodds, Ronald. *The Brave Young Wings*. Stittsville, ON: Canada's Wings Inc., 1980.

Edwards, Suzanne K. *Gus: From Trapper Boy To Air Marshal*. Renfrew, ON: General Store Publishing House, 2007.

Fitzsimons, Bernard, ed. *Warplanes and Air Battles of World War I*. New York: Beekman House, 1973.

Franks, Norman. *Osprey Aircraft of the Aces: Albatros Aces of World War I*. Oxford: Osprey Publishing, 2000.

_____. *Osprey Aircraft of the Aces: Sopwith Camel Aces of World War I*. Oxford: Osprey Publishing, 2003.

_____. *Osprey Aircraft of the Aces: Sopwith Triplane Aces of World War I*. Oxford: Osprey Publishing, 2004.

Fredette, Raymond H. *The Sky on Fire: The First Battle of Britain 1917–1918 and the Birth of the Royal Air Force*. Washington, DC: Smithsonian Institution Press, 1991.

Funderburk, Thomas R. *The Fighters: The Men and Machines of the First Air War*. New York: Grosset & Dunlap Publishers, 1965.

Gilbert, Martin. *The Battle of the Somme: The Heroism and Horror of War*. Toronto: McClelland & Stewart, 2006.

Graves, T.B.A. *"Unsung Hero": The Combat Diary of Raymond Collishaw*. Liskeard, Cornwall: MVR Publications, 1988.

Hart, Peter. *Aces Falling: War Above the Trenches, 1918*. London: Phoenix, 2008.

_____. *Bloody April: Slaughter in the Skies Over Arras, 1917*. London: Cassell, 2006.

Johnson, J.E. *Full Circle: The Tactics of Air Fighting 1914–1964*. New York: Ballentine Books, 1964.

Keegan, John. *The First World War.* Toronto: Vintage Canada, 2000.

Kilduff, Peter. *Richthofen: Beyond the Legend of the Red Baron.* New York: John Wiley & Sons, Inc., 1994.

Lake, Deborah. *The Zeebrugge and Ostend Raids 1918.* Barnsley, South Yorkshire: Leo Cooper, 2002.

Lee, Arthur Gould. *No Parachute: The Exploits of a Fighter Pilot in the First World War.* London: Arrow Books, 1969.

Levine, Joshua. *On a Wing and a Prayer: The Untold Story of the Pioneering Aviation Heroes of WWI, in their Own Words.* London: Collins, 2008.

Mackay, James and John W. Mussell. *The Medal Yearbook: 2001.* Devon: Token Publishing Limited, 2001.

Mathieson, William D. *My Grandfather's War: Canadians Remember the First World War, 1914–1918.* Toronto: Macmillan of Canada, 1981.

McCaffery, Dan. *Air Aces: The Lives and Times of Twelve Canadian Fighter Pilots.* Toronto: James Lorimer & Company, 1990.

McWillians, James and Steel, R. James. *Amiens Dawn of Victory.* Toronto: Dundurn Press, 2001.

Molson, Kenneth M. *Canada's National Aviation Museum: Its History and Collections.* Ottawa: National Museum of Science and Technology, 1988.

O'Kiely, Elizabeth. *Gentleman Air Ace: The Duncan Bell-Irving Story.* Madeira Park: Harbour Publishing, 1992.

Perkins, Dave. *Canada's Submariners: 1914–1923.* Erin, ON: The Boston Mills Press, 1989.

Pershing, John J. *My Experiences in the World War: Volume I and II.* New York: Frederick A. Stoles Company, 1931.

Roberts, Leslie. *There Shall Be Wings: A History of the Royal Canadian Air Force.* Toronto: Clarke, Irwin & Company Limited, 1959.

Rochford, Leonard H. *I Chose the Sky.* London: William Kimber, 1977.

Romanov, Prince Dimitri. *The Orders, Medals and History of Imperial Russia.* Denmark: Balkan Heritage, 2000.

Shannon, Norm. *From Baddeck to the Yalu: Stories of Canada's Airmen at War.* Ottawa: Esprit de Corps Books, 2005.

Shores, Christopher and Hans Ring. *Fighters Over the Desert: The Air Battles in the Western Desert June 1940 to December 1942.* London: Neville Spearman, 1969.

Snowie, J. Allan. *Collishaw and Company: Canadians in the Royal Naval Air Service, 1914–1918.* Bellingham, WA: Nieuport Publishing Inc., 2010.

Stone, Norman. *The Eastern Front 1914–1917.* London: Penguin Books, 1998.

Titler, Dale M. *The Day the Red Baron Died.* New York: Bonanza Books, 1970.

Wise, S.F. *Canadian Airmen and the First World War: The Official History of the Royal Canadian Air Force Volume I.* Toronto: University of Toronto Press, 1980.

Websites

www.nanaimo.ca, Nanaimo's Historical Development and A Historic Timeline for Nanaimo. Accessed May 20, 2008.

INDEX

Numbers in italics refer to photos and their captions.

OF RELATED INTEREST

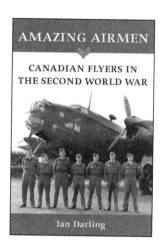

Amazing Airmen
Canadian Flyers in the Second World War
Ian Darling
978-1554884247
$24.99

Canadian and British airmen engaged in fierce and deadly battles in the skies over Europe during the Second World War. Those who survived often had to overcome incredible obstacles to do so — dodging bullets and German troops, escaping from burning planes and enduring forced marches if they became prisoners.

In one story, a tail gunner from Montreal survived despite being unconscious when blown out of his bomber. Another story describes how the crew of a navigator from Ottawa used chewing gum to fill holes in their aircraft. And another tells how a pilot from northern Ontario parachuted out of his plane and became the target of a German machine-gunner, but within hours 120 Germans surrendered to him.

These painstakingly researched stories will enable you to feel what now-aging veterans endured when they were young men in the air war against Nazi Germany.

Dancing in the Sky
The Royal Flying Corps in Canada
C.W. Hunt
978-1550028645
$28.99

Dancing in the Sky is the first complete telling of the First World War fighter pilot training initiative established by the British in response to the terrible losses occurring in the skies over Europe in 1916. This program, up and running in under six months despite enormous obstacles, launched Canada into the age of flight ahead of the United States.

The results enabled the Allies to regain control of the skies and eventually win the war, but at a terrible price. Flying was in its infancy and pilot training primitive. This is the story of the talented and courageous men and women who made the training program a success, complete with the romance, tragedy, humour, and pathos that accompany an account of such heroic proportions. A valuable addition to Canada's military history, this book will appeal to all who enjoy an exceptional adventure story embedded in Canada's past.

Visit us at
Dundurn.com | Definingcanada.ca | @dundurnpress | Facebook.com/dundurnpress